THE
TELL IT! Manual

The Complete Program for Evaluating Library Performance

Douglas Zweizig

Debra Wilcox Johnson

Jane Robbins

with Michele Besant

American Library Association
Chicago and London
1996

Project editor: Louise D. Howe

Cover design: Tessing Design

Printed on 50-pound a pH-neutral stock, and bound in 10-point C1S cover stock by Edwards Brothers, Inc.

The paper used in this publication meets the minimum require-ments of American National Standard for Information Sciences—Permanence of Paper for Printed Library Materials, ANSI Z39. 48-1992. ∞

Library of Congress Cataloging-in-Publication Data

The TELL IT! manual : the complete program for evaluating
   library performance / Douglas Zweizig ... [et al.].
      Includes bibliographical references and index.
      ISBN 0-8389-0679-6
      1. Libraries—United States—Evaluation.   2. Libraries—
   Evaluation.   I. Zweizig, Douglas.
   Z678.85.T45   1996
   027.073—dc20   95-26323

Printed in the United States of America.

00 99 98 97 96   5 4 3 2 1

Contents

Contents

Preface

This manual is the result of a project initiated in 1992 by the Office of Library Programs in the U.S. Department of Education, funded under the Higher Education Act, Title II-B, Research and Demonstration Program. The "Evaluating Library Programs & Services" project was carried out through a contract with the School of Library and Information Studies at the University of Wisconsin–Madison.

Ray Fry, who was Director of the Office of Library Programs at that time, explained the purpose of the project in this way:

> Over the years, little emphasis has been placed on the quality of program evaluation. Without useful evaluation, we lack evidence about either the value of specific library programs or the impact of libraries on society. In these days of scarce resources, it is increasingly important for libraries to demonstrate that the programs and services they offer make a positive difference in people's lives. . . . While the purpose of the manual is to promote better evaluation, the purpose of evaluation is to promote better programs and services. By providing information for decision making, evaluation becomes an essential component of the planning process.

The "Evaluating Library Programs & Services" project developed a planning and evaluation approach, using the acronym TELL IT!; conducted numerous national and regional institutes for librarians from a variety of library types; assisted groups of libraries in planning cooperative services; and, over the course of the project, developed the text for this manual. We have tried to provide in this manual the ingredients that a librarian would need to design evaluations for services and programs and could use to train colleagues in evaluation approaches.

This manual on the planning and evaluation of library services has received critical support from the Office of Library Programs, from the chief officers of state library agencies, from the hundreds of librarians attending institutes, from an active advisory committee representing a variety of library perspectives, and from the attentive editors at the American Library Association. All of these sources of support have strengthened this manual through expressions of needs, testing of evaluation and training approaches, and review of the manuscript in various forms; infelicities that remain are the responsibility of the authors.

Douglas Zweizig
Debra Wilcox Johnson
Jane Robbins

PART ONE

TELL IT! A Framework
for Planning and Evaluation

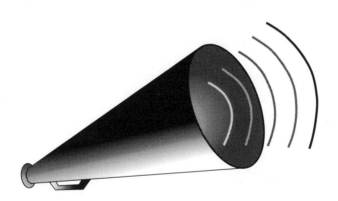

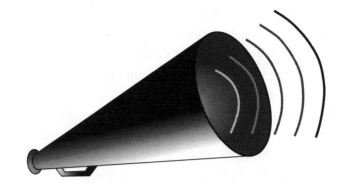

CHAPTER 1

Overview of TELL IT!

Douglas Zweizig

Whether or not a library formally evaluates its services, evaluations are being conducted of those services all the time by everyone who has any interest in those services: users, taxpayers, teachers, library staff, funders. This means the issue is not whether evaluation is going to take place—because it's constantly taking place. The issues are whether a library is going to *learn about the information gained* through those evaluations and whether a library has an opportunity to *affect the kinds of evaluations* that are conducted. For example, will the basis for evaluation be how cheap a service is or will it be how many people are being served? If the library staff are not players in the evaluation activities taking place, they may not learn of evaluation results until decisions based on those results have been made. In a community, public officials may be evaluating how crucial various civic services are—and may conclude that a cut in public library services will harm the community less than a cut in other services. If the staff of that public library is not out in front in evaluating the contributions made by its services and is not communicating those results to city officials, then the decisions for budget cuts may be made before the library has a chance to participate in the discussions. A university administrator has described the university library as a "bottomless pit" into which large amounts of money disappear with little evidence of benefit. Librarians in universities would do well to make the contributions of their collections more evident.

In a similar way, if the library is not actively engaged in evaluation, it may lose the opportunity to affect *how* it will be evaluated. If the library has communicated its goals to public officials, then it has helped to shape how it will be evaluated. A library whose community agrees that it should be an Independent Learning Center, for example, will be able to get agreement on how its services should be assessed—number of reference questions, number of booklists or pathfinders prepared, and so on. In the state of Ohio, when it became clear that funding for public libraries in that state was going to be provided through appropriations directly from the state legislature, Ohio librarians got out in front of the inevitable legislative evaluations that would occur by developing new standards for public library services in Ohio. That standards document put forth the terms by which library services in Ohio could be evaluated. The Ohio library community has taken the initiative to carry out periodic evaluations of the services in the state so that they could report to the legislature on progress being made.

A state university library in the sixties persuaded its board of regents to support the development of an automated circulation system by framing the terms of their case: "We can save 250,000 hours of faculty and student time by eliminating the delays related to the present overloaded system."

Libraries in all situations and of all types can take similar initiatives to learn from their own evaluations and to communicate the information gained to those most concerned.

In addition to active planning and evaluation making good sense, it has become a part of federal law in the *Government Performance and Results Act of 1993*. This Act, to become fully effective by the year 2000, requires an annual performance plan from each federal agency that:

- establishes performance goals

- expresses goals in measurable terms

- describes resources needed to meet goals

- establishes performance indicators

- provides a basis for comparing program results with performance goals

- describes means used to verify and validate measured values

- provides for the establishment of:

  strategic planning

  performance measures

It can be expected that this federal initiative will affect the expectations of agencies at all levels of government, including libraries of many types.

Although the major theme of this manual is evaluation, evaluation is so intimately bound with planning as to be almost a single term, "planningandevaluation." The approach to planning and evaluation taken in this manual is captured in the working definition of planning being used:

PLANNING
is
a series of
successive approximations
to a moving target.

Planning is not seen as an activity that will result in a static plan for a library, but as a process of continuous consideration of what the library is and where it is going. Each time the library engages in planning, it approaches its target more and more closely. And, because the demands on a library and the context in which it exists change rapidly (that is, the target moves), an approach to planning must allow the library to be aware of and to adapt to those changes. A second implication of this definition is that planning must be inexpensive and easily used. The evaluation part of this joint process is checking on and reporting on progress toward the target or the vision.

A planning and evaluation process or framework is like a recipe. There are many recipes for chocolate cake. Some recipes are elaborate and call for separating eggs and sifting dry ingredients. Some are simpler and call for starting with a box of cake mix. One recipe could be as simple as: go into a convenience store and look for a package labeled "Chocolate Cupcakes." Just as there is no one way to end up with chocolate cake, there is no one way to plan; there are many recipes for planning. But a planning process or framework is useful because it *reminds us of what should be in place* in order to plan—in a recipe, it is the list of ingredients; in a planning framework, it's information and people you may need—and of the *steps to be followed* in order to produce the desired product—a cake or a plan.

We have already observed that a planning and evaluation approach must be handy and inexpensive. It is also important to take a "no fault" approach to evaluation. As the Context Input Process Product (CIPP) approach puts it:

The purpose of EVALUATION
is not
to prove, but
to <u>im</u>prove.

Therefore the emphasis in any evaluation activity is on what can be *learned* in order to improve services in the future. In fact, it might be useful to think of evaluation as synonymous with learning. In our everyday activities, this is how we use evaluation: we learn from it. We decide from our experience at a restaurant to be sure to go there again (or not to go there again). We use our evaluations to improve our future experience. The goal of this manual is to help evaluation be as useful and natural an activity in library services as it is in daily life.

While a "no fault" approach is important, it is also important to make evaluations as accurately and candidly as possible in order to be able to learn from them. A fifth-grade school teacher reflects while having to assign a failing grade: "If she was not honest, she would never have tangible evidence of progress or decline." (Tracy Kidder, *Among Schoolchildren*. Boston:

5

Houghton Mifflin Co., 1989.) Even though the immediate news from an evaluation may be bad, it is important to locate accurately where things stand so that performance can be adjusted.

For this sourcebook, we are using the TELL IT! framework to organize our thinking about planning and evaluation; this chapter introduces that framework and explains some of its meaning. The TELL IT! framework consists of six steps in a planning process and simple explanatory sentences for each step. The approach is intended to be as simple as possible and to consume as little time as possible. The "plan" for a library project could be written on the back of an envelope as a result of staff discussion.

The basic framework for TELL IT! is:

Talk about the vision

Explore alternatives and design your approach

Learn from what's happening

Let people know what happened

Integrate results with ongoing services

Think about how it all worked **!**

At each of the steps of the process, some phrases are provided to suggest how the results of that step might be communicated:

Talk about the vision
> The difference we want to make is….
> For these reasons….

Explore alternatives and design your approach
> The best way to do this would be….
> For these reasons….

Learn from what's happening
> The way we'll check on progress is….
> We can correct for problems by….

Let people know what happened
> The way we'll document the difference we've made is….
> We'll communicate the difference by….

Integrate results with ongoing services
>   We'll take what we learned and relate it to the library as a whole by....
>   The best way to integrate learnings would be....

Think about how it all worked
>   Improvements to be made in performance....
>   Improvements to be made in planning....

!

The remainder of this chapter describes the activities that can occur at each step and the products of each step.

TALK ABOUT THE VISION

This step reminds us to emphasize the difference we want to make with our proposed service. Emphasizing the difference the service can make is a way to connect with those who have a stake in the success of library services: the community residents, university officials, users of the service, and so on. The *Talk about the vision* step reminds us to clarify in our own minds the difference we want to make and to communicate that vision to those who work with us, to those who fund us, to those who are served by us.

The partial sentences after the step, "The difference we want to make is...." and "For these reasons....," suggest an outline for communicating about this step. Evaluation approaches that would support clarifying the vision for the project could be: focus group interviews used to determine service needs from people in the community, or use of existing data, such as census data or registration information, to determine trends that require a library response.

In clarifying and communicating the vision, a library may want to use standard planning statements such as mission, roles, goals, and objectives. These statements are all different ways of expressing the vision of the library—the ends toward which the library is working. The *vision* captures the state of society that is desired by the library's planners. The *mission* is an expression of the library's purpose and service priorities for the current period. It will be most useful if the mission is specific to a given library community served and to a particular time. A *role* expresses an image for a service emphasis. Roles characterize different purposes for services or responses to needs in the community and have been used most frequently in public libraries. For example, in a particular public library, "Preschoolers' Door to Learning" or "Popular Materials Library" might be chosen as roles. Roles speak to what kind of library a user can expect; they are expressions of the identity of the library. A *goal* is a statement of a specific direction in which the library intends to move. It is an expression of aspiration and, as used here, is not expected to be fully achieved. A goal is an "unreachable star" for which the library is reaching. An *objective*, on the other hand, states how far in the desired direction the library plans to move by what time. An objective should be achievable and capable of being evaluated. That is, it should be possible to determine whether you have achieved an objective or not.

These planning terms all state how a library intends for things to be different, and the distinctions among them are not always easy. Vision tends to have a societal focus, while mission has more of a library-centered emphasis. As can be seen from the examples in the "Planning Terms" chart, these planning statements have a hierarchy to them, with a vision being the broadest statement and an objective being a specific statement of a difference to be achieved by a definite date. It is not a requirement of planning that a library use all of these kinds of planning statements, but they may be useful in capturing and communicating the planning decisions made. (These terms are defined in somewhat different ways by different planning approaches and in different types of libraries. While it is not possible to obtain agreement on their usage, we will use them in this manual in accordance with the "Planning Terms" chart.)

Planning Terms

Terms	Definitions	Examples
Vision	A desired state of affairs; has a societal focus	*Community residents will find information they need to function fully in society.*
Mission	The business the library is in; its purpose & priorities	*This library will address the needs of our citizens for prompt and accurate information.*
Role	A concrete image for a library service emphasis	*Independent Learning Center*
Goal	A direction in which the library wants to proceed	*To provide our users the information they need when they need it.*
Objective	How far the library intends to proceed—measurable, attainable, understandable, time based	*To increase Subject Fill Rate from 75% to 85% by July 1, 199_.*

EXPLORE ALTERNATIVES AND DESIGN YOUR APPROACH

This is the place in planning at which the shift is made from ends to means. *Talk about the vision* focuses on where the library is heading and why. The second step deals with how the library is going to get there. In working toward a vision, there are a variety of activities from which to choose. It is useful to explore the full range of possible activities so that the "best" choice can be among those considered and so that you can speak to why other alternatives have been rejected for now.

For example, if a college library wants to assist faculty in grant writing, it could initiate a newsletter of sources of support and tips in grant writing, could designate a member of the reference staff to become expert in researching grant sources, could add grant location and grant writing materials to the collection, and so on. This step in planning is to inventory the possible ways to achieve the vision—by exploring alternatives—and to select or create an approach that will work best for the project—design your approach. The usual way to do this is to evaluate the alternatives against some criteria, such as expected effect of each alternative, cost, staff training needed, time required to implement, and so on. Having done this, the planners can fill in the statements listed after this step: "The best way to do this would be...." and "For these reasons...." That is, they can *document* that the best way to work toward the vision would be the selected activity and can give the reasons for its selection.

An evaluation approach that would support exploring alternatives could be a quick survey to other, similar libraries to inquire about solutions that worked for them, or focus group interviews with librarians who have provided services to the client group you want to serve.

LEARN FROM WHAT'S HAPPENING

In carrying out a project, activities need to be monitored to see that tasks are completed on time and that planners are alerted to any adjustments needed in order to continue to approach the vision. The ways in which the process of the project should best be monitored will be very individual to the project and the setting, so little can be prescribed in advance.

Evaluation approaches that may be used are observation to ensure that implementation steps are being carried out or focus groups of those carrying out the project to identify things learned and potential problems.

This step reminds planners that there needs to be a way of evaluating the process of the project and that the plan should include ways of completing the statements: "The way we'll check on progress is...." and "We can correct for problems by...."

LET PEOPLE KNOW WHAT HAPPENED

When a project is completed, there are many benefits to informing people about what was accomplished. The staff involved in the project can gain a sense of fulfillment from a summation of the project. The community receiving service can be reminded of the contribution to the community from its library. The officials providing funding can gain evidence to use in allocating future funds.

9

Among the evaluation approaches that can help document the contributions of the project are focus group interviews, evaluations of projects by peer librarians, and surveys designed to obtain a fast response. Chapter 12, "Evaluation Methods," provides an overview of the range of evaluation techniques.

In planning the project, it is useful at the beginning to design how the final assessment will be done. In the TELL IT! model, we are reminded to say: "The way we'll document the difference we've made is…." In addition, the results of the evaluation should be made known to a variety of audiences. As a reminder of who should receive the information and how that should occur, we have the statement: "We'll communicate the difference by…."

These first four steps in the model deal with the project itself: clarifying the vision, selecting the activities, monitoring progress, and documenting effects. There is a convenient break in the TELL IT! acronym between the TELL and the IT! to signal that the last two steps are outside the project itself. These steps deal with the larger issues of how the project ties in with other library functions, and with reflections on the process of planning and evaluating.

INTEGRATE RESULTS WITH ONGOING SERVICES

Special projects are usually funded in order to provide start-up costs and experience, with the expectation that activities that are found to be workable and beneficial will become part of business as usual. We know that too often, when the special funding ends, the project dies with it. This step is a reminder for special projects that a plan for the integration of services should be part of the initial project planning. This plan can be expressed by completing the sentences: "We'll take what we learned and relate it to the library as a whole by…." and "The best way to integrate learnings would be…."

THINK ABOUT HOW IT ALL WORKED

Planning and evaluation are ways that an organization learns. This step is a reminder to pay attention to what can be learned from the project, both in its planning and in its execution so an organization can benefit from the experience. Therefore, notes can be made of "Improvements to be made in performance…." and "Improvements to be made in planning…." The things that are learned from this project may be of greatest use to the library itself or they may be important to share also with other libraries attempting similar efforts.

We can see from this quick run through of the TELL IT! framework that the approach builds on familiar planning and evaluation steps. This model, however, emphasizes the vision—communicating the ends a project is working toward and the contributions of the project to the community or institution. We are hopeful that this framework will be a useful way of organizing planning and evaluation elements you are already familiar with as well as ones that may be new for you.

The ways in which the TELL IT! approach compares with other approaches used in libraries is illustrated in the table on the following page. This comparison can help make the steps of TELL IT! familiar. It also shows graphically, by the blanks in that row, that the planning approaches available for libraries today have not dealt with the need to integrate special library programs and services into the ongoing services of the library.

FEATURES OF TELL IT!

We have used the analogy of a recipe to talk about planning and evaluation processes. Recipes have different features—some chocolate cakes are light sponges with butter cream icing, some are heavy flourless chocolate jolts. Planning processes also have their individual features, and it may be useful to point to a few of the features of the TELL IT! approach.

- TELL IT! focuses on evaluation. It tries to maximize the learning that can occur from a project at each stage of its development and execution—both the learning for the library and the learning for the community.

- TELL IT! is "planning lite." TELL IT! is not intended to substitute for *Planning and Role Setting for Public Libraries,* or other library planning models but gives a planning approach that can be used for a specific service or program or can be used as a "front-end" for an overall planning process. A library may develop a comprehensive plan using an approach such as *Planning and Role Setting for Public Libraries* and could use TELL IT! as a framework for communicating portions of the plan to the community or other stakeholders.

  "Planning lite" also means minimalist evaluation. What we mean by minimalist is that a library does as *little* planning and evaluation as it can. For a minimalist evaluator, planning and evaluation are not seen as ends in themselves but as means to higher quality and more cost-effective services. Of course, we also mean that planning and evaluation are occurring constantly—that they are an integral part of business as usual, a natural part of any decision-making in a library.

  By advocating minimalist evaluation, we are not suggesting that librarians avoid evaluation but that evaluation becomes an easy and natural part of the way the library functions. We should consider which evaluations are critical, what would be the cheapest way to obtain the information, and how often evaluations need to be conducted. As an example of effective minimalist evaluation, we might cite the example of a public library serving a well-educated community whose staff determined that a sign of quality service for that community is that at any time the library is open, at least two books currently on

11

the *New York Times Book Review* Best Sellers list should be available for circulation in the new books section. The staff in this library routinely check whether this level of service is being provided throughout the day, as they walk past the new books section to retrieve a reference tool or as they walk to their breaks. This evaluation does not require any elaborate study. If a staff member notes that two such books are not present among the new books, immediate action is taken to process returned books or to order more copies of the currently popular materials. Through this device, staff in this library can be sure that they consistently provide the kind of service they think important. As a simple evaluation approach, TELL IT! is intended to encourage this type of frequent and easy evaluation.

- TELL IT! has a societal focus. In keeping with the call for information on impact, TELL IT! has a societal rather than institutional focus. In determining the library's direction and in documenting results of service, TELL IT! reminds us to do so in terms of the vision for the community. It emphasizes the *contributions* that services can make for their communities and the importance of *communicating* those contributions to a variety of audiences.

- TELL IT! emphasizes communication. Communication both within the library and with the community is an activity required at all the steps of the process. It is particularly important in the *Talk about the vision* and in the *Let people know what happened* steps.

- TELL IT! is about learning. The TELL IT! approach reminds the planners to learn both from the direct outcomes of the project—"what happened"—and from the *process* of conducting the project—"how it all worked." In addition, it reminds the planner/evaluator to use what was learned to improve existing services in the *Integrate results with ongoing services* step.

From the many options available for organizing planning, the TELL IT! approach was developed because it emphasizes the *contributions* that services can make to communities and the importance of *communicating* those contributions to a variety of audiences. The following chapters of this section provide more information on each of the steps of the approach.

Comparison of TELL IT! with other Planning and Evaluation Approaches

TELL IT! A Framework for Planning and Evaluation	*Planning and Role Setting for Public Libraries, 1987*	CIPP Context Input Process Product model	Related terms from other approaches
Talk about the vision	Preparing to plan Looking around Developing roles and mission Writing goals and objectives	Context Evaluation: *What's out there?*	Assessing needs, opportunities, barriers; Visioning; Setting targets; Designing the ends; *PLAN*
Explore alternatives and design your approach	Taking action: identify and select activities to meet each objective	Input Evaluation: *What to do about it?*	Designing the means Designing the services *DO*
Learn from what's happening	Taking action: manage implementation, monitor implementation process	Process Evaluation: *Are we doing it?*	Implementation *DO*
Let people know what happened	Review and recycling	Product Evaluation: *Did we do it?*	Find the benefits Review Diagnosis; *TEST*
Integrate results with ongoing services			
Think about how it all worked	Review and recycling Planning to plan		Meta-review; *CHANGE*

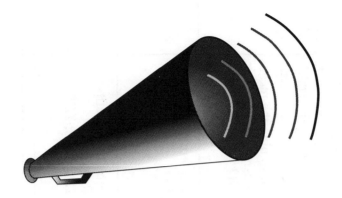

CHAPTER 2

Talk about the Vision:
The Heart of Your Library

Jane Robbins

WHAT IS VISION?

Vision has been described by many management authors, consultants, and speakers. For some, institutional vision is best described as:

- an expression of value

- an idea for a preferred future

- a focus, a concept, or a reason

- a center for self-motivation

- a desired state of affairs with a societal focus

- an expression of the *impact* of what an organization does.

For others the more accurate description is:

- a philosophy or credo

- an inward gyroscope

- an invisible grace

- a force stored in the heart.

Organizational vision should not be confused with organizational mission. Mission statements address the business that an institution is in, what an organization does, while vision statements express the motivation for that business. Mission is the outward and visible sign, while vision is the inward and spiritual grace.

Whatever the definition or description, it is clear that all organizations that achieve greatness are guided by a vision that is easily communicated and broadly shared among those who work for, or with, as well as use, the organization. An organization loses ground when a vision cannot be articulated for it, when its vision becomes cloudy, or when multiple differing visions come into conflict. Everyone associated with an organization needs to share in the organizational vision because vision forms the bond which holds any great organization together and supports its accomplishments.

A library's vision needs to be on the one hand *strategic*—that is, an aid in staying focused on users and in staying focused on how the library contributes to individual fulfillment and achievement and to societal betterment. On the other hand, vision needs to be *lofty*—that is, an expression of optimism and greatness that captures the imagination and engages the spirit. Vision expresses values, and centers efforts on contributions. It empowers through integrity. It values competitors as well as coworkers while pursuing organizational mission.

Vision is important because it is what makes those who are not users of the library into supporters of it; vision manifests library service as a public benefit. Vision for the library is what makes people think of phrases such as "informed citizenry," "the heart of the university," and "children with a joy for learning" when they think of their library. A library with a staff who shares a vision is staffed by people who clearly believe in their work and can articulate this in public.

FOUR STEPS TO CREATING A VISION

Introduction

Creating a vision is an act of leadership. The director of the library does not have to be the one who has the initial creative spark that ignites the visioning process, but it is essential that the director supports and nurtures an environment in which those who have productive vision can share it and can bring others within its empowering force. Creating a vision is not a simple task.

Only rarely will it be possible for the first statement of vision to be sufficiently articulated as to capture the imagination and energy of all who come in contact with the library. While one way to begin the visioning process locally is to borrow another library's vision statement, it should not be expected that such borrowing will result in a shared vision for the borrowing library. An example of one public library's vision statement follows. It is offered here not necessarily as an exemplar, but as an example:

> The Library will offer materials and services to assist in reaching the following vision:
>
> • Children, regardless of their social status, will enter school ready to learn. Once enrolled in school they will make the most of the educational opportunities available. All children will develop a lifelong love of reading and learning.
>
> • Everyone in our community not only will know how to read, but will take advantage of the benefits reading can bring. Area residents will regularly use information to improve the quality of their lives (personal and job-related).
>
> • The area will have a healthy economic climate, with successful local businesses and a fully employed workforce.
>
> • The community will understand and respect people's differences, and will value and support strong and healthy families.
>
> • The community will have a high degree of citizen participation in government and in cultural and other activities which add to the quality of life.

A shared vision cannot be imposed upon a library; it will be necessary to work at creating one. It is reported by those who consult with organizations that are having trouble creating a shared vision that vision inspiration and articulation often happens at unexpected moments. Vision articulation has happened in the middle of a staff meeting called for a totally different purpose and during a librarian's talk at a Lions Club meeting. Working at creating a vision for a library is a requirement because it is vitally important that the library's contribution to the community it serves be understood. No library can be a great library if vision for it is lacking.

STEP 1
Sensing the Environment(s)

This step requires curiosity and attentiveness to what is happening in all the relevant environments of the library. Politics, economics, demographics and technological realities and possible futures need to be in the mind of the visionary. While it is important to once again remember that a vision needs to be strategic, it is also important that it not be constrained by short-term focusing. In this step of looking around, or scanning the environment, the purpose is to be open to insight and inspiration.

16

As an example of looking around, a visionary might review our federal government's National Education Goals. Briefly, the goals state that by the year 2000:

- all children in the U.S. will start school ready to learn;

- the high school graduation rate will increase to at least 90 percent;

- U.S. students will leave grades 4, 8, and 12 having demonstrated competency in challenging subject matter including English, math, science, arts, foreign language, history and geography, civics and government, and economics;

- the nation's teaching force will have access to programs for the continued improvement of their professional skills and the opportunity to acquire the knowledge and skills needed to instruct and prepare all students for the next century;

- U.S. students will be first in the world in math and science achievement;

- every adult will be literate and will possess the knowledge and skills necessary to compete in a global economy;

- every school in the U.S. will be free of drugs, alcohol, and violence and will offer a disciplined environment conducive to learning;

- every school will promote partnerships that will increase parental involvement and participation in promoting the social, emotional, and academic growth of children.

Clearly, several of these goals have the potential for inspiring vision in librarians that serve preschoolers, students of any age, and the general public. Another written source of potential for inspiring vision is Amitai Etzioni's *The Spirit of Community: Rights, Responsibilities, and the Communitarian Agenda*. In this book, Etzioni, the founder of the Communitarian movement, a renowned professor and former White House Fellow, calls for a reawakening of our allegiance to the shared values and institutions that sustain us. He calls for the people of our nation to remember the basic truths of our democratic social contract. The public library visionary could find much in the Communitarian agenda as inspiration.

STEP 2
Creating the Vision

Together, library staff and others with a "stake" in the future of the library, having learned from the result of the scanning process, design a mind picture of the library thriving in the face of change. (The model on the following page describes the stakeholders for federally-funded public library programs.) Shared motivational focuses that empower the act of creating a vision are:

- We value above all our ability to serve users.

- We are committed to ethical service.

Stakeholder Model

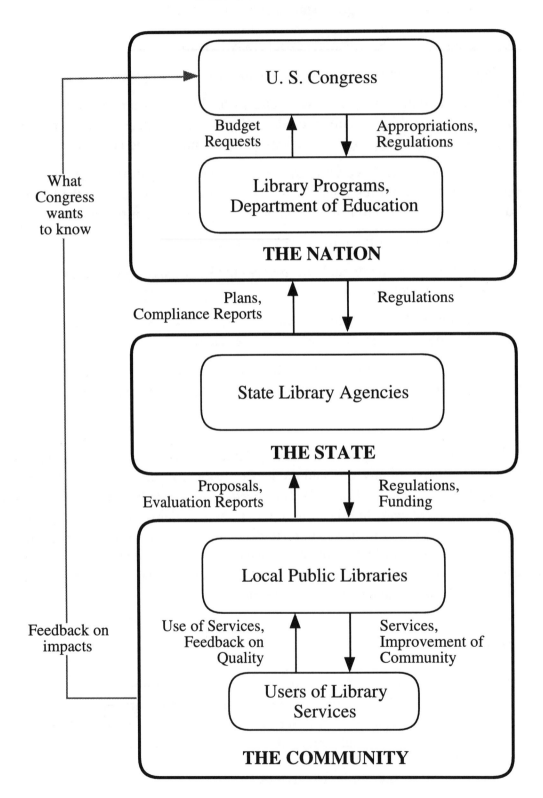

- Our interactions with everyone who comes in contact with the library must reflect the high standards we profess.

- We think "we" not "I."

- Our services will look good as well as be good.

Staff who are involved in the creation of the vision will be likely to understand it, to be committed to it, and to behave in accord with it.

STEP 3
Sharing the Vision

Because the fundamental purpose of a vision statement is to explain desired impact—that is, the contributions to society that the library expects to make—it is important to use the statement as a basis for all communication efforts. Publicity and public relations opportunities should be used to convert the idea(s) of the vision statement into pictures and phrases. All the library's plans and actions should clearly derive from it. Library staff, users, funders, board members, faculty, and supporters—the library's stakeholders—should all be equipped to communicate the vision at any opportunity.

STEP 4
Focusing Today's Activities in Accord with the Vision

The vision statement forms the *why* that undergirds the library's planning activities. It is the focus for role setting, for mission, goals, and objectives development, and provides the focus for the measurement of the inputs, processes, and outputs of the library's services. The vision statement also leads to the development of measures of impact. For example, before a library had envisioned that it had a role in contributing to a community in which "all adults were literate so that they could compete in a world economy and exercise the rights and responsibilities of citizenship," it might have focused its attention on: 1) measuring the number of students who entered their adult literacy program, and 2) counting the number of people who completed it. After developing such a vision the library might study the activities of the literacy program participants in terms of those who had become employed or had obtained more demanding work, or who had begun to serve on local boards or committees, or who had become citizens and voters.

CONCLUSION

Talk about the vision, as the first step in the TELL IT! approach, calls our attention to the necessity of clarifying our purposes before we begin to think about activities or about evaluation. On completion of this step, the library staff will be able to state "The difference we want to make is...." and to explain "For these reasons...."

It is well to think of vision as a lighthouse that gives direction rather than as a destination. Vision, while it has many outcomes that are practical, is in itself not practical; it is idealistic, maybe even spiritual. Vision suggests that nice people finish first. Vision is enlightened self-interest. Vision is empowering. Go forth and create some.

REFERENCES AND FURTHER READING

Brassier, Ann. "Strategic Vision: A Practical Tool." *The Bureaucrat* 14 (Fall 1985): 23–26.

Collins, James C., and Jerry I. Porras. "Organizational Vision and Visionary Organizations." *California Management Review* 34 (Fall 1991): 30–52.

Etzioni, Amitai. *The Spirit of Community: Rights, Responsibilities, and the Communitarian Agenda.* New York: Crown Publishers, 1993.

Wilson, Ian. "Realizing the Power of Strategic Vision." *Long Range Planning* 25 (October 1992): 18–28.

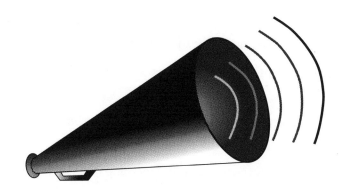

CHAPTER 3

Explore Alternatives and Design Your Approach

Douglas Zweizig

The TELL IT! approach places great emphasis on vision. It is vision that justifies the worth of a service or project; it is vision that serves as a guide for all the decisions that follow. When we are deciding how to implement an activity, these decisions need to fit the focus of the vision and the definition of the mission or the activity may go astray, may begin to work toward other visions than were intended. Robert Townsend at the time he was Chief Executive Officer at Avis kept a sign by his phone that read, "We rent cars." The reason for this sign with the mission is that in the conflicts and pressures of the workday, it was possible to forget what the purpose of the company was and to make decisions that would compromise or contradict that purpose. So it is not only important to determine a vision for the library; it is also important to recall that vision regularly and to check the activities against it.

This second step of the TELL IT! approach deals with taking action to work toward the selected vision. It reminds us that we should not simply begin to carry out the obvious or familiar approaches to the vision, but should *deliberately consider* the alternative ways that could be used to pursue that vision and to select the approach that will work best.

The first task at this point is probably to brainstorm the ways in which the library might work toward the selected vision. If a library has selected a goal of helping children in the community to start school ready to learn, there are a large number of possible ways of working toward that goal. Possible approaches might include:

- providing "newborn kits" to new parents at the hospital that would introduce library services and communicate the importance of reading to children;

- taking programming to daycare homes and centers to reach preschoolers in the community;

- writing a regular newspaper column on new materials of value for preschoolers;

- training all library staff in the skills needed to serve preschoolers and their caregivers;

- redesigning the children's room to provide a more inviting environment for parents and preschoolers.

The point here is not to recommend any of these approaches, but only to illustrate that for any vision the library is pursuing, a variety of alternative ways of approaching the vision can probably be identified. The act of listing alternatives will suggest additional approaches that might not have come to mind initially. Generating activities can be done alone, but it is probably best done in a small group. The suggestions of one person are likely to trigger ideas from others in the group. The list of serious contenders for approaches to be used should include a variety of approaches, and the number of alternatives should be manageable (at least four and no more than ten).

The possible approaches (in this example, newborn kits, daycare programming, new materials column, staff training, and room redesigning) can be assessed against some criteria in order to allow the selection of an approach or combination of approaches to use. A familiar example of this process is found in the issues of *Consumer Reports* when they report on the evaluation of a product. The product may be lawn mowers—machines for the purpose of maintaining the length of your grass. The report will list the alternatives, the different makes of lawn mowers, down the left-hand column of the page and will list criteria for evaluating the different makes along the top. The criteria might include price, width of cut, ease of height adjustment, safety, and comfort of use.

Likewise, the different ways that improved service might be provided for the children in the community can be evaluated against criteria. The criteria that might be used include:

- the cost of providing the service;

- the number of preschoolers who would be reached;

- the likelihood that the approach would be successful in helping children start school ready to learn;

- the likelihood that caregivers would respond to such a service;

- the number of staff required to implement the approach.

The decision of which criteria are to be used to evaluate possible approaches should be made by those doing the planning. The criteria will differ depending on the activities to be evaluated. Again, this process will work best if there are at least four criteria and no more than ten. Each of the possible approaches can be evaluated against each of the selected criteria. A small group may again be useful since the ratings will be assisted by the combined judgment of knowledgeable people. It is probably not useful to attempt to determine ratings precisely; costs, for example, may not be known at this stage. But it should be possible to rate the alternatives against each other and to determine which alternatives will be most costly and which less costly. A rough rating scale such as "high, moderate, low" or "positive, negative" can be used to rate the alternatives as illustrated on the decision chart on the following page.

Determining the "best" alternative is a creative act, not a mathematical solution. For some libraries, cost may be the primary criterion; for others, it may be the likelihood of success. The point of this step is to support a discussion among the staff of what approaches can be taken to pursue the vision and a selection of the approach or combination of approaches to take.

Criteria will probably not be equally important. The number of preschoolers who would be reached, for example, may be the most important criterion; for this project, perhaps cost is not so important. So at some point in the discussion, it may be useful to identify the most important criteria and to use them first in deciding among alternatives.

There are two important advantages of determining the approach to take through a deliberate process. The first advantage is accountability. A library staff that has carried out the kind of discussion that this step recommends will be able to account for its selection of an approach. It will be able to explain what alternatives were considered and why the selected approach is best for the library to use at this time. When a public official asks about an alternative that she thinks might be cheaper, the library can respond with its evaluation of that alternative against the other possibilities and can explain the ways in which the selected approach was rated higher.

The second advantage is that this process provides a back-up plan in case things do not work out with the selected approach. If, for whatever reason, the preferred approach is no longer feasible, other alternatives have already been evaluated, and the second best plan can quickly be identified and implemented. Fastening too early on a single solution prevents easy movement to an alternative solution.

The product of this step will be the plan—a statement that describes what will be done, by whom, in what order, and by what time to carry out the selected approach. At this point, the library staff should be able to complete the statements:

The best way to work toward this vision would be....
(Listing the selected approach.)

For these reasons....
(Describing the evaluation of the approach by the criteria.)

and should be ready to carry out the service as designed.

DECISION CHART

Possible Approaches	Criteria	Cost	Number of preschoolers reached	Likelihood of success	Likelihood caregivers would respond	Staffing requirements
		High - Low	High - Low	High - Low	High - Low	High - Low
Newborn Kits						
Daycare Programming						
New Materials Column						
Training Staff						
Redesigning Room						

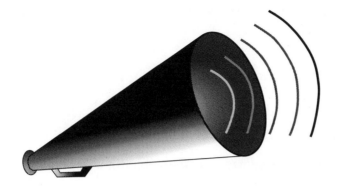

CHAPTER 4

Learn From What's Happening

Douglas Zweizig

Our definition of planning (a series of successive approximations to a moving target) acknowledges that, as the bumper sticker says, "Things Happen," that mid-course corrections are going to be required in order to stay in pursuit of the vision. External events like large bequests or budget cuts, internal changes like fatigue or additions to staff happen. Staff who understood the vision at the beginning of the project (e.g., "to bring the library to the nonusers in the community") begin to shift their focus to other ends (e.g., making sure that new borrowers have adequate identification). The alternative selected for your plan turns out to cost much more than anticipated or not to be ready by the time required. Things happen, and therefore adjustments will be necessary to keep steering in the desired direction.

This step is a reminder that you will need a plan to deal with change in the middle of things. There are two ways in which you can plan to cope with the inevitable changes that will occur:

- you can draw up a schedule of activities that should occur with times for completion and responsibilities assigned, and

- you can think ahead to how you will identify and adjust to the inevitable surprises that will occur.

25

You are reminded of the first task by the sentence to complete: "The way we'll check on progress is...." This requires that you have some means of monitoring the progress of the project. The simplest form would be

- a listing of the tasks to be completed,

- in the order in which they need to be completed,

- with a deadline for each task, and

- with an individual assigned as responsible for completing the task.

A form such as this Project Monitoring Form could be used to alert those involved of the tasks and deadlines and to record the completion of tasks.

Project Monitoring Form

TASK		PERSON RE-SPONSIBLE	PRODUCT	DATE **TO BE** COMPLETED	DATE COM-PLETED	WHAT WAS LEARNED	SERVED THE VISION? (Y/N)

The tasks should be listed in the order in which they should be performed, with tasks with the earliest "dates to be completed" occurring first. For each task, an individual should be listed as responsible for its completion. A product for each task will help in being clear about whether a task is completed or not. Products may be such things as a copy of the invoice for materials ordered, a report on the program that was held, a copy of the news release that was created. The product should be something naturally associated with the task and should require little extra effort to produce. (The products for the tasks will help in the writing of the final report for the project.) The completion of each task should be reported to the overall manager for the project, and that person should note the date on which the task was reported as complete. The completion of tasks can be occasion for "headlines" in staff newsletters or for notices on a bulletin board. In addition, there are spaces for noting what was learned as that task was being checked off as complete and for verifying that the task did serve to advance the vision for the activity.

All that is required for monitoring, then, is to check regularly on the Project Monitoring Form to make certain that things are happening on schedule. A pattern of tasks being completed on schedule would indicate that things are going according to plan; a pattern of tasks being completed late indicates that some correction needs to occur or the overall project is in danger of failing to realize the vision. A review of the things learned will indicate whether things learned at each step have resulted in improvements or whether the same lessons come up over and over again.

Of course, it is likely that things will not conform to the original plan, so there is a need to have a plan for responding and adjusting. The sentence beginning "We can correct for problems by…." provides a place to describe just how that will happen. Devices for adjusting to challenges can be:

- decisions to change can be made by the individual responsible for the project;

- problems encountered need to be brought to a staff or advisory committee;

- back-up plans could already be in place to respond to some predictable problems (for example, the alternatives that were contenders for carrying out the plan could be turned to if the chosen alternative turns out not to work);

- a specialist acting as a consultant for the project could be asked to recommend responses.

The point of thinking out in advance how needed changes will be made is so that problems will not result in paralysis but will trigger a problem-solving process that has already been thought out. Then energies can be spent in solving the problem rather than deciding at that time who should do what in order to produce a solution.

Learning from what happens and adjusting to it can also help with fear of evaluation. No one wants to learn at the end of a project year that the project was conducted badly or did not achieve what it was supposed to. If ongoing evaluations are being made of the progress in carrying out the tasks and in pursuing the vision, then problems can be identified early and corrected before the final evaluation results need to be reported to those who review the programs. Learning from what's happening—also known as process evaluation—can give those carrying out the project a feeling of control over what happens and can increase the chances that the project will produce the impacts that were desired.

> *Activities* for this step are designing a simple method for monitoring progress, and a process for making adjustments as needed. Example monitoring methods would be schedules and checklists.

> *Products* of this step could be periodic progress reports.

The point of "Learn from what's happening" is to ensure that the project is on course toward the vision. This step should not become an end in itself but should be carried out in the most modest way possible. If it is being done right, the staff carrying out the project are hardly aware it is being done.

27

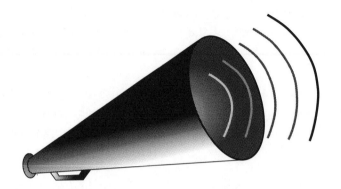

CHAPTER 5

Let People Know What Happened: Telling the Story

Amy Owen

In the TELL IT! model of evaluation, the fourth letter, "L," represents "Let people know what happened." Communicating the results of an evaluation is empowering in at least three ways. First, it requires you to plan early in the evaluation process how you will document the results of the evaluation, thus assuring that you have a story to tell. Second, it is central to the next step in the model: integrating what you have learned into the library's ongoing activities. Third, "telling the story" communicates the results to a wide audience: library users, the library community, decision-makers, and the library staff. In short, no evaluation, however elegantly planned and executed, will make the slightest difference if you do not tell the story.

WHAT'S THE STORY?

In his book *The Reflective Practitioner*, Donald Schön describes one of the hallmarks of any professional: the ability to name and frame a problem. "Telling the story" requires library managers to name and frame the results of their evaluation. This process recapitulates much of what has gone before in evaluation. "Telling the story" includes communicating the vision which prompted and justified the evaluation, why the process used was chosen, and how the evaluation was carried out. Most importantly, "telling the story" includes what the library has learned, what decisions have been made, and how library services will improve.

WHO IS THE AUDIENCE?

To "tell the story," you must determine who wants to know and who should know. Think broadly; in general, we do ourselves a disservice by not communicating enough. There are many audiences for the results of an evaluation project, and although not every evaluation needs to be communicated to all audiences, each deserves careful consideration.

Internal audiences *may be* the easiest to reach and inform. Project staff and library administration, obviously, want to know and should know. Too often, however, the general staff is left to rely on the grapevine or, worse, left completely in the dark to wonder what is going on. Consider how the findings of your evaluation or the changes that result from it could affect the work of others on the library staff. Even if the impact appears to be slight, talking about evaluation encourages others to think about evaluation in relation to their own work and to operate in a more productive and constructive framework.

External audiences for evaluation include professional peers, accrediting agencies, the state library agency, the federal government, and the like—the latter especially if the project was financed with state or federal funds. Library supporters (faculty, trustees, members of friends groups, library users) are external audiences that usually are very interested in how the results of an evaluation will improve library services. Other external audiences include the news media, the general public, and foundations or other funding bodies.

However, the most significant audience for your story may well be the government officials responsible for the library's budget. "Telling the story" to these officials (elected or appointed) can result in increased credibility for the library—a credibility that translates into solid support when budgets are determined.

WHAT FORMAT IS BEST?

Formats can be sorted into four basic categories by creating a matrix of formal/informal and oral/written. Examples of each are shown in the chart below. In selecting which format to use, the most important rules to keep in mind are:

- Match the format to the audience's needs

- Communicate the user point of view whenever possible

- Use clear, expository narrative that focuses on results, decisions, and impact

- Use graphs and charts and other visual materials whenever possible

Communication Formats

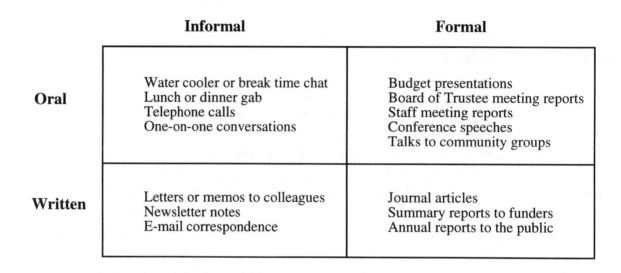

	Informal	Formal
Oral	Water cooler or break time chat Lunch or dinner gab Telephone calls One-on-one conversations	Budget presentations Board of Trustee meeting reports Staff meeting reports Conference speeches Talks to community groups
Written	Letters or memos to colleagues Newsletter notes E-mail correspondence	Journal articles Summary reports to funders Annual reports to the public

WHO NEEDS TO KNOW WHAT?

The central question in "telling the story" is: "Who needs to know what?" Each potential audience has its own special interests. Just as you may not wish to spend endless hours viewing *all* the home videos your neighbor shot on a recent family vacation, each of the potential audiences for the library's evaluation may not wish to hear all the details. This is especially important to remember when trying to reach external audiences and decision-makers. Consider the following tongue-in-cheek rules in such situations.

RULE 1
The More Important the Individual, the Less They Want to Know

We all instinctively know that most bosses (including elected or appointed officials) have limited time and patience for twenty page, much less two hundred page, reports. They want answers to three basic questions: "So what?" "What now?" and "How much?" Such individuals will be grateful for clarity and brevity. They will be favorably impressed in direct proportion to your ability to translate the evaluation results into concrete improvements with a low cost price tag or no cost.

RULE 2
Tailor the Message to the Individual or Group

In much the same way that individuals have different styles of learning, they also have differing styles for acquiring information. Use your imagination to help you understand what your audience or listener needs or wants to know and how you can make your message meaningful. For example, budget analysts tend to be impressed with cost analyses and clear, objective data. Politicians prefer anecdotes (preferably about one of their own constituents) and statements of impact. News media representatives are also interested in the human angle and impact, but will be looking for forecasts, good quotable material, or "hooks" to help them frame the issue for the general public. Professional peers are the audience with the most patience for information about the "how's" of your evaluation study. Finally, staff are primarily interested in one thing: "How will this affect my job?"

RULE 3
Sing Their Song

Keep in mind that even your boss has a boss—someone who must be pleased, someone who creates an agenda or sets priorities which must be honored. Determine what themes, goals, slogans, or targets are dominating public discourse in your area or are used in determining priorities for public funding. Then think of these public themes as musical themes or the tune of a song and deliberately set the words of your story to that song. This will help even strong library supporters better represent the library's services, its goals, and aspirations at higher levels of government or in the public arena.

RULE 4
Tell the Full Story

Even though your message may be brief, be sure to include enough information about each phase of the evaluation process to allow your audience to see the full picture. This does not mean that all aspects of the evaluation need equal attention. For communicating with officials and decision-makers, devote at least half of your message to the impact of the evaluation. Let them know what difference this will make in library services or activities, what impact the population served will observe, what improvements will result. Divide the other half of your message among three topics: the original vision (why the study is important); the results of the study (what you have learned); and how you conducted the study.

WHAT ABOUT BAD NEWS?

Sometimes evaluation results in bad news. For example, a good evaluation study may document that something hasn't worked or that things have not improved, or it may raise unanswered questions. A library opponent may conduct a study of his/her own that "proves" that the library is inefficient, spends too much money, or gives poor service when compared to another "like" library. Or alternatively, controversy over a library policy or funding issue may thrust the library into a difficult situation.

When the "bad news" is an internal matter held largely between the library staff and board or supportive local officials, keep the following tips in mind.

Make sure you've done it right. Is your study methodologically correct? Do the numbers add up? Sometimes simple omissions or errors can drastically affect the results.

Identify external factors which may have influenced the results. Assume that an evaluation study shows that the library's performance on a specific output measure has not improved. In such a case, a major decline in library funding, a loss in library staff, a closure due to remodeling or a disaster, a dramatic increase in workload or other similar factors could call for a very different interpretation of the study's results. The "bad news" could be a success story in disguise.

Understand the methodology you've used. Many evaluation methods rely on sampling or surveying. While results from samples are usually expressed as a single number (e.g., a 92% Fill Rate), they are actually ranges (i.e., 92% Fill Rate plus or minus some percentage—the confidence interval). An apparent decline in the library's "score" may simply be a shift within the confidence interval. (If the results of the samples taken have a confidence interval of ±5%, then a score of 92% one year and a score of 88% in a following year cannot be said to be different. If the confidence interval had been ±2%, then we could say that the scores had declined.)

Seize the initiative in a positive manner. Define the library's response proactively. Determine what steps can be taken to turn the situation around, to respond to the problem at hand, and to change and improve the situation. A positive, constructive, forward-looking plan of action will win support. Whining, excusing, and blaming only worsen the situation.

Learn to play the numbers game. Library critics often make invidious and unfavorable comparisons. However, few libraries are exactly comparable. Each library tends to have a unique service profile, differing user characteristics and different government financial support practices. A careful examination of the source and basis of your critic's numbers will usually uncover to what extent your library really is comparable to the library or group of libraries with which it is being compared.

When "bad news" is played out in a public arena with broad media coverage and angry constituents or officials, libraries would do well to follow models for response used in the corporate world.

Face the adversity head on. Don't delay or deny. Acknowledge the situation and move ahead in a proactive manner.

Know the facts and tell the truth. Don't equivocate or lie. If you need time to assemble information, say so; then do it.

In confrontational situations, speak to the reasonable person in the audience. Don't repeat negative phrases or "hook" terms used in questions. Even if your questioner is hostile, your audience is broader than one individual. A mature, thoughtful response will earn respect.

Be positive, be positive, be positive. Know your message and the library's vision. Use questions as an opportunity to make that statement; you are not obligated to answer on the limited terms posed by your questioner. Take time to think before responding; there is no penalty for taking a few seconds to marshal your thoughts.

In continuing situations, line up personal and professional support. Take care of your own need to work through panic, anger, and self-reproach in private with a trusted friend or colleague. Dealing with your own emotional reaction "offstage" will help you better represent the library "onstage." You can then do a better job of helping to move the library through the process of assessing the facts, setting immediate short-term goals, identifying allies, weighing choices, rebuilding the confidence of library staff, acting decisively, and communicating publicly.

IN THE LAST ANALYSIS

In the last analysis, it is not surprising that a review of "telling the story" has led from simple decisions to preparation for potentially difficult public responses. It is not surprising because evaluation presupposes a willingness to change, a willingness to ask hard questions and to make difficult decisions. For these reasons, evaluation and planning are political. They are complementary processes designed to help library managers make a difference in the quality and extensiveness of the services received daily by library users.

REFERENCES AND FURTHER READING

Carr, Harold. "Communicating During a 'Crisis'." Address on December 2, 1986 in *Vital Speeches of the Day* 53 (February 1, 1987): 248–50.

Feinberg, Mortimer R., and Bruce Serlen. "Crash Course in Crisis Management." *Working Woman* 1 (January 1987): 24–26.

Lukaszewski, James E. "Managing Bad News in America." Address on March 15, 1990 in *Vital Speeches of the Day* 56 (July 1, 1990): 568–73.

Schön, Donald. *The Reflective Practitioner: How Professionals Think in Action*. New York: Basic Books, 1983.

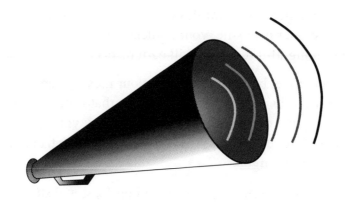

CHAPTER 6

Integrate Results with Ongoing Services
and
Think About How It All Worked

Douglas Zweizig

The first four steps of the TELL IT! approach deal with the project itself: clarifying the vision, selecting the activities, monitoring progress, and documenting outcomes. The break in the TELL IT! acronym between the TELL and the IT! signals that the last two steps are outside the project itself; they deal with the larger issues of the place of the project in the library and with reflections on the project as a whole.

INTEGRATE RESULTS WITH ONGOING SERVICES

We all know of too many examples of library programs and services that were developed because of special funding or special need and that were abandoned at the end of the project as the library went back to business as usual. Of course, this is an important disappointment. Projects are often funded in libraries in order to allow for the development of new solutions to persistent problems. These include reaching users that are somehow not served well by traditional services, creating new services using advanced technology, or bringing special areas of collections up to date. The reason for carrying out special projects such as these is so that the service level of the library will be permanently improved. However, too often the experience is that the service quality returns to its previous level when the project ends—the new users lose the attention they had gained; the technology continues to advance but the library doesn't keep up; the new materials begin to become dated but there is no plan to keep the collection refreshed. Unless attention is given to reaping the results of projects and to learning from them, their contribution to the library and to the practice of library service in other libraries will not be realized.

This step is a reminder that what is learned from these efforts can benefit the library as a whole. Using this step allows us to act on those lessons to improve library services by:

- making the special service part of normal business,

- taking some project management feature to improve the management in existing departments,

- letting other librarians know about the experience with the project through a presentation at the state association meeting or an article in a system newsletter.

There are a number of things that can be done to increase the chance that the good things from a project will not be lost when the funding ends.

Continually involve the staff who would need to implement the integration of the results. Even though only a small number of staff may be directly involved in the project, involving the other concerned staff in the design of the project (evaluating alternatives and approaches) and keeping them informed of the progress of the project will help them to integrate the beneficial portions of the project.

Plan for integration from the beginning. If the need for integration is kept in mind from the beginning, the project will be more likely to be carried out in a way that will lead to integration. For example, one of the criteria to be used in evaluating alternatives is the degree to which the selected alternative could become part of a new "business as usual" for the library. Plans can be made at the beginning for how the decision to integrate results will be made: how successful elements will be identified and who will make the decision.

Budget for integration. Even though much of the development work may be done during the project, there will be some costs and effort associated with the changes required to integrate the new service. Thinking ahead to the resources needed for integration at the end of the project can make that integration possible.

Communicate with decision-makers throughout the project, especially those with budget authority, so that they can anticipate the contribution this service can make as part of the library's normal service.

Start with a *smaller* demonstration project that financially is more in reach for the library to continue.

Build alternative funding sources during the life of the project, so that continuation funding is in place when the project funding ends.

When developing a project, link it to existing, strong services rather than emphasizing differences or the "special" nature of the new services. The project's services will be more likely to be seen as part of the library's regular offerings.

Activities at this step might include convening a meeting of those in the library who might incorporate features of the service into their normal practice or writing a report for the library (or for other, similar libraries) on the successful features of the project. The product of this step could be a *plan* for the changes to occur in the library as a whole.

There are many benefits to be gained from considering which elements of a project to integrate into the operation of the library, but these benefits will not be gained if advance thought is not given to integration. For this reason, the TELL IT! model reminds us to record: "We'll take what we learned and relate it to the library as a whole by…." and "The best way to integrate learnings would be…."

THINK ABOUT HOW IT ALL WORKED

This step is one of *reflection* on the program or service being evaluated in order to attempt to gain as much as possible from what has been learned about providing such a service and about conducting such a project. The audiences for this step are the people who carried out the project and those who might carry out such projects in the future. The results of this step should answer such questions as: what went well, what problems were encountered and how were they resolved, and what methods of managing the project were found to be useful.

The factors that might be considered at this step are of two kinds: those that have to do with the performance of the service and those that have to do with the management of the project. On performance of the service, consider:

• techniques that were found to be particularly effective;

• learning that occurred as a new service program was developed;

• details that should be remembered when carrying out such a program, e.g., remember to find co-sponsors for adult programs.

On the planning and management of the service, consider:

- hints for keeping a project on schedule

- ways of monitoring the budget to maintain control of expenses

- methods found useful for assessing the effectiveness of services.

The activities for this step could include such approaches as a review of the project by an individual, group meetings of the staff who were involved, or informal surveys of the people who were involved in the project. Key questions for this step are: who is in a position to provide information about the experience of this project and what would be the best way to gain that information.

The materials produced during the course of the project—the periodic reports on progress, the communications on the outcomes, the original plan—will all be grist for this reflection on how it all worked. To help ensure that such material is available for the review, a project notebook could be kept to organize all the materials produced as the project progresses—from the original project proposal to the final report, including progress reports, fliers for programs or other project publicity, memos, staff logs, newspaper clippings, and so on. These materials will help to jog memories as the people involved try to recall their experiences.

Products of this step could include informal notes on things to remember next time or a formal report to the staff or the library board of recommendations for the conduct of future projects. For purposes of clarity, it will probably be best to separate the reflections on how it all worked into the two types suggested:

Improvements to be made in performance. . . .

Improvements to be made in planning. . . .

PART TWO

Designing Evaluation Training

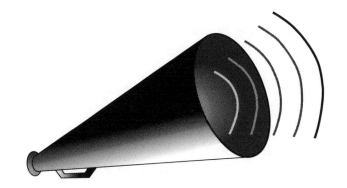

CHAPTER 7

Overview of Adult Learning

Robert O. Ray

BY WAY OF INTRODUCTION . . .

The TELL IT! model includes a number of assumptions and actions that have grown from the ideas of many people. The vision expressed by TELL IT! is predicated upon the assumption that all who have participated in this effort found it worthy—that it is a viable vision. This shared vision is needed as a basis for training in evaluation.

For this chapter, the assumption is made that a vision for evaluation of library services and programs is in place and that what is needed at this point is some information about how to bring that process to life. Training is one of the key ingredients that will determine the effectiveness of implementing the vision, and this effort now falls to the person responsible for implementation of outcomes. The purpose of this chapter is to present a number of suggestions and concepts that might be useful in accomplishing that task. Some attention is given to the nature of learning in adulthood and some guiding questions are posed for consideration. Finally, the chapter presents some strategies for effective training instruction along with references for further reading.

TRAINING

As with most topics it's important to start with a common understanding of concepts. For the purpose of this section "training" refers to the process of helping people acquire both the understanding of and expertise for effective evaluation of library projects, programs and services. "Evaluation" refers to processes used to determine the effect of an action. There is no one way in which this is best done. Both training for evaluation and evaluation design are multifaceted and multidimensional, defying a "one approach fits all" mentality. Both training and evaluation involve interactive processes calling upon knowledge and expertise of the learner, in a particular context using relevant processes. This interactive model forms the basis of the information on training for evaluation which follows.

Interactive Model for Adult Education

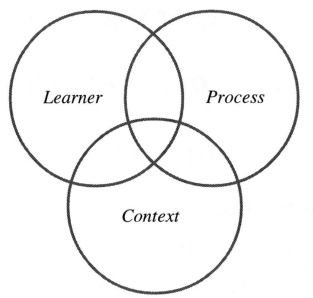

DESIGNS FOR TRAINING IN EVALUATION OF LIBRARY PROGRAMS AND SERVICES

The Learner

To begin the discussion of training, the first item of focus is understanding the adult as a learner. There are many approaches to how adults receive, process, interpret and use information. The table on the following page gives a brief synopsis of several schools of learning theory along with the key points one might consider when designing a training program.

Each of these approaches offers another way, or "lens," for viewing learners. The rest of this section briefly explains each of these perspectives. Readers are also encouraged to review Bigge and Shermis' *Learning Theories for Teachers* for greater depth on theories of learning.

Among those who sought to understand learning in a scientific manner was an early group who became known as the behaviorists (e.g., Watson, 1928; Thorndike, 1949; Skinner, 1974). Their traditions draw heavily upon the principles of empirical observation and ignore the internal process of thinking since it cannot be observed. To the behaviorist, learning occurs when a behavioral change is observed in the individual. The key component in this behavioral change within the person is due to some external manipulation of environment which makes the change possible. A key assumption is that it is the environment which presents a stimulus provoking a particular response in the learner. Thus, if change in behavior is desired, changing the environment leads to a particular reward which the learner finds desirable. It is necessary to find the right inducement to get the behavior wanted.

Theories of Learning

Conceptual School	Key Writers	Key Questions	Emphasis for Learning Process
Behaviorist	Watson, Thorndike, Skinner	What are the rewards?	Focus on environmental manipulation to bring about behavior
Cognitivist	Lewin, Ausubel, Gagne	Do I understand?	Focus on development of content and promoting insight
Developmentalist	Piaget, Erickson	Am I ready for this?	Focus on understanding level of readiness
Humanist	Maslow, Rogers	Am I secure enough to do this?	Focus on support and development of the individual
Social Learning	Bandura, Rotter	Will there be a supportive environment?	Focus on development of collaborative environment

A second group of learning theories comes from the perspective of cognitive psychology (e.g., Lewin, 1936; Ausubel, 1968; Gagne and Briggs, 1979). This school of thought tends to focus on the development of individual understanding to bring about learning. The assumption made here is that an individual who is comfortable in understanding information presented is open to change in knowledge and behavior. As a trainer using this approach, there is considerable attention focused on reducing knowledge into understandable components in order to facilitate actions based upon comprehension of information.

Those who believe that learning is dependent upon the stage of development in the learner are most obviously the developmentalists (e.g., Piaget, 1966, 1952; Erikson, 1978). Developmentalists hold the view that people develop along relatively predictable paths and that their success at learning depends upon their stage of social and intellectual development. For the most part these models assume that particular types of learning cannot effectively occur unless the individual is at a point of personal readiness. The task of the trainer using this approach to adult learning is to understand the level of development in the clientele participating in training.

Humanistic theories of learning are predicated on making the learner comfortable in learning the knowledge presented (e.g., Maslow, 1970; Rogers, 1983). The assumption is that the individual as a learner must be comfortable with self and internally motivated for the acquisition of knowledge to be effective. The trainer employing this approach is supportive of the individual and focused on encouragement to learn by developing self-assured behavior (confidence) within the person. Learning depends upon the individual's level of self-perceived abilities to achieve some outcome.

The environmental circumstances of a learner are key concepts for those in the social learning school of education (e.g., Bandura, 1977; Rotter, 1954). Key to learning under this conceptual base is the support of and modeling of behavior by others. A key assumption is that people are more likely to learn something if those around them are modeling the practice under consideration. The trainer's task under this perspective is the creation of collaborative networks and environments where people can consult each other toward the achievement of some goal. Although empowerment has some interesting connotations in education, it is one of the primary goals of social learning theory. In our present circumstance, the outcome would focus on the power to develop, implement and conduct evaluation of programs and services using expertise and skills found among the learners.

Intertwined with concepts of learning is the notion that situations of learners also greatly influence their interest and outcomes of any training activity. This facet is covered in the next section.

The Context

Training programs often are mandated experiences. The choice of participation is limited, and rejection of invitations to participate may often be seen to have punitive consequences. If the motivation to attend a training session comes from an external source, resistance and reluctance are more likely to occur than if the motivation comes from more internal interest. There are some very good reasons for resistance. Some of the very real concerns can be manifest in comments such as the following:

- "If people want to train me, I must not be doing a very good job."

- "There is so much going on here that I can't afford to take time away for training which someone else believes I need."

- "Why do I need to know this anyway? I have an evaluation statement in my comprehensive plans."

- "Our agency budgets are too small and I can't afford the expense personally, so who will pay?"

- "My background in evaluation is limited; I'd rather just be a 'librarian' and leave the evaluation to someone else."

- "Whose idea was this anyway? I know it wasn't mine because I have enough to do already."

All of these are legitimate concerns on behalf of those who are the target of professional development activities. The trainer must be able to recognize these problems and not simply ignore them as irrelevant. The trainer must become a sales representative convinced of the value in this product. Some suggestions for the trainer to consider in developing this approach are as follows:

- Help people understand the purpose of evaluation in very personal terms (e.g., it might be a way to help increase funding support for programs).

- Develop choices and/or options for learning and practicing evaluation skills and techniques. Not everyone has to go to the same spot at the same time, do they?

- Give people some basic tools for evaluation that are simple and relevant to their circumstance. Are you helping them meet their own needs or yours?

- Give people skills to develop techniques, collect information, analyze information, and make sense of the work. A mandate without a technique is going to be a very difficult product to sell.

- Have a response to how data are to be used after collection. So many times information is collected and sits or goes into a "black hole." Be clear about what will happen.

- Be prepared to talk about the resources that will be needed to conduct these evaluations. Nothing occurs free of cost. Will you be able to help people understand resources available and how they might be used to accomplish the ends?

The above is not an exhaustive list of contextual questions, concerns or observations that are likely to arise but they are representative of the issues one faces as a trainer. It is not a pleasant experience to face learners who are resistant from the beginning. It is most advantageous to spend time preparing the process of training before implementation of the event.

The Process

Given the training task at hand and knowing something about the learner who lives within a particular context, the next major task is to determine an appropriate training strategy. Some basic questions for consideration include some simple logic that often gets overlooked. For example:

- Is there a clear understanding of the need for training? What's the objective?

- Who is the target for training and why them?

- Are you the one who needs to deliver the training or are there other options? Can you hire someone with the expertise? Can the training occur by phone conference, or e–mail, or some other means?

- Where will the training occur and why there?

- When should the training occur? How fast does it need to happen?

Once these basic questions are addressed and the training agenda has been set, there are a number of facilitation techniques that fit certain goals better than others. While there are many resources available on how to lead learning groups, one of the most useful tools can be found in Apps' book *Mastering the Teaching of Adults*. The following list paraphrases a few of the suggestions he makes.

If the training is dissemination of information or skill development, some of the techniques for teaching include:

Lecture—Yes, it has its drawbacks, but it also has a purpose in the transfer of information. The effective trainer, however, must be well versed in how to construct a good lecture.

Interview—Invite a well-informed guest and interview that person or group by way of guided discussion in front of the training clientele.

Field trip—Going to a site where the desired result may be seen and providing understanding of how that process came to exist. This observation needs to be structured.

Print materials—A good handout with sufficient information and "white space" can facilitate learning by guiding instructional exercises or by aiding note-taking.

Interactive computer programs—Increasingly available, a good program allows instant feedback on success at the mastery of a desired skill.

Demonstration—Have one trainer train another by showing a successful technique.

Internship—It's possible for one individual to learn from the successes of others by simply spending time with them.

If the goals of training are for more in-depth understanding of an issue or topic some techniques which have been useful include forum presentations and simulations.

- Forum presentations that are well constructed present multiple sides of an issue and allow discussion to occur but may or may not lead to a specific conclusion. Similar techniques to obtain a depth of knowledge include buzz groups and group discussions.

- Simulations and role-playing have an element of taking positions which represent possible conflicting views. They promote awareness by placing people into shoes they may not normally fill.

An obvious warning is needed here as these activities must be well constructed or some serious conflicts could occur and damage would outweigh the benefits of such activities. Apps (1991) suggests a number of other approaches that may be useful; those listed above seem to have considerable use within the TELL IT! project. For a more academic treatment of teaching adults, readers are encouraged to review Hayes' monograph on *Effective Teaching Styles*.

SUMMARY

This chapter presents an overview of the concepts of adult learning as they relate to training programs on the evaluation of library services and programs. An effective training program needs to consider the complexities of adult life in its design. More specifically, it is important to understand how adults learn and how their circumstances may affect their learning interests and abilities. Finally, an effective training program needs time and careful preparation if it is to meet specified goals of the learner or the agency. Effective training is not decided and delivered at the whim or fancy of those who are in leadership.

REFERENCES AND FURTHER READING

Apps, J. W. *Mastering the Teaching of Adults*. Malabar, Fla.: Kreiger Publishing Company, 1991.

Ausubel, D. P. *Educational Psychology: A Cognitive View*. New York: Holt, Rinehart & Winston, 1968.

Bandura, A. *Social Learning Theory*. Englewood Cliffs, N.J.: Prentice Hall, 1977.

Bigge, M. L. and S. S. Shermis. *Learning Theories for Teachers*. 5th ed. New York: HarperCollins, 1992.

Erikson, E. H. *Adulthood*. New York: Norton, 1978.

Gagne, Robert M., Leslie J. Briggs, Walter W. Wager. *Principles of Instructional Design*. 4th ed. Fort Worth: Harcourt Brace Jovanovich College Publishers, 1992.

Hayes, E., ed. *Effective Teaching Styles*. San Francisco: Jossey-Bass, 1989.

Lewin, K. *Principles of Topological Psychology*. Translated by F. and G. M. Heider. New York: McGraw-Hill, 1936.

Maslow, A. H. *Motivation and Personality*. 2nd ed. New York: Harper & Row, 1970.

Piaget, J. *The Origins of Intelligence in Children*. New York: International Universities, 1952.

Piaget, J. *Psychology of Intelligence*. Totowa, N.J.: Littlefield Adams, 1966.

Rogers, C. R. *Freedom to Learn for the 80's*. Columbus: Merrill, 1983.

Rotter, J. B. *Social Learning and Clinical Psychology*. Englewood Cliffs, N.J.: Prentice Hall, 1954.

Skinner, B. F. *About Behaviorism*. New York: Knopf, 1974.

Thorndike, E. L. *Selected Writings from a Connectionist's Psychology*. New York: Appleton-Century-Crofts, 1949.

Watson, J. B. *The Ways of Behaviorism*. New York: Harper & Row, 1928.

The following chart is consistent with the theoretical context of this chapter and is a distillation of adult education literature and experience:

Ten Things You Already Know about Training

1. Adults bring lots of experience to any training, so trainers build on and take advantage of this. Adults' experiences can be integrated into the training and related to new learning.

2. In contrast to youth in school (or adults who return to college), adults' involvement in training is a secondary, not primary role or condition. It is not an end in itself, but relative to something else—in this case, work.

3. Adults are oriented toward application of the learning—now or perceived to be useful in the near future. This means the learning needs to be "relevant" or more problem–centered rather than subject–centered.

4. Adults generally learn best by doing, especially if behavior change is desired. This suggests participatory learning.

5. Adults can take responsibility for their own learning, so part of "doing" is setting their own learning goals and assessing progress toward those goals. In this context, training is guidance.

6. Learning most likely occurs when the learner feels respected and accepted.

7. Learning occurs at different paces. The larger the group, the more likely learning will be happening at different rates. For this reason, additional readings, opportunities to network, or videotaping for future review support training.

8. Adults have different learning styles or ways of learning. For example, some people do best when the abstract concepts come first, followed by discussion and then application. Others have the opposite style. Another view of this is learner preferences for a training approach, such as visual, kinesthetic, or auditory. One observation related to the issue of learning style: trainers tend to teach in their own preferred learning styles.

9. Learning is sometimes a painful process. People may prefer the pain of the familiar to the pain of the unknown. Learning does imply giving up or adjusting old ways of thinking, doing, or valuing.

10. The motivation of the learner is critical to the success of the training. Adults with a "felt need" learn best. They are aware that a gap exists between where they are now and where they want to be; training is seen as a viable way to close that gap. This helps to explain the dilemma of mandated or "strongly encouraged" attendance at training. Critical to this issue is the realization that learning occurs inside the individual and is not controlled by the trainer.

—Debra Wilcox Johnson

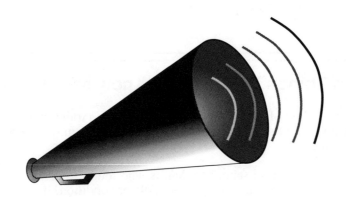

CHAPTER 8

Planning Training Activities: A Checklist

Ruby A. Licona

When planning for a training activity, whether it will be a half-day workshop or a five-day clinic, it's good to have a framework with which to start. This avoids having seemingly inconsequential, but potentially serious, details fall through the cracks. Presented here is a basic checklist which can be used as a memory-jogger by individuals planning training activities. It is intended as a reminder to use on an as-needed basis, not as an all encompassing, expert list.

NEEDS ASSESSMENT

Before planning any training activity, there are several evaluative steps that will help the trainer design training that is needed and useful. Looking around at the particular environment helps to establish both the current status and the desired status. In other words, there needs to be an assessment of the situation or context for the particular training process being planned.

- Is training needed?

- What kind of training is needed?

- What outcome or learning is desired?

- Who needs the training?

- Who can do the training?

- Is there someone in-house who can do it?

- Will an outside trainer be needed?

- Will the training be of interest to anyone outside the organization?

- What kind of funding is available?

- What are the possibilities and what are the limitations?

Once it has been established through an evaluation process that a training activity is necessary or desirable, a checklist helps to proceed in an order which ensures success. There are many details that must be considered in planning training, and a trainer is well-advised to develop a strategy to prevent losing control of some of them. Also, if a well-developed plan is being followed, it is easy to substitute changes and be aware of the impact these will have on the rest of the process. Depending on the nature and scope of the training activity, an informal run through a checklist may suffice. Something on a grander scale needs a more formal, written plan. Presented here is a very basic checklist that includes suggestions for the types of issues that need to be considered for each category.

PURPOSE

A primary concern when planning a training activity is to consider the training goals and objectives. Write a statement of the purpose(s) of the training in terms of the learning to be achieved considering three categories: gaining knowledge, changing attitudes, and learning new behaviors. Assuming that some kind of needs assessment has taken place, this section of the plan can spell out what needs to be taught, why and to whom. Describe specific, attainable, measurable objectives which are learner-focused. In other words, deal with what the learner will gain from this exercise and how her/his proficiency will manifest itself in the end.

- Briefly describe any attitudinal or proficiency changes that will occur as a result of the training, what new abilities are to be gained, and how they will be measured.

- Ensure specificity by carefully selecting action verbs that cannot be misinterpreted or misunderstood, i.e., "will be able to conduct a basic evaluation process..." rather than "will understand how an evaluation process...."

- Try to show how the objectives will meet the needs identified by the original needs assessment. How will the group or institution benefit from presenting this particular training?

RATIONALE FOR INSTRUCTIONAL APPROACH

Rationale is an explanation of why this particular training activity is being proposed for this audience at this time using these techniques. It may be stated in terms of the efficiency of the particular training approach, the level of difficulty of the topic, the improvements that could result, or other reasons for the specific activity. It is appropriate in this section to delineate the specific techniques that will be used. How, where, and when will the information be imparted? All of these details can be introduced in the rationale and elaborated on in a later part of the plan.

BUDGET

A primary consideration in planning for training activities is knowing how much money is available and exactly where it comes from. In fact, it is extremely important to have a full understanding of all budget matters before any training commitments are undertaken. If more than one institution is participating in the process, it's important to know what each one's monetary commitment is. Consider the following examples that may have an effect on the budget:

- What is the cost of the training event?

- How much money is available?

- Where is the money coming from?

- What are the spending restrictions?

- Who is authorized to spend?

- Will some of the costs be covered by registration fees?

- Is money available up-front or do receipts have to be presented for reimbursement?

- Will there be mailings that will require postage money?

- Will the budget cover clerical staff to help with any advance work?

- Does the funding restrict who can participate?

PARTICIPANTS

When deciding on a training activity, the number and type of participants are factors to consider. Regarding the number of participants:

- What are the funding constraints?

- How will participants be recruited? Selected?

- How many participants can be accepted?

Some training activities are practical for groups of a certain size and others are not, so a decision about the number of participants that can be accommodated is necessary at the outset of planning. The size of the group will determine such things as whether or not a particular technique is to be used, e.g., the logistics of getting 300 people assigned and into small-group activities are fairly formidable and might make a different learning tool or technique more desirable. Certainly the number of participants will be a deciding factor in arriving at decisions such as the size of facilities needed, the types and numbers of trainers/speakers to be used, or the kinds and amounts of supplies necessary.

Types of participants and group dynamics are also factors that should be considered in planning training. If participants are from a known group, e.g., your home institution, it is a good idea to take advantage of prior knowledge of individuals in determining group compositions. For example, if the organization is divided into feuding factions, don't plan anything that will exacerbate the situation or create further competition and animosity. Consider such things as whether it is advisable to integrate groups or create separate learning opportunities for each. Is the training of a sensitive nature such that things like ethnicity, gender, age or job classification should be a consideration in determining group composition? Of course, these variables are more easily dealt with when one is working within a particular institution. With state level activities, one can try to be aware of these factors, but cannot really do much to control for them ahead of time (unless, of course, the training activity is being planned with a particular audience in mind and registration will be limited to a particular group).

For any type of training, it is a good idea to consider ahead of time the level of experience, understanding and preparation of the participants. In some circumstances it can be very intimidating for novices to have experts taking over in a group, while, at other times, it can prove to be very useful. Consider whether a mix of experience will be useful or detrimental to the overall process. If a more homogeneous group is desired, the publicity for the training needs to be clear about who the target audience is.

TIME FOR THE ACTIVITY

An estimate of the time required for the training activity will aid in planning a particular event. This involves not only the planning for the segments of the program, but also such things as determining which dates will allow for the most participants to take part. If participants are coming from out of town, is it necessary for them to arrive the night before the program? Or, if it is a multi-day program, can some activities begin in the late afternoon or evening of the travel day? Does the day of the week selected for the program affect the kind of travel rates the participants can get?

As for planning time segments for the program, one needs to consider what kind of travel time is needed to go from room to room if there will be different activities being presented in different locations. Consider even the most mundane questions, e.g., is there enough time being allowed for breaks, and are there enough stalls in the bathrooms or will participants need to stand in lines and, therefore, need more time? Develop a day-by-day grid of all the activities that must be accounted for. Make certain that enough time is allowed for each segment, but also make certain that segments aren't too long. There needs to be enough time allowed for each presentation to address the topic, but not so much time devoted to any one thing that people will lose interest.

INSTRUCTIONAL APPROACH

When planning training activities, especially for a large group, it is important to remember that different people have different styles of learning. Try to present ideas in a variety of ways in order to meet various needs. As much as possible, plan different approaches: individual paper and pen exercises, small group discussions, larger group discussions, lectures, demonstrations, role playing, working in pairs, and/or other combinations of methods. When planning time segments, it is also important to lay out methods of presentation. Consider the content of the program and determine how best to present it. Try not to repeat methods from one session to the next. Just as it is important to not let any one topic drag on for too long, it is equally important to select techniques which are appropriate for the ideas being presented. Think about how the schedule could be changed if planned activities are not working. Consider some of the following:

> *Lecture/Speech*—Can the information best be imparted using a straight lecture format? Is the nature of the topic such that it is fact-filled and best presented by a single resource person?

> *Rebuttal Team*—If a formal lecture is presented, should there be an audience response team or a formal panel to question or respond to the resource lecturer?

> *Panel Discussion*—Is the nature of the information to be imparted such that it can be broken up and presented by several individuals and then discussed among them?

If there will be follow-up activities, what pattern will they follow?

> *Group Discussions*—Is it best to the give learners an opportunity to discuss new concepts in small group situations? Will they absorb the information better if they can discuss it immediately after they hear it?

> *Question Period*—Will there be sufficient time for individual questions and follow-up? Can these questions be voiced at any time or must they be kept until the end? Will they be asked directly or will they be screened by a moderator?

Small Group Activities—Can the new information be reinforced with specific individual involvement? Will games, role-playing, exercises and round-robin discussions or simulations strengthen the learning process? Does each group need a facilitator to keep them on task?

What kinds of learning aids will be used?

Films or Live Presentations—Is there a film available or a skit that can be used to more clearly present the new information? Are there other audiovisual aids that can be employed?

Manuals and Workbooks—What kinds of tools can the participants take away to help them remember and work through the process they have just learned?

Worksheets and Instruction Sheets—Are participants learning a new process for which they will need pictures and instructions later? What will they need help remembering?

All of the above are but a few examples of the kinds of things to consider when planning the format for a training activity. The intended audience, their learning styles, the content to be presented, and the facilities available influence the choice of format for training.

ROOM ARRANGEMENT

Different size groups and different activities require different arrangements of chairs and tables to facilitate instruction. Determine what methods of instruction will be used and then make certain that seating is arranged appropriately. If participants will need to take a lot of notes, then make certain that a classroom arrangement with comfortable writing surfaces is available. If most of the presentations are to take place at the front of the room, then don't place people at round tables where they have to crane their necks to see the speakers. On the other hand, if people are going to be assigned to groups for small group discussions/ activities, then they can be at tables in groups of six to ten. Consider whether tables are really needed for writing or holding materials, or is it better to just have chairs in a circle? Is the entire group small enough so that all the training can take place around a conference table? Or is a round table best so that participants can make eye contact? Planning a room arrangement comes down to looking at the whole situation with a very practical eye and then developing a "best-fit" environment.

SPECIAL SUPPLIES AND EQUIPMENT NEEDED

It is important to know what supplies are needed to support the suggested training—pencils, notepads, handouts, easels and newsprint pads, marking pens, masking tape, blackboards and chalk, etc. It is also good to plan for any special audiovisual equipment that may be required. If renting a facility for the activity, check the contract to see whether needed equipment can and will be provided. Is the equipment included in the price of the rental? Is there an additional charge to rent the equipment, or can you bring in your own? Finally, is the equipment in good working order?

Contact presenters to determine whether their portions of the program will create any special requirements. Enough details are needed to make certain the situation is completely covered. If funding is a problem, try to find donors for small items like pencils and note pads. Also, try to find donors to fund different segments of the program if it is appropriate in the given situation.

ADVANCE PREPARATION

For some training activities, there are things that may have to be done in advance: individuals assigned to groups, tables labeled, handouts prepared, packets collated, and supplies assembled. Plan ahead. Will there be registration packets sent out or will they be given out the day of the training? Can any of the details be included with the registration? Do participants need to be notified ahead of time to bring certain items with them? Try to plan out the logistics well enough that last minute preparations can be avoided.

As a part of advance preparation, visit the facility where the training will take place. Check details such as:

- Lighting and location of electrical outlets.

- Ventilation and temperature.

- Accessibility for the physically challenged.

- Nearness to restrooms.

- Acoustics and noise from adjoining meeting rooms.

In addition to an advance scouting trip, it's also advisable to check the room right before the event to check on such things as audiovisual equipment, correct seating arrangement, water for speakers and participants, and any other details that can potentially affect the success of the activity.

DIRECTIONS

Whether a trainer comes from within the sponsoring organization or from the outside, it is of the utmost importance that everyone involved be very clear about exactly what is expected. Step-by-step instructions are needed for how training should proceed: how the session will be introduced, what needs to happen in what order, how learning will be confirmed at the end of each session. Take steps to ensure that the trainer is fully cognizant of the goals and objectives of the training activity. Also, the needs of the trainer have to be recognized and met. Be certain to discuss all aspects of what will take place during the training so that there are no last-minute surprises. Examine all of the above points with the presenter(s) to ascertain that no important details are being overlooked. Provide trainers/speakers with full details regarding:

- Time, date and location of presentation.

- Length of presentation and specific topics to be covered.

- Nature of audience.

- Information about any special interests or needs of participants.

- Contract details—fees and expenses to be paid.

- Arrangements for travel and hotel accommodations.

- Permission to tape/publish presentation.

- Commitments of their time other than the actual presentation.

Directions for participants are also critical. Develop ahead of time a list of all the information they'll need, produce the necessary documents, and send them out sufficiently early to be effective. Are there helpful hints to provide regarding travel, hotel arrangements, availability of parking, or timetables? At the actual training, is punctuality essential? Make certain that participants understand this ahead of time. Are people to be assigned to particular groups? Will it affect the success of a session if they don't show up for their assigned groups but go with a friend to a different group instead? No instructions are too trivial to bother with if disseminating them will help ensure success for the planned training activity.

EVALUATION

It's important to determine from the outset how success of the planned training activity will be measured.
- Will there be a written evaluation?
- Will there be participant observers?

• Who is responsible for evaluation?

• To whom are evaluation results to be reported?

As well as reporting the results of a particular training activity, it is appropriate to determine what could be done differently another time and what additional activities are recommended. If good evaluation materials are developed and presented, it's that much easier to get funding and approval for the next training activity. (See Chapter 9, "The Evaluation of Continuing Education.")

REFERENCES AND FURTHER READING

Creth, Sheila D. *Effective On-the-Job Training: Developing Library Human Resources*. Chicago: American Library Association, 1986.

> Written to help avoid a "seat of the pants" approach to employee training and learning. Gives good overview of the training process and has a particularly clear and complete section on planning for training. Exercises which accompany the reading provide a useful hands-on approach to this subject.

Hart, Lois B., and J. Gordon Schleicher. *A Conference and Workshop Planner's Manual*. New York: AMACOM, 1979.

> This is an older publication; however, it contains much information that will not go out-of-date, such as room arrangements and hints for negotiating site contracts. It also provides many forms which are useful in the workshop planning process. Written for the workshop coordinator, this workbook presents a committee approach to planning workshops which can be adapted for use by an individual.

Sullivan, Maureen, ed. *Developing Library Staff for the 21st Century*. New York: Haworth Press, 1992.

> Presents chapters by various contributors. Gives good background and ideas on why training programs for library staff are important. More philosophical than hands-on in approach.

PLANNING TRAINING ACTIVITIES: A CHECKLIST

Needs Assessment—Where are the potential participants in terms of training? Where do they want to be?

Purpose—What are the goals and objectives of the particular training being proposed? What will be accomplished?

Rationale—Why is this particular training activity proposed for this audience at this time using these techniques?

Budgets—How much money is available? Where is it coming from? What are the spending restrictions? Who is authorized to spend the money?

Participants—Estimate the number and types of participants in order to determine size and kinds of facilities and supplies necessary. This will also be important in determining the trainers needed and the activities that will be appropriate for a particular group.

Time for Activity—How much time is needed for the activity and what are the related details? Are the activities planned appropriate for the amount of time available? What other time constraints need to be considered? Can the objectives be achieved within the time frame proposed?

Instructional Approach—What form will the training take in light of the topic and nature of the audience? What details of the planning will be affected by it?

Room Arrangement—What types of room arrangements are needed to facilitate instruction?

Special Supplies Needed—What supplies are needed to carry out the planned activities?

Advance Preparation—What details do trainers and participants need to be aware of ahead of time? What mailings need to be done? What equipment and supplies need to be made available?

Directions—What instructions should be given to trainers? What special instructions and needs do the trainers have? How will learning proceed? What do the participants need to know?

Evaluation—How will success be measured? How will learning be assessed? Is additional training necessary? Are there suggested follow-ups?

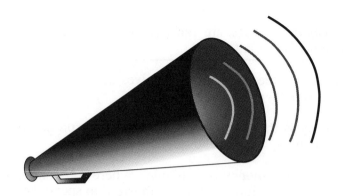

CHAPTER 9

The Evaluation of Continuing Education

Debra Wilcox Johnson

PURPOSES OF TRAINING

Training is done for a variety of reasons related to learning. When designing training activities, including evaluation of these events, it is critical to keep in focus the purpose behind each activity. Although a variety of purposes are attributed to training, they generally may be grouped into three categories: gaining knowledge, changing attitudes, and learning new behavior. These three purposes are equivalent to the categories of outcomes desired from training.

Gaining knowledge, either concepts or facts, is the most generally recognized goal of training. The level of knowledge gained varies, however, along a continuum of general orientation to a topic or issue to becoming expert in a subject. A frequently cited purpose of training is to "raise awareness," which is closer to the orientation side of this knowledge continuum. When designing evaluation of training for this purpose, the focus would be on assessing the extent of knowledge gained. The closer the purpose is toward "expert" knowledge, the more likely it is that specific knowledge gains would be documented by testing.

Changing attitudes encompasses modifying values, beliefs, or feelings. Deeply held values or beliefs will be the most difficult to change or adjust, while feelings are less strongly held points of view. Attitude change entails rethinking currently held views, introducing alternative viewpoints, or thinking or forming attitudes in areas not familiar to training participants. Related to the purpose of changing attitudes is training that is motivational or inspirational—to help create enthusiasm on an issue or for a service or product. When designing evaluation of training in this category, attention centers on differences in feeling about the topic or issue.

Learning new behavior is synonymous with gaining new skills or enhancing existing abilities. As is the case with gaining knowledge, the degree of skill change varies with the design of the training. This continuum ranges from learning the basic steps to mastery of a process or technique. The level of proficiency gained is affected by the length of the training and repetition and practice built into the training. When learning new behavior is central to the training, it may mean changing in two ways: learning the new skill and "unlearning" the old skill or habit. When learning new behavior becomes the primary training goal, the provider needs to clearly define what competencies make up the skill in order to assess the impact of the training. These new competencies or skills can be observed by evaluators or self-assessed by learners. Ultimately, application of the new skill or a behavior change in the workplace is the desired outcome from the training.

Once the primary purpose of the training is clear, then planners can talk about to what degree and in what areas the learning might occur and choose a training design that accomplishes these ends. The three categories of purposes—gaining knowledge, changing attitudes, and learning new behavior—are interrelated, but each event or portion of an event has one primary desired result. Some argue that these purposes represent stages of learning, i.e., that one must change attitude prior to changing behavior. Others argue that once a new behavior is internalized, attitudes change. There are proponents for each view, suggesting at the least there is an interdependence between the different purposes.

WHY EVALUATE?

As training opportunities have increased, many evaluation strategies (including a plethora of questionnaires) have resulted. This may have led to a common response to the question of why evaluate—"because everyone does it." While this may be restated as "it's good continuing education practice," this is not a sufficient reason by itself for doing the evaluation. The first and foremost reason for evaluating is to measure changes or impact in the three areas described in the previous section in order to improve future training events.

Providers also evaluate in order to communicate with different constituencies about the training. When measuring change, providers consider different stakeholders, such as funders, instructors, employers, and consumers. The key question in this instance is: "Who needs to know the results of the training?" If the results of the evaluation are not used or are not useful, it suggests a rethinking of the rationale behind the evaluation and the techniques being used.

Besides measuring outcomes, evaluation of training becomes a needs assessment tool. In this case, questions about future topics of interest, the design of the workshop, and location and facilities help in planning future events.

Another justification for evaluating training is to assess the match between the expectations of participants and what actually occurred. This feedback helps the trainer make adjustments in future events, either in the training or in the stated purposes of the training. The results in this kind of evaluation also serve as a check on the match between what is advertised by the provider and what is actually being delivered.

An important reason to evaluate training is to determine if the training is affecting the problem that initiated the training in the first place. This takes the trainer back to the question of the purpose(s) of the training in relation to the specific topic for the training event. This further suggests that the "true measure" of success may come from the workplace rather than at the immediate conclusion of the training.

Perhaps the ultimate reason for evaluating training is to answer a user-focused question: "Do people receive a higher quality of library service as a result of a particular continuing education activity or program?"

WHAT DO YOU WANT TO KNOW?

As suggested in the previous section, the training provider has a long shopping list of potential evaluation questions. In order to keep training evaluation focused and efficient, the provider or instructor will need to clarify what is the most important information to gather about the training event or program.

As a basic level, two categories of information may be gathered: the number and nature of participants. The latter translates into a profile of attendees along a number of dimensions. Some of the most frequently reported are: frequency of attendance at training events, level of staff (e.g., clerk, library assistant), years of education, years of library work, type of library, and gender. The provider needs to assess the value of such questions in relation to each event or in the context of an entire continuing education program.

If a desired outcome of the evaluation is change or learning, this suggests some assessment of the current state of knowledge, skills, or attitudes at the start of the training. This results in questions about perceived level prior to the training or some form of actual assessment of current levels of competency or currently held attitudes.

Course quality is a frequently used category for training evaluation. It is important for the provider, since a perception of poor quality by participants reduces the likelihood of future attendance. Quality is usually reported from two perspectives: the attendees' and the provider's. Among the factors used to define quality are: knowledge of the presenter, style of the presenter, handouts or supplemental materials, training methods used (e.g., lecture, discussion), and length in relation to the amount of information covered. Of particular concern is judgment on the content or extent of coverage and the level of the presentation for a given audience. Another useful question in this category is a comparative one: "Compared to previous workshops offered by (name of provider), how would you rate the quality of this workshop?"

As discussed in the previous section, another area for evaluation is expectation. Often this translates into a question about reasons for attending or a rating of the stated learning objectives by participants. Actually, the various stakeholders in the training have different expectations. Knowing these different expectations prior to conducting the training allows the provider to gather the needed information to speak to these different expectations. For example, the expectation of some participants may be very low since they were required by their employers to attend. In contrast, the expectation of change may be very high from the employer's standpoint. A clear match between expectations of the provider, trainer, and participants will result in the most consistent evaluation results. The more diverse the audience, the more varied will be the responses to the question of match between expectations and what was delivered.

As has been emphasized throughout this chapter, the primary category for information gathering relates to the purposes of the training. This goes back to the three areas of learning: gaining knowledge, changing attitudes, and learning new behaviors. Once the purpose(s) of the training have been clearly defined, then evaluation can occur along those dimensions. In addition, the evaluation focuses on the degree of change in any of the three categories. For example, the purpose of the training may be primarily to learn the basic steps of using electronic mail. The degree to which participants can recall the steps or demonstrate their abilities to carry out these basics is the focus for the evaluation. The kind and amount of learning that occurs is central to training evaluation.

Related to measuring learning is a question about the long-term impact of training. While participants may give very high marks for quality and demonstrate effectively their new knowledge or skills, the question remains: "What effect did the training have on the workplace?" This suggests follow-up evaluation of training or assessment by supervisors of the perceived changes as a result of the training.

Other areas for evaluation include environmental factors (e.g., room, food) and needs assessment (e.g., future topics, speakers). If evaluation does not occur immediately after the event, the overall evaluation results are less likely to be influenced by the environmental factors.

EVALUATION METHODS

Basically, the choices of training evaluation methods are the same as those for any type of evaluation: numbers gathering, questionnaires, interviews, and observation. "Testing" as a technique derives from these, as the test may be a written instrument, oral interview, or observation of a new skill. How to use these methods are discussed in the next part of the manual. This section addresses these methods in relation to continuing education.

The most frequently used method for evaluating training is the written questionnaire, usually to the exclusion of other approaches. This self-reported form of evaluation tends to use two types of questions: a rating scale and open-ended questions. In addition, sentence completion can be used to assess the impact of training. For example, "I learned the most from . . . ." or "I plan to . . . ." Asking for words descriptive of what was learned or about the quality of the training is another possible approach. The key to using questionnaires is to assess carefully what is the most important information needed in order to keep the questionnaire user friendly. Providers want to avoid this result: "What I liked least about this workshop . . . was filling out this form."

Another issue related to questionnaires is when to administer the form. If the desire is to assess participants prior to the training, an instrument might be sent to participants ahead of time or administered at the start of the training. The most frequent approach is to collect evaluation forms at the end of the training event. Another option is to mail questionnaires to participants after the event, either as a follow-up to the one used at the training or as the only form used. While the follow-up questionnaire has the advantages of filtering out some of the environmental factors and allows for participant reflection and possible application from the training, the response rate can be lower than desired. Follow-up with non-respondents by telephone can improve the response rate.

Observation is an evaluation method that can be either informal or structured. Informal observation is a natural and ongoing assessment of training. Very few providers are ever surprised by the overall evaluation results gathered in writing. Structured observation, however, details what types of behavior are being examined, such as notetaking, questions raised, or level of participation. It allows the provider or an outside observer the opportunity to listen and record behaviors of participants and the trainers in a systematic way. A participant observer (i.e., someone attending the training and assisting in evaluation) can observe unobtrusively and provide both the learner and provider viewpoints. Briefly sharing the observer's conclusions at the end of training with participants can lead to a verbal evaluation by learners in response to the observer's comments.

Interviewing is underutilized as an evaluation technique in continuing education. One form of this approach is selecting a small group of participants to "debrief" after the training. Follow-up telephone interviews can seek information about the effects of the training for a selected sample of participants. For a provider who offers a continuing education series, the focus group interview allows for assessment of the overall program, rather than of an isolated event.

Two other strategies used in training evaluation are journals and "letters to self." For longer training (i.e., longer than one day), participants are asked to keep a journal during the event. The content of the journals is used by the participant to provide information for the training evaluation (in whatever form).

The "letter to self" derives from the concept of action plans. One of the concerns of training is what happens back at the workplace after the training. Asking participants to set a plan for using the training results helps build commitment for change. As a reminder of their action plans, participants write letters to themselves, which are mailed after a set period of time to the participants. The time the letters are returned is a good time to administer a follow-up questionnaire or conduct telephone interviews, since the letter serves as an opportunity for further reflection on the impact of the training.

One issue related to methods is the question of how often does the evaluation need to occur. Does every event need to be evaluated (especially with something offered frequently) or can selected events be used for evaluation? A rotation of methods used for evaluation also supplies some variety for the provider and participants, with the potential result of more complete responses by participants or fresh perspectives for the provider. The question of frequency also relates to the timing of the evaluation. As noted above, follow-up evaluation provides a clearer picture of the longer term impacts from training. In the desire to be more efficient in evaluating training, using a sample of participants for the evaluation will reduce effort and can still provide an evaluation picture for the provider.

FACTORS AFFECTING TRAINING OUTCOMES

By considering the factors that affect the outcomes of training, the results of the evaluation can be further interpreted. The ideal would be for the provider to have total control over the outcomes; reality, however, poses a different scenario. Besides the efforts of the provider and trainer, learners and other factors contribute to the ultimate success of training events.

The provider has the most control over the design, content, and marketing of the training. Most critical is developing a format that is appropriate to the topic, meets the purposes of the training, and is adaptable and flexible in meeting learners' needs. The trainer needs to exhibit a comfort level with the style of the workshop and be fully briefed on the nature of the audience by the provider. Attention to these factors, and those elements described in the chapter, "Planning Training Activities: A Checklist," take care of the provider/trainer side of the equation for successful training.

An evaluation model that only considers the provider/trainer side, however, does not take into account the other factors that will affect the evaluation results. Among these factors are audience diversity, the match between expectations and what is delivered, and the group dynamics. The receptivity of the library to the person who returns from a training event also affects the learner's perception of the value of training. If the library exhibits a willingness to listen to or use the information from the training, this will positively affect the training outcomes. Further, environmental factors influence the evaluation results, such as the facility, location, weather, competing events, and amenities (chocolate being a highly rated one). The provider control over some of these other factors is more limited.

Finally, there are factors that relate to the learners themselves. Participant differences in preferred learning style, level of expertise in or understanding of the topic, motivation, and interest in the topic explain much of the variance in the outcomes of training. Other learner factors influencing outcomes include: what happened to participants prior to coming to the training, the ability to apply or use the information at the workplace, the reasons for attending (required vs. choice), self-awareness of the need for training, and perceived benefits of the training.

The range of learner-based factors explains why there are not "perfect" evaluations or outcomes from training. The key in the evaluation is to gather information about the most critical learner factors in order to distinguish the results of the evaluation. For example, differences in training results could be attributed to reasons for attending or interest in the topic. This comparison among groups allows the provider and trainer to rethink training strategies for individuals that exhibit some of these factors. It also broadens the view of success, since the tendency is to report only overall evaluations without consideration of learner differences.

SUMMARY

The most important ideas about evaluating training have been addressed, but it is useful to highlight the key points. Determining the purpose(s) of training is the critical first step in evaluation. From this, clarity on what outcomes are desired can be obtained. Second, the provider chooses the most useful and insightful kinds of information to collect. This may result in more efficient data collection or greater variety of information about training activities. Third, evaluators need to use a variety of methods and times to conduct the training evaluations. Finally, consider the training results in light of factors that affect those outcomes.

Along with documenting learning outcomes, changing and improving training is a desired result from the evaluation process. In order to learn from the evaluation, the process needs to be more customized to each event to answer questions related to both outcomes and improvement of training.

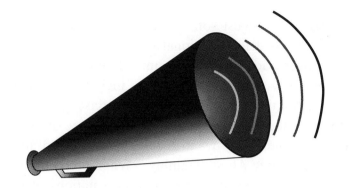

CHAPTER 10

Training Outlines and Guidelines

Debra Wilcox Johnson

Training modules are outlined in this chapter to help trainers visualize the different ways in which TELL IT! might be presented. Each of the six modules includes the following sections: a time frame, focus of training, outline of training, key readings for preparing presentation, hand-outs, overheads, and exercises. The first part of this chapter covers guidelines for training with TELL IT! as they relate to these training modules. These are derived from training experiences with TELL IT! in a variety of settings.

TRAINING GUIDELINES FOR TELL IT!

Training is not a simple matter of taking a prepared outline and notes and then presenting the information. Training blends content with the personal style, experience, and beliefs of the trainer and the nature of the learners. These proposed training modules, this manual, and other resources on evaluation serve as a starting place for a trainer. What results is much more personal than is suggested by this training packet. Customizing the outlines and content is the challenge for the

Information in this chapter is drawn from a training packet developed in May 1995 for the State Library of Florida by Debra Wilcox Johnson. Used with permission of the State Library of Florida.

trainer. Each trainer will want to use examples from state or local practice that participants will find relevant.

The training modules suggest some handouts, overheads, and exercises, but the trainer will want to explore the manual for additional possibilities. The manual includes camera-ready pages for handouts and overheads. Although a limited number of overheads were suggested, it is expected that some trainers will expand on these to include duplicates of the handouts and outlines of key points of the training. In addition to the exercises used in the training modules, other approaches can be found in the methods chapters in Part Three of the manual.

As an overview, trainers may want to read Chapter 7 on adult learning and review the "Ten Things You Already Know About Training." When preparing for any of the training modules, the manual provides the basic content for the presentations. Part One focuses on the TELL IT! model, Part Two on training in general, and Part Three on evaluation methods and training suggestions related to the methods. This section of this chapter shares additional ideas about training that have been effective in other TELL IT! workshops and presentations.

PERCEPTIONS OF EVALUATION

A discussion of the audience's perceptions of evaluation is a useful beginning, since it gives the participants a chance to air concerns early in the session (when you still can address them). A whimsical approach to this topic is to note that some people suffer from "valuephobia." This is defined as an irrational fear of evaluation, often manifested in unreasonably strong dislike or opposition to evaluation.

Possible *exercises* include:

- discussing an overhead of the list of "Some Reasons for Doing Evaluation";

- using a written instrument (for example, "Breakfast Ticket") and reporting back the results later in the workshop;

- having participants introduce themselves and say the first thing they think upon hearing the word evaluation; and

- brainstorming a list of reasons for evaluation.

The different approaches have different strengths. Use of the list as a discussion starter is interactive. A list of negatives associated with evaluation could be developed as a contrast to the more positive list provided here. This allows the trainer to speak directly to the concerns people have about evaluation.

A written form soliciting words and thoughts on evaluation makes individuals think for themselves and gives them time to reflect on the issues. It also allows for anonymity. If reported back to participants, the results can be a useful discussion starter. For a large group, randomly select a sample of responses in order to provide initial feedback to the participants quickly. Use of an exit form (see "The Key...") allows providers to compare the two sets for differences, one measure of change.

The word association exercise is much more interactive (and therefore less predictable) and helps the trainer build rapport with the group. It is often lighthearted while at the same time raises the pros and cons of evaluations. For unusual word associations there is often an "evaluation tale" connected. Sharing these "tales" gives the trainer a chance to propose alternatives or point to related topics coming up later in the training. This training starter allows the trainer to expand on points along the way, including presenting positives when the associations lean toward the negative side. This process leads to broad coverage of the topic of evaluation within the unique context of a single training event.

A brainstorming session has some of the same strengths as the word association exercise, but can be done more quickly (especially if the group is large). The brainstorming may lead to two lists—positive and negative. The trainer needs to be ready to incorporate both in the discussion. The list provided here could be used as a visual at the close of the exercise to summarize key points from the discussion.

SOME REASONS FOR DOING EVALUATION

- Someone required it

- Monitors progress to allow for program adjustment

- Provides baseline information for comparison over time

- Aids with decision making to:

  Adjust a program

  Continue a program

  Discontinue a program

  Allocate funds among programs

- It's part of planning

- Makes more systematic our natural tendency to assess

- Allows a library to affect how it is evaluated

- Aids communication with different stakeholders (i.e., staff, funders, users)

- Assures participants have a voice in a program

- Provides insight and information that can lead to answers

- Gives a fresh perspective

- Provides supporting information for grant proposals

- Gives a view of what's working and what's not

- Tests assumptions about approaches or client groups

- Documents outcomes or impacts

- Makes sense of messes

The purpose of EVALUATION
is not
to prove, but
to <u>im</u>prove.

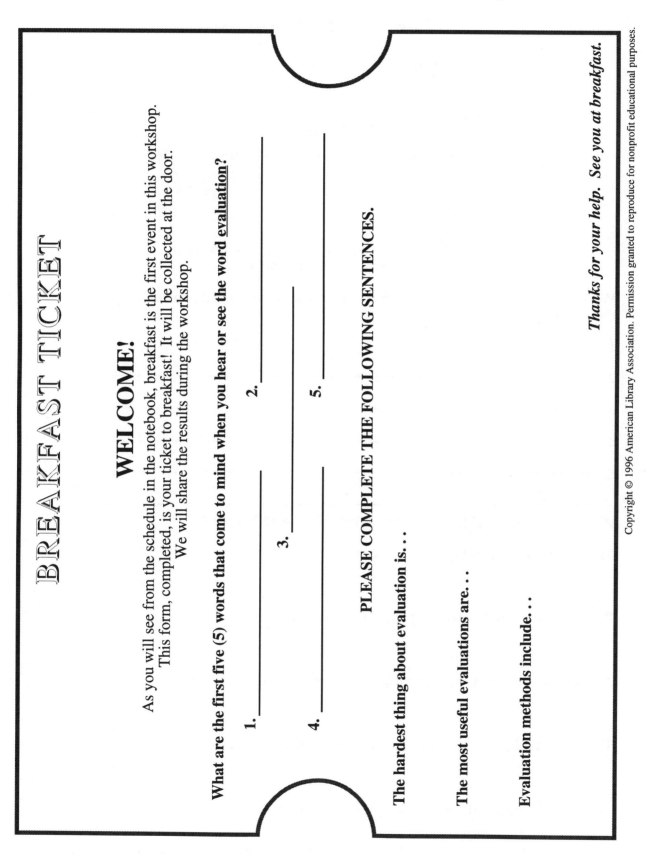

BREAKFAST TICKET

WELCOME!

As you will see from the schedule in the notebook, breakfast is the first event in this workshop. This form, completed, is your ticket to breakfast! It will be collected at the door. We will share the results during the workshop.

What are the first five (5) words that come to mind when you hear or see the word <u>evaluation</u>?

1. _____

2. _____

3. _____

4. _____

5. _____

PLEASE COMPLETE THE FOLLOWING SENTENCES.

The hardest thing about evaluation is. . .

The most useful evaluations are. . .

Evaluation methods include. . .

Thanks for your help. See you at breakfast.

THE KEY TO THE DOOR OUT!

This form will be your key to exit the final session.
It will be collected at the door as you leave.

What are the first five (5) words that come to mind when you hear or see the word <u>evaluation</u>?

1.

2.

3.

4.

5.

PLEASE COMPLETE THE FOLLOWING STATEMENTS.

My understanding of evaluation was helped by . . .

Barriers to my understanding of evaluation were . . .

An evaluation technique that caught my interest was . . .

Topics that might be included in the next workshop are . . .

What surprised me the most about this workshop was . . .

OVERVIEW OF TELL IT!

The manual provides extensive text to support this overview, as well as graphics that can be used as overheads and handouts. Chapters 1–6 and Chapter 11 provide the background information. In addition, it is useful to translate the TELL IT! model into a series of questions. One approach is:

T	Where are we going?
E	What will we do to get there?
L	Are we doing it?
L	Are we there yet?
	Who needs to know?
I	What have we learned? What changes can be made?
T	How did the planning and evaluation process work?
!	

Another useful starting point is to point out that we "naturally" evaluate all the time, e.g., what we are wearing, how well someone is doing something. The purpose of TELL IT! is to make that natural instinct more systematic and regular in order to document and communicate the library's successes.

By using the TELL IT! Framework Worksheet (p. 106), a practical *exercise* is to have individuals or a small group with similar interests complete this form. For the full day module that is organized around the steps in the model, the trainer would introduce each step and then break into small groups to work on the appropriate part of the worksheet. The groups could share back with the large group after each step or at the end of the "TELL" part of the model. The trainer will want to work through a few examples of this worksheet to be able to assist the small groups with possible responses.

STAKEHOLDER CONCEPT

Underlying the TELL IT! model is the concept of stakeholders. This means that multiple constituencies have a "stake" in the library and its services. When planning and evaluating services, it is important to keep in mind the concerns and perspectives of the various stakeholders. The ability to talk about program success in terms of different stakeholders' perspectives is part of telling the story of the library's efforts. Because you express the benefits and results of your services from their perspectives, the stakeholder feels the library speaks directly to their concerns.

The list of possible stakeholders is extensive, but the basic definition for stakeholders includes three groups: agents, beneficiaries, and victims (as defined in Egon G. Guba and Yvonna S. Lincoln. *Fourth Generation Evaluation*. Newbury Park, Calif.: Sage, 1989).

Agents—Those involved in producing and implementing—funders, decision makers, providers of supplies/materials, personnel involved in the project.

Beneficiaries—Those who benefit from services—including the targeted population(s) for a given service and indirect beneficiaries (those with relationships with beneficiaries and those who gain because the beneficiaries gain).

Victims—Those negatively affected—including groups who are excluded, those losing power or prestige, and lost opportunities. When program decisions are made, who is left out?

A quick *exercise* that can be used to illustrate this concept is to brainstorm on stakeholders for a given service or project. This can be done in the large group by calling on volunteers for suggestions. If the responses are very generic, e.g., the whole community, ask for stakeholder groups within the community.

Another useful *exercise* is to identify a list of stakeholders and then ask how each group can be motivational; the exercise can provide a powerful statement of what our communities can be. "Vision without action is just a dream. Action without vision is just spending time."—Joel Barker.

TALK ABOUT THE VISION

Providing sample vision statements can be very helpful. One readily available example is the federal National Education Goals (or Goals 2000). Check with local service groups, colleges, or public schools for other examples.

An *exercise* to use for this step is for participants to articulate possible elements of a vision statement for a community. Some possible discussion starters include: What does your community value? What do people want this community to be like? Areas to probe for include: youth, employment, environment, attitudes, politics, education, leisure, and access to services and/or information. Another way to expand a vision statement is to consider different stakeholders—what would be their main concerns for the future?

A vision is not a problem statement, but a statement of hope. It can derive from problems in the community—e.g., educational difficulties, violence, poverty—and what the library has learned about the community through needs assessment. But the vision is the desired state, as seen in the National Education Goals. It may not be immediately obtainable.

A critical point to make with participants is that the vision is not about the library directly. It is community focused, not library focused. Based on the vision for the community, the next step is to describe what the library can do to contribute to the vision of the community. This is translated into a mission and library priorities.

The most persistent error that occurs in training on the first step in the TELL IT! model is that the trainer focuses exclusively on the topic of vision. This is partly because the vision portion is a relatively recent development in planning and evaluation. In reality, this first step goes beyond vision. It includes needs assessment (community analysis) and setting priorities (goals and objectives). The key result of the "Talk about the vision" step is the determination and articulation of desired outcomes by the library. This means the library sets strategic directions for the library or for a given service. A vision statement alone, without the library-focused steps of determining desired outcomes, will make it difficult for libraries to carry out the rest of the steps in the TELL IT! model. In Chapters 1 and 11, the manual relates the TELL IT! model to the more familiar public library planning process; this may be a useful comparison for public library audiences.

Articulating the desired outcomes seems to be the hardest part of evaluation. A sample worksheet has been developed for this packet as a possible training *exercise*. Participants can select their own services or projects to work on or the trainer can use pre-prepared scenarios (see the handouts and exercise sections of the training modules).

EXPLORE ALTERNATIVES AND DESIGN YOUR APPROACH

This is a familiar part of planning for most people—what to do to achieve the desired outcomes. In grant writing, this includes the implementation and budget sections of a proposal. The key point in this step is change—or at least openness to new ways of accomplishing the library's priorities. The manual suggests that decision makers first think about what criteria to use to evaluate alternative approaches and offers a sample decision chart (p. 23). One discussion *exercise* is to ask participants to suggest possible criteria for assessing design approaches for a desired outcome, e.g., encouragement of reading families, improved reference accuracy, or reaching remote library users.

Creativity is key to this exploring step in the process. Another way to consider the wide range of potential service responses is to use a services matrix. Using Margaret Monroe's four service categories, a "Services Matrix" can be constructed to illustrate the different ways user groups can be served by the library. The four service functions are defined as:

Information—Providing information in a variety of formats, with services ranging from simple ready reference questions to information and referral services.

Advisory—Providing guidance to readers, viewers, and listeners on the selection of materials. The services range from displays and bibliographies to selective dissemination of information and bibliotherapy.

Instruction—Supports the learning mission of libraries by assisting users in becoming "information literate." This includes identifying, locating, and interpreting information. Services range from basic signage and handouts to point-of-use instruction to independent courses for credit.

> ***Stimulation***—Incorporates creating a climate of use through outreach services and accessible facilities and services and stimulating use through external public relations.

Services Matrix

	User Groups	Programming	Collections	Technology
Information				
Advisory				
Instruction				
Stimulation				

Developed by Debra Wilcox Johnson, Johnson & Johnson Consulting, 1015 Holiday Drive, Waunakee, WI 53597. (608) 849-7286.

The type of services offered in each area are affected by targeted user groups, programming, collections, and technology. From the Services Matrix, planners can fashion a unique pattern of services.

LEARN FROM WHAT'S HAPPENING

This is essentially the monitoring and formative evaluation step in the TELL IT! model. It suggests two things: 1) that evaluation information is collected throughout the life of a project or throughout a planning cycle and 2) that evaluation information can be used to help keep a project or service "on track" toward reaching the desired outcomes. The problem with evaluation in the past is that it was very centered on the "end" of a project or planning cycle. This does not allow for program adjustment and improvement throughout that period. For grant or short-term projects, the summary evaluation comes too late to redirect program activities and resources. It is sometimes necessary to collect baseline information at the beginning in order to show changes at the end of the project or planning cycle. In addition, monitoring usually includes tracking a timeline for activities and fiscal management.

LET PEOPLE KNOW WHAT HAPPENED

The trick of training in this step is to realize that two basic functions occur within this phase. First, in order to let people know what happened, a summary evaluation needs to be done. That becomes the first half of this step: determining what outcomes resulted. Based on the vision and library priorities, what actually happened? It is at this step that the trainer covers the various evaluation methods (see later section in this chapter). This is traditionally referred to as summary evaluation.

Before the library can make full use of the evaluation information, it is critical to summarize the results into easily understood and communicated forms. While the staff most closely linked to a service might want a long, detailed report, many of the stakeholders will not need or want that depth of information. Even for staff, the need is to synthesize the results into manageable units. One approach is to look for "themes" that emerge from the results. The information gathered from the various data sources and using a variety of evaluation methods can be linked together through these organizing themes or categories. It is this step—making sense of the results—that is often missed in the TELL IT! process. Without this step, use of the results is limited for decision making or communicating, and it makes it difficult to carry out the second element of this step of the model—telling the story.

The "telling the story" component is more clearly linked to the name of this step, "Let people know what happened." Since the TELL IT! model is predicated on communication with stakeholders throughout the process, the key activity here is communicating back the results of evaluation to the multiple stakeholders.

THE ROLE OF TELL IT! IN GRANT WRITING

The TELL IT! model is applicable to the whole library, a selected service, or for a grant project. In linking TELL IT! to proposal writing, consider the following outline of how it fits with different sections of a grant.

T   *Needs assessment or problem statement*—What data gathering methods were used to document need? Provide evidence of stakeholder involvement in project planning or awareness of the multiple perspectives connected to the problem or need.

   Goals and objectives—Critical to completing the evaluation section, since this contains the statements of desired outcomes. Relate goals and objectives to the stakeholders' concerns and vision for the community.

E   *Implementation and staffing*—Explore alternative approaches to meeting the need. What will be done and who will carry out the work?

   Budget—The resources to carry out the alternative chosen *and* to conduct effective evaluation.

L   *Evaluation*—Includes monitoring the project, a timeline for gathering evaluation throughout the project, and collecting baseline information at the start of the project. How will you make mid-course adjustments?

L   *Evaluation*—Results in a summary of what progress was made toward the desired outcomes. Details what methods will be used, when will the information be collected, and who is responsible for the evaluation.

        Implementation—How will the project be publicized? How will the results of the project be communicated?

I   *Project continuation*—How will it be integrated if it is successful? How does the project fit with existing services?

T   *Evaluation*—Reflect on how success was defined. What evaluation strategies were useful for documenting that success? Were results as expected?

        Project continuation—In order to continue, what adjustments to the process would be needed? Reexamine desired outcomes.

!

Using stories from grant reviewing on the weaknesses of the evaluation component can help to reinforce the value of evaluation in the grant proposal and, ultimately, in the project. The trainer can emphasize the need of the funder to have impact information to keep funding projects as further incentive for improved evaluation elements in proposals.

EVALUATION METHODS

The manual provides an overview of each of the methods, first with a summary chapter (Chapter 13) and then individual chapters on methods (Chapters 14–20). This becomes the basis for presentations about method, although for the training modules offering more in-depth coverage of the methods, additional reading may be needed. This will be affected by the trainer's own experience with each of the methods. While all the methods need to be introduced, there has been significant interest in focus groups and questionnaires. More time may be needed for these topics given the level of interest of the group.

When talking about methods, two key points can be made: 1) that the methods are not new, and 2) that although presented at the fourth step in the model, the methods are the same for needs assessment and formative evaluation. It also is beneficial to include mention of the advantages and disadvantages of each approach. Sometimes over-enthusiasm for one approach by a participant can lead to inappropriate use of a technique, i.e., it doesn't gather the kind of evaluation information needed. A key point in the presentation of methods is that not one method will work in all cases and for all stakeholders. Supplementing the presentation with actual samples of "good practice" aids understanding of the approach by participants. The manual also includes examples of the methods.

Training *exercises* in each of the methods are found at the end of each of the specific methods chapters in the manual. In addition, having small groups work from library scenarios allows for practical, hands-on application on the evaluation techniques. This can happen in two ways. One approach is to use the scenarios to develop an overall evaluation strategy. The two key questions in this exercise are: 1) what results or changes do you expect from your project or service? 2) how can you collect the information needed to document the impact of the service or project? The second approach is to present scenarios and then specify an evaluation technique to be applied. The two that work best for this are focus group interviews and fast response surveys. Sample exercises using both these approaches are included in this manual. In both cases it is critical to debrief from the small groups. The most effective approach is not to have each group share everything they did. Rather, ask each group for one or two answers or examples from the techniques they tried. Vary the kind of information asked from each group to cover the key points linked to the method or choosing appropriate methods.

For the full-day training modules, one interesting *exercise* is to assign the group to "evaluate" lunch, each using a different technique. Immediately following lunch, the group can share how they approached their assignments and reflect on the strengths and weaknesses of each approach. One side benefit of this exercise: it reinforces the need to be clear about what questions you want answered in an evaluation *prior* to collecting information. Since the assignment was only to "evaluate lunch," people will focus on different aspects, e.g., food, ambiance, service. The trainer does not want to spend a great deal of time debriefing, but it does help to reorient people following the lunch break.

Two final notes of caution about training in this area. First, just because people are familiar with a method (e.g., questionnaires) does not mean they are good at these techniques. With the more familiar techniques, the trainer needs to remind people of the weaknesses of the approach and flaws to watch for in the method. Second, proficiency in any of the methods, even in a full-day training module, is not a likely outcome. One or two-day training on each of the methods is more likely to lead to proficiency. Understanding of the basic steps of each approach and when the method might be used is a reasonable expectation from the shorter training sessions. The hands-on exercises help show the application of the method. Participants gain the basics, but need to be urged to read more about the method and to experiment with the approaches in order to build their skills in the different techniques. The manual chapters and suggestions for further reading can be helpful for this. On the plus side, participants are more aware of the alternative approaches to use and are not as reliant on only one method for needs assessment or evaluation.

Choosing Evaluation Methods

In most cases, the time is too limited for extensive discussion of this topic. Instead, this subject is interspersed with the presentations of the different evaluation methods. In the process of describing advantages, disadvantages, and uses of each method, learners are being given clues about the appropriateness of each method. For the longer training modules, the exercise on designing an evaluation strategy also requires participants to consider the issue of choosing methods. In the debriefing discussion that follows this exercise, the trainer can fold in additional comments on things to remember when choosing a method. The "Factors to Consider When Choosing an Evaluation Method" can be a handout for those modules that emphasize the evaluation methods.

SUMMARY OF KEY POINTS

With the longer training modules, there is a need to reiterate the key points covered during the training. This reinforces the learning that has already occurred and later can serve as an orienting device when participants return to their notes or begin to apply what they have learned. The points chosen for this summary are derived from the emphases placed by the trainer(s) at the event.

As a way of reinforcing the main points, the trainer can use a story or example to reinforce the key points. For example, using a story of a trip allows the trainer to explain the TELL IT! steps in a more recognizable way. Another type of story might be a quick application of the model to a specific service, so that people have a "real" example of how the TELL IT! model might work.

Two other approaches to the summary might be considered. One is to use a "participant observer." Prior to the training, someone would be asked to present a summary of the key points at the end of the event. During the training, the observer draws his/her own conclusions about the key points and then shares them with the group. If needed, the trainer can briefly expand on or highlight some of the areas noted by observer.

A second approach would be to "debrief" the audience in order to identify the key points covered that day. The trainer becomes facilitator and asks, "What are some of the key things you learned today (or were reinforced for you)?" This oral summary can be supplemented with comments from the trainer to assure that the most important elements are highlighted in this summary. This and the former approach also serve as a form of evaluation of the training. Participants are telling the trainer(s) what they found the most useful or enlightening.

TRAINING MODULES

TRAINING MODULE I
Reasons to Evaluate and Overview of TELL IT!

Time frame: One hour. Can be expanded by one-half hour for more in-depth coverage on making use of evaluation results and additional questions and discussion.

Focus of training: Module I raises awareness about the need for and value of evaluation and the necessity of communicating evaluation information. Participants will become familiar with the TELL IT! process.

Outline of training:

10	minutes	Defining success
10	minutes	General characteristics of TELL IT!
25	minutes	Overview of the TELL IT! process
5	minutes	Making use of evaluation results
10	minutes	Questions/discussion (at end or interspersed during hour)

Key readings for preparing presentation: Chapter 1
Chapter 5
Chapter 10
Chapter 11

Handouts: TELL IT! model (p. 97)
Comparison of TELL IT! with other Planning and Evaluation Approaches (p. 13)
Comparison Chart of Evaluation Methods (pp. 122–24)

Overhead: Comparison to PLA Planning Process (p. 105) [If public library audience]

Exercises: None, although if the time allowed is longer than one hour, you can query the participants on how different stakeholders might define success for the library (or a given service).

TRAINING MODULE II
TELL IT! and Grant Writing

Time frame: One hour. Can be expanded by one-half hour for more in-depth coverage on evaluation methods.

Focus of training: Module II links TELL IT! to grant writing and would most likely be used as part of a larger workshop on grants. In addition to introducing TELL IT!, the steps in the model are related to the sections of the grant proposal. This type of presentation allows for reinforcement of the need for improved evaluation strategies in grant proposals.

Outline of training:

5	minutes	Role of evaluation in grant writing
10	minutes	Overview of the TELL IT! process
30	minutes	Review of evaluation methods
5	minutes	Application of TELL IT! to the grant application
10	minutes	Questions/discussion (at end or interspersed during hour)

Key readings to prepare for presentation: Chapter 1
Chapter 13
See the section "The Role of TELL IT! in Grant Writing" in this chapter.

Handouts: TELL IT! model (p. 97)
Comparison Chart of Evaluation Methods (pp. 122–24)

Overheads: Sample evaluation tools (e.g., focus group interview schedule, fast response survey) to support overview of the methods. Draw from the manual or from examples of "good practice" in grant proposals and reports.

Exercises: None, although if the time allowed is longer than one hour, you can query the participants or brainstorm on evaluation methods that might relate to the grant categories.

TRAINING MODULE III
Overview of TELL IT! and Defining Desired Outcomes

Time frame: Half day (three hours plus break)

Focus of training: Module III centers on the first step in the TELL IT! process, "Talk about the vision." This step incorporates the decision making that is the basis for effective evaluation. Participants will become familiar with TELL IT! as an evaluation process and will enhance their abilities to develop outcome statements for library or service. Following a basic introduction to evaluation methods, participants will be able to link potential evaluation methods to desired outcomes.

Outline of training:

15	minutes	Perceptions of evaluation
30	minutes	Overview of the TELL IT! process
55	minutes	What difference will we make? Defining desired outcomes
45	minutes	Brief overview of methods to help document the desired outcomes
30	minutes	Linking evaluation methods to outcomes
5	minutes	Summary of key points
		[Questions/discussion dispersed throughout the training]

Key readings to prepare for presentation: Chapter 1
Chapter 2
Chapter 10
Chapter 11
Chapter 13

Handouts: TELL IT! model (p. 97)
Comparison Chart of Evaluation Methods (pp. 122–24)
Determining and Evaluating Desired Outcomes (p. 99)
Factors to Consider When Choosing an Evaluation Method (p. 133)

Overheads: Comparison of PLA planning process and TELL IT! (p. 105) and sample(s) of impact areas and definitions of success (see manual for suggestions or draw from examples of "good practice" from local projects).

Exercise: Use the "Determining and Evaluating Desired Outcomes" exercise in the manual. Follow the steps on the handout for an explanation of the exercise. Form small groups and have participants choose a service area for practice on at the session or pre-assign to groups. As part of the registration for the training, people can indicate their preferences for topics. Debrief the group after the first two steps of the exercise and after the third step to reinforce learning and emphasize good examples.

TRAINING MODULE IV
Choosing Evaluation Methods

Time frame: Half day (three hours plus break)

Focus of training: Module IV builds comprehension of the TELL IT! process and essential understanding of key evaluation methods for documenting progress. Participants develop the basic skills needed to select among evaluation methods.

Outline of training:

20	minutes	Perceptions of evaluation
30	minutes	TELL IT!: An introduction
80	minutes	Evaluation techniques
45	minutes	Choosing methods to document outcomes
5	minutes	Summary of key points
		[Questions/discussion dispersed throughout the training]

Key readings to prepare for presentation: Chapter 1
Chapter 10
Chapter 11
Part III, Chapters 13 and 14, using Chapters 15 through 21 as needed to supplement the information on the individual methods.

Handouts: TELL IT! model (p. 97)
Evaluation Methods chapter (pp. 113–24)
Tip sheets for each method (pp. 154, 175, 187, 212, 222, 236, 246)
Factors to Consider When Choosing an Evaluation Method (p. 133)
Developing an Evaluation Plan (p. 134)

Overheads: Sample evaluation tools (e.g., focus group interview schedule, fast response survey) to support overview of the methods. Draw from the manual or from examples of "good practice" in grant proposals and reports.

Exercises: Form small groups to conduct the exercise on developing an evaluation plan. Use the instructions as listed on the sheet.

TRAINING MODULE V
Developing Evaluation Skills

Time frame: Full day (six hours plus breaks and lunch)

Focus of training: Module V concentrates on evaluation methods. As context, participants will gain a basic understanding of the TELL IT! process and how to make use of evaluation results. Essential skills in the different techniques will be developed, and participants will have the opportunity to apply evaluation methods.

Outline of training:

20	minutes	Perceptions of evaluation
30	minutes	TELL IT!: An overview
180	minutes	Evaluation techniques
75	minutes	Choosing evaluation methods
45	minutes	Telling the story with evaluation information
10	minutes	Summary of key points
		[Questions/discussion dispersed throughout the training]

Key readings to prepare for presentation: Chapter 1
Chapter 5
Part III, Chapters 13 through 21
Supplement with readings from the bibliography
    as needed.

Handouts: TELL IT! model (p. 97)
Chapter 13 and comparison chart (pp. 122–42)
Tip sheets for each method (pp. 154, 175, 187, 212, 222, 236, 246)
Factors to Consider When Choosing an Evaluation Method (p. 133)
Focus Group Interviews (p. 186)
Fast Response Questionnaires (p. 160)
Developing an Evaluation Plan (p. 134)

Overheads: Sample evaluation tools (e.g., focus group interview schedule, fast response survey) to support overview of the methods. Draw from the manual or from examples of "good practice" in grant proposals and reports.

Exercises: Designing a focus group interview schedule or a fast response survey. The principle behind this exercise is to give hands-on experience in the design of these kinds of evaluation tools. See exercise handouts for description of steps. Also can use the "Developing an Evaluation Plan" exercise. This exercise allows participants to build skills in linking desired outcomes and evaluation methods. See exercise handout for description of steps.

TRAINING MODULE VI
Applying TELL IT!

Time frame: Full day (six hours)

Focus of training: Module VI allows participants to internalize the steps of TELL IT! Participants gain the ability to apply the full TELL IT! process to the library or a specific service, while gaining a basic understanding of the evaluation methods.

Outline of training:

15	minutes	Why evaluate?
15	minutes	Introduction to TELL IT!
80	minutes	Talk about the vision
45	minutes	Explore alternatives and design approach
25	minutes	Learn from what's happening
140	minutes	Let people know what happened
15	minutes	Integrate the results
15	minutes	Think about how it worked
10	minutes	Summary of key points
		[Questions/discussion dispersed throughout the training]

Key readings to prepare for presentation: Part I of manual, Chapters 1 through 6.
Chapter 11. This chapter includes suggestions
for training at each step of the process.
Chapter 13
Review of methods chapters in Part III as
needed to support your presentation.
Review relevant sections of *Planning and Role
Setting for Public Libraries.*

Handouts: TELL IT! model (p. 97)
Chapter 13 and comparison chart (pp. 122–42)
Tip sheets for each method (pp. 154, 175, 187, 212, 222, 236, 246)
TELL IT! Framework Worksheet (p. 106)
Determining and Evaluating Desired Outcomes (p. 99)
Factors to Consider When Choosing an Evaluation Method (p. 133)
Services Matrix (p. 76)

Overheads: Comparison of the PLA planning process with TELL IT! (p. 105), the decision chart (p. 23), and samples of methods from manual or other "good practices."

Exercises: This training uses the TELL IT! Framework Worksheet as an ongoing exercise throughout the workshop, with an opportunity to work on the T, E, and second L steps of the model. Small groups can choose service areas or be pre-assigned. As part of the registration for the training, people can indicate their preferences for topics. The trainer will have the small groups work after an introduction to each of the steps in the model. The "Determining and Evaluating Desired Outcomes" can be used as a supplement to the first and fourth steps in the model. It is recommended that the trainer debrief after "Talk about the vision" and "Let people know what happened," using examples from the groups to reinforce the key points at each of these two critical steps. Following the "Explore alternatives" step, the trainer can ask for a few comments or questions on the process, rather than spend extensive time for discussion.

CHAPTER 11

Training in the TELL IT! Approach

Douglas Zweizig

The TELL IT! planning and evaluation approach is much like a pilot's preflight checklist. That is, TELL IT! provides reminders to those engaged in planning and evaluation that can help prevent common planning and evaluation errors, such as failing to define the purpose and therefore not being able to evaluate the effects, or seizing on a particular activity or solution before clarifying the difference you want to make. The purpose of training in the TELL IT! approach is

- to help participants understand the significance of the steps,

- to enable them to apply the steps in practice, and

- to help them to internalize the steps so that TELL IT! functions as an automatic framework whenever planning of programs and services occurs.

The familiarity with the steps begins to occur with the first introduction of the TELL IT! approach. The material for communicating this is provided in Part One of this manual, particularly in the first chapter in which the approach is introduced, a rationale for using the approach is provided, the steps are explained, features of this approach are listed, and a comparison with other familiar planning and evaluation approaches is made. The figure on page 97 of this manual can be reproduced as a handout or overhead transparency to introduce the approach. In addition, the "Terms Used in the TELL IT! Approach with Examples" graphic found on page 98 can be used as a handout, a transparency or transparencies, or as the basis for a presentation to illustrate how the approach works with some example program and service areas.

The most difficult part of planning is specifying the outcomes that are intended to result from activities. The exercise, "Determining and Evaluating Desired Outcomes," (page 99) focuses attention on the areas in which impact is desired, the nature of success in those areas, and the means to collect evidence of success. The exercise is intended to be used at several points in the course of a TELL IT! workshop.

The examples on "Measuring the Impact of Regional Library Services" (Examples A through D) and "Measuring the Impact of Public Library Services" (Examples E through H) were developed by Sandra Nelson of the Tennessee State Library and Archives for use in training in that state. These examples can be studied to prepare to instruct others in applying TELL IT!; some could be duplicated or adapted as examples for participants.

Page 104, "Ends and Means in TELL IT!," provides an illustration of the relationships between ends and means in the first four steps of the TELL IT! approach. "Talk about the vision" refers to the intended end of the program or service while "Let people know what happened" reports on the achieved end of the project. "Explore alternatives and design approach" deals with the intended means of carrying out the program or service, and "Learn from what's happening" documents the achievements of the means. Participants may have questions about the relationship between the planning model in *Planning and Role Setting for Public Libraries* and the TELL IT! approach. The graphic on page 105, "Planning Cycles: *Planning and Role Setting for Public Libraries* and TELL IT!," shows the planning steps in the *Planning and Role Setting* planning cycle and how the steps of TELL IT! compare. While the steps do not match exactly, the overall logic of the planning and evaluation approaches is similar for each.

While a lecture or reading can be used to introduce TELL IT! to participants, other chapters in Part Two remind us that adults learn in a variety of ways and that lectures and readings have limited effectiveness. This chapter provides a number of additional ways of helping participants in training to be able to apply the TELL IT! approach in practice. Understanding of the approach will be aided by the use of a feedback form that participants can fill in after being introduced to the model. This form asks participants to consider each step and to suggest examples or applications of the step and to identify areas that need clarification. Then it asks for some overall reactions to the approach.

This sheet should be provided as a work form with white space after each of the indented lines. Trainers can review these forms in order to learn of suggestions that participants have and to identify the areas that need clarification in the next session.

TELL IT! APPROACH FEEDBACK SHEET

Talk about the vision

The difference we want to make is....

For these reasons....

> *Additional ways of explaining this step or examples to use:*
> *Things to clear up:*

Explore alternatives and design your approach

The best way to do this would be....

For these reasons....

> *Additional ways of explaining this step or examples to use:*
> *Things to clear up:*

Learn from what's happening

The way we'll check on progress is....

We can correct for problems by....

> *Additional ways of explaining this step or examples to use:*
> *Things to clear up:*

Let people know what happened

The way we'll document the difference we've made is....

We'll communicate the difference by....

> *Additional ways of explaining this step or examples to use:*
> *Things to clear up:*

Integrate results with ongoing services

We'll take what we learned and relate it to the library as a whole by....

The best way to integrate learnings would be....

> *Additional ways of explaining this step or examples to use:*
> *Things to clear up:*

Think about how it all worked

Improvements to be made in performance....

Improvements to be made in planning....

> *Additional ways of explaining this step or examples to use:*
> *Things to clear up:*

Thoughts on the overall approach

> *I think the TELL IT! approach will help to:*
> *The biggest remaining question I have about TELL IT! is:*

Groups that have some familiarity with TELL IT! might be asked to suggest tips or reminders for those using the TELL IT! steps. At a workshop, participants were divided into six small groups with each group given some examples of possible tips for using TELL IT! and asked to think of others for the use of one of the TELL IT! steps. Below is the list of what the groups reported.

TELL IT! Tips

Talk about the vision

- Think about what will be different for the clients

- Brainstorm possible visions

- Prioritize alternative visions

- Brainstorm with a variety of groups/stakeholders/cooperating agencies

- Distinguish between vision and mission

- Agree on definition of vision (talking about vision? or a problem?)

- Make benefits of clear vision obvious

- Make understandable to different parties; avoid jargon

- Have info about community to help determine "appropriate" vision

- Think about what your "bottom line" is

- Remember you need "buy-in" with vision

- Think: about users/new users, "big," "different," "inspiring"

- Link values to vision: make the implicit explicit

- In thinking about the vision, it may be possible to use sentence completions, such as:

    "A good public library is/concentrates on _____."

    "A good public library user is _____."

    "My library is most like a _____, but if I had my way it would be a _____."

Explore alternatives and design your approach

- Use nominal group technique to generate a list of alternative approaches

- Think of the criteria that might be used by different stakeholders to evaluate alternatives

- KISS: Keep It Simple Stupid; doesn't have to be complicated; consider ease

- Create matrix

- Prioritize consideration

- Create scenarios of possible futures

- Consider unique aspects of the community (e.g., multilingual)

- Consider what worked before and why

- Discuss alternatives/designs with key informants from community

- Be up-front about what you may have to give up to do alternative; tradeoffs

- Identify barriers (eg., tight deadlines); Identify resources (e.g., staff)

- Identify current focus and compare with where you want to be—the difference may point to an alternative

Learn from what's happening

- Put regular appointments in your calendar for when progress will be monitored

- Think about who can best tell you how things are going; delegate monitoring and reporting back clearly (get to people doing tasks)

- Think about what's working and what's not working

- Consider what may have changed (contextually) that requires rethinking means/ends

- Talk to customers about what they think is happening/what they are learning

- Allow all individuals involved to express in their own terms what's been learned and develop group consensus

- Collect appropriate, measurable and concise data

- "Listen to what you hear; look at what you see"

- Reassure that change is OK—learning is expected—fine tuning is good —"learning is our friend"

- Monitoring ability of staff to change/adapt to improve project

- Avoid micro-planning of whole project—identify phases, detail first couple of steps, check in later and plan further

- Plan to have a "Rah-Rah" session (motivational meeting) at the low point in "roller coaster" of change (initial excitement worn off, "needs" of daily work drowning you—could be a lot of friction)

Let people know what happened

- Think about what will be evidence of working toward the vision

- List which people need to learn of what happened

- Think about various ways to inform different stakeholders

> Media—all forms
>
> Newsletters
>
> Annual reports
>
> Interagency meetings
>
> General networking—talk it up ("each one tell one" model)
>
> National library literature
>
> Conference
>
> Teleconference
>
> Poster sessions
>
> Posting to LIBNET or statewide network
>
> Sell it with TELL IT!

Integrate results with ongoing services

- When designing the project, plan how it can be integrated if successful

- Think about who needs to be involved to make integration occur

- Identify which aspects of project/service were successful/should be integrated

- Ask where does project/service fit within existing programs/library/community

- Raise awareness of project—both internally and externally

- Rotate "regular staff" into "project staff"

- Weed unneeded projects/services to make room for the new

- Get project on the agenda; keep it in focus

- Add to your goals and objectives/long range plan/budget

- Be "realistic in planning"

- Be able to articulate clear vision

- Be able to articulate how project is a *replacement* or *enhancement*

Think about how it all worked

- Reflect on what "success" means for this project

- List things to remember for the next time you conduct a project

- If to be continued, what changes need to be made (brainstorm adaptations)

- Review materials used

- Think back to beginning—are results expected?

- Get input on project from different perspectives (staff, users, funders)

- Identify possible future projects that "branch off" from current project

- Reexamine objectives—were they real?

- (Re)Examine external factors you didn't anticipate

- Reflect on how results affect vision/long and short goals

- Make time for reflection

- Make up "next time" sticky notes to tag documents for next planning session

- Celebrate

- Review "results" again at later date…and again at a much later date

---

Small groups, made up of three to seven people, are an ideal setting for applying newly learned concepts. Small groups can be given the assignment of filling in a TELL IT! Framework Worksheet (on p. 106) for a particular area of program or service focus, such as services to prisons or to support a particular unit of a curriculum. The area of focus can be assigned to the group, or the group can select an area as its first task. The group task is then to start at the top of the form and to fill it in with a particular program or service in mind.

For purposes of learning TELL IT!, the groups should try to quickly decide on an area to make a difference. In using TELL IT! to plan actual services in a library, the discussion of just what difference the library seeks to make can be lengthy, but in the training setting, more of the time should be spent trying out all of the steps of the approach. Groups can fill in all but the last step, "Think about how it all worked," at this time. Being reminded of the last step at the beginning, however, increases the likelihood that the learning from carrying out the plan will be used to improve performance and planning.

As groups are working to fill out the worksheets, the trainer(s) should circulate among the groups to listen to discussions, to clarify instructions, and to sense when the groups are done. After groups have filled in their worksheets, they may share the plans with one another in a large group session. The more important learning to reinforce, however, is the experience with the approach. The trainer should ask some of the same questions that appear on the TELL IT! Approach Feedback Sheet:

"In what ways did the TELL IT! approach help you in planning this service?"

"At which points did you bog down? What helped you progress?"

"Where did you have disagreements about what the TELL IT! approach intended?"

"In what areas did you feel the need for additional guidance from the approach?"

An alternative exercise for applying TELL IT! in a workshop setting is planning and evaluating the experience in attending a workshop or conference. Page 107 provides a TELL IT! worksheet that has been adapted for this purpose. This exercise can be done as an individual exercise with the trainer asking for example visions, approaches, and observations. For groups who are acquainted with TELL IT!, the form could be sent at the time of preregistration. Some coaching tips for helping people fill this out:

- In thinking about the vision for attending the conference, consider who cares about what you get out of the conference: the stakeholders.

- In exploring alternatives, brainstorm a number of quite different approaches; deliberately list an alternative that's whimsical, such as "sitting in the hotel lobby to see who comes by." It's important to be creative in generating alternatives, to have a rich list of candidate approaches.

- For learning from what's happening, think about how often to check for progress.

- At each step of the worksheet, be sure to check back with the vision to ensure that the activities and evaluation match the original intent.

Pages 108 and 109 contain instructions and a form for an exercise in exploring alternatives and designing an approach. This is best done as a small group exercise. A minimum of an hour should be allowed for the determination of a vision, the identification of alternative means to approach that vision, the evaluation of these means against selected criteria, and the selection of an approach to take. The groups should be reminded that the purpose of the exercise is to try out the process and that the particular area of service is relatively unimportant. To support discussion, groups should be given newsprint pads on easels. Group recorders can be given a blank chart on transparency material and a pen for recording the group's decisions for presentation to the large group. Discussion in the large group can focus on what things the facilitator did to assist the process of the group, what hints could be offered to other groups making similar decisions, whether the approaches decided upon were superior to the ones that came first to mind for providing service in this area of vision.

A final group or individual exercise would involve taking a plan or proposal for a library program or service and analyzing it for the information called for in TELL IT! For example, the proposal could be searched for information to complete the sentence in the first step, "The difference we want to make is…." and then for information to complete the second question, "For these reasons…." The discussion could address not only what information is present in the proposal but what kinds of information might be provided to fill in the sentences. By working with real examples, the TELL IT! approach can be tested for its applicability, and the participants can also increase their sense of how evaluation fits within the parts of a standard proposal. Again, large group discussion questions can center on how the TELL IT! approach helped in analyzing a proposal, in calling attention to needed information, and in ensuring that the proposal could speak to the impact of the program or service.

TELL IT!
A Framework for Planning and Evaluation

T alk about the vision

The difference we want to make is:

For these reasons:

E xplore alternatives and design your approach

The best way to do this would be:

For these reasons:

L earn from what's happening

The way we'll check on progress is:

We can correct for problems by:

L et people know what happened

The way we'll document the difference we've made is:

We'll communicate the difference by:

I ntegrate the project with on–going services

The way this project will relate to the library as a whole is:

T hink about how it all worked

Improvements to be made in performance:

Improvements to be made in planning:

!

TERMS USED IN THE TELL IT! APPROACH WITH EXAMPLES

Term	Definition	*Example 1*	*Example 2*
Vision	A desired state of affairs; has a societal focus	*Community residents will find information they need to function fully in society.*	*Creation of a learning society. Children have a joy of learning.*
Role	An image for a library service emphasis	*Independent Learning Center*	*Preschoolers' Door to Learning*
Mission	The business the library is in: its purpose & priorities	*This library will assist the needs of our citizens for prompt and accurate information.*	*This library seeks to instill in children a love of learning.*
Goal	A direction in which the library wants to proceed	*To provide our users the information they need when they need it.*	*All children entering school will be ready to learn.*
Objective	How far the library intends to proceed— •measureable, •attainable, •understandable, •time based	*To increase Subject Fill Rate from 75% to 85% by July 1, 199_.*	*To increase by September 1, 199_ the percentage of children entering school ready to learn from __% to __%.*
Inputs	Resources used to provide a service	*Book collection Staff training*	*$ for HeadStart # of preschool programs # of children's services staff*
Process	Activities carried out to produce outputs	*Selection procedures Staff practices*	*Enrollment in preschoolers' program Integration with other programs*
Outputs	Measures of the amount of service provided	*Title, Subject & Author, and Browsers' Fill Rates*	*# completing preschoolers' program # of preschoolers attending programs*
Impact	How things have changed for the users or in the community	*Users report that they are more effective in fulfilling community, occupational, or family roles because of info obtained through the library. People in speeches give the library credit for providing info for speeches or otherwise supporting success.*	*1st grade teachers can begin at a more advanced level. Fewer children kept back from progressing to 2nd grade. Parents report that children are excited about learning.*

DETERMINING AND EVALUATING OUTCOMES

This exercise allows you an opportunity to develop a basic outline of an evaluation plan for a specified service or project. This process involves three components:

1) determine areas of impact for a given project or service,

2) define success for each of these impact areas, and

3) identify evaluation methods to document the desired outcomes.

There is not a "science" to completing the first two steps in this exercise. Some questions to consider in the process of completing these steps are listed below.

- What are possible impact areas? Some possibilities include:

    User/participant behaviors

    User/participant attitudes

    User/participant knowledge

    Staff behaviors, attitudes, and knowledge

    Collaboration

    Use of library services and/or collections

- What difference will your project make for users? For the community? For the library?

- Consider the different stakeholders of your project or service. How would each group define success for this service or project?

- Sentence completion can be helpful here. Three possibilities:

    Good *name of service or project* is _____

    Name of service or project currently is _____

    Name of service or project will be _____

FOLLOWING THE PRESENTATION ON "What difference will we make?"....

1. List the possible areas of impact for a given project or service.

2. Define success for each of these impact areas. Be specific about the outcomes desired in each of these areas. There may be more than one outcome for each impact area. For planning purposes, these can translate into goals and objectives.

FOLLOWING THE OVERVIEW OF EVALUATION METHODS....

3. Link evaluation methods to each impact area that can document the desired outcomes.

Developed by Debra Wilcox Johnson, Johnson & Johnson Consulting, 1015 Holiday Drive, Waunakee, WI 53597. (608) 849-7286.

MEASURING THE IMPACT OF REGIONAL LIBRARY SERVICES

	Example A	*Example B*
Community need	*People in non-metropolitan areas do not have convenient access to all of the information they need.*	*Geographically isolated Tennesseans do not have easy access to recreational and informational print materials.*
Vision	*All citizens of Tennessee have the information they need to function effectively in society.*	*All citizens will have access to materials they need to meet their recreational and informational needs.*
Role	*Library Development*	*Direct Service*
Mission	*The Tennessee Regional Library System will assist local/county governments to establish public library services.*	*The Tennessee Regional Library System will provide books and materials to areas unserved by public libraries.*
Service goal	*Every Tennessean will have access in his/her county to a full-service library that meets the state standards.*	*Citizens in geographically isolated parts of the state will have reasonable access to materials which meet their recreational and educational needs.*
Objective	*By 1997/98, 80% of the libraries in this region will meet or exceed the standards for their service populations.*	*By 1997/98, 90% of the people living more than 20 minutes from a public library in this region will have easy access to a deposit collection of materials.*
Evaluation method	*Analysis of public library statistics.*	*Analysis of library locations and bookmobile stops.*
Impact being measured	*Number of regional residents who have access to a full-service library that meets standards.*	*Percentage of regional residents who have convenient access to basic library materials.*
Activities	• *Identify the libraries that do not meet standards.* • *Recruit teams of one staff member and one trustee from each such library to be responsible for coordinating the library development plan.* • *Plan regional and state training for the development teams.*	• *Identify areas that are more than 20 minutes from a public library.* • *Locate an appropriate site for the deposit collection.* • *Determine the types of materials the users of the collection want/need and select them.*

SOURCE: Sandra Nelson, Tennessee State Library and Archives

MEASURING THE IMPACT OF REGIONAL LIBRARY SERVICES

	Example C	*Example D*
Community need	*People in non-metropolitan areas do not have convenient access to all of the information they need.*	*Geographically isolated Tennesseans do not have easy access to recreational and informational print materials.*
Vision	*All citizens of Tennessee have the information they need to function effectively in society.*	*All citizens will have access to materials they need to meet their recreational and informational needs.*
Role	*Library Development*	*Direct Service*
Mission	*The Tennessee Regional Library System will assist local/county governments to establish public library services.*	*The Tennessee Regional Library System will provide books and materials to areas unserved by public libraries.*
Service goal	*Every Tennnessean will have access in his/her county to a full-service library that meets the state standards.*	*Citizens in geographically isolated parts of the state will have reasonable access to materials which meet their recreational and educational needs.*
Objective	*By 1997/98, the per capita support from local sources for public library services will have increased 20%, from $___ to $___ in this region.*	*During 1997/98, circulation of materials from deposit collections in geographically isolated areas will increase from 5% of overall regional circulation to 7% of the overall regional circulation.*
Evaluation method	*Per capita allocation from local sources.*	*Percentage of overall circulation.*
Impact being measured	*Local support for libraries.*	*Use of materials in deposit collections.*
Activities	• *Work with each library board to develop a long-range plan to increase funding.* • *Help local library staff develop PR materials.* • *Train library staff and board members to make effective budget presentations.*	• *Develop and administer a reader's interest survey to users at deposit stations.* • *Revise the bookmobile collection development plans in response to survey results.*

SOURCE: Sandra Nelson, Tennessee State Library and Archives

101

MEASURING THE IMPACT OF PUBLIC LIBRARY SERVICES

	Example E	*Example F*
Community need	*Children and young adults are not learning the skills they need to function effectively in a global economy.*	*Many children enter school without the skills they need to succeed.*
Vision	*All children and young adults will receive a quality education and graduate with the skills required to succeed personally and professionally.*	*All children will develop the social and language skills they need to succeed in school.*
Role	*Formal Education Support*	*Preschooler's Door to Learning*
Mission	*The library will assist children and young adults to meet their educational objectives.*	*The library will encourage young children to develop an interest in reading and learning.*
Service goal	*Children and young adults will have the information they need when and where they need it.*	*Children in "at risk" homes or otherwise unserved will be identified and given the special attention they need to succeed.*
Objective	*During 1997/98, the percentage of children and young adults who use the public library to find information needed to complete their homework will increase from 15% to 25%.*	*During 1997/98, 50% of the preschool children whose mothers receive ADC will attend at least one program sponsored by the library (on- or off-site).*
Evaluation method	*Fast response survey in schools in the spring of 1998.*	*Output Measure: Program Attendance per Capita (modified to measure mothers who receive ADC and not the entire population of the service area).*
Impact being measured	*Increase in the number of children and young adults finding the homework help they need at the library.*	*Increase in the number of "at risk" preschool children who are introduced to the pleasures of reading through library programming.*
Activities	• *Meet with teachers and school media personnel to encourage them to tell the library about upcoming assignments.* • *Visit the schools to encourage students to use public library resources to complete their homework.* • *Design and administer the fast response survey.*	• *Determine the number of mothers who receive ADC.* • *Determine locations for the planned programs that would be most convenient for the target audience.* • *Work with the appropriate agencies to publicize the program.* • *Plan and present programs that will encourage mothers to read to their children.*

SOURCE: Sandra Nelson, Tennessee State Library and Archives

MEASURING THE IMPACT OF PUBLIC LIBRARY SERVICES

	Example G	*Example H*
Community need	There are too few cultural and re-creational activities for the residents of the community.	In a rapidly changing environment, people have difficulty updating their skills and knowledge.
Vision	All people in the community will have the recreational and cultural opportunities they need to enhance the quality of their lives.	All people in the community will have the information they need to succeed personally and professionally in a rapidly changing environment.
Role	Popular Materials Center	Independent Learning Center
Mission	ʟe library features a variety of current high-demand, high interest materials in a variety of formats.	The library supports individuals pursuing a program of learning independent of any formal education provider.
Service goal	Residents will have the materials they need to support their recreational and cultural needs.	Residents will have the materials they need to support their independent learning activities.
Objective	During 1997/98, 90% of the people who use the library "looking for something interesting" (browsing) will find something that meets that definition.	During 1997/98, 75% of the people who use the library will find materials on the subject they are looking for.
Evaluation method	Output Measure: Browsers' Fill Rate	Output measure: Subject Fill Rate
Impact being measured	Percentage of library users who find materials that meet their recreational or cultural needs.	Percentage of library users who find materials they need to support their independent learning activities.
Activities	• Weed the fiction collection regularly. • Create attractive displays highlighting new or interesting books. • Use circulation figures as a guide for allocating materials budgets. • Consider shelving genre books together (mysteries, etc.). • Prepare bibliographies with the theme "If you liked _____ try these books."	• Provide users with a computerized library catalog that includes both local and statewide holdings. • Use circulation figures and Interlibrary Loan (ILL) requests as guides when allocating the materials budget. • Publicize ILL as a method for obtaining materials not owned locally.

SOURCE: Sandra Nelson, Tennessee State Library and Archives

ENDS AND MEANS IN TELL IT!

	Intentions	Achievements
Ends	Talk about the vision	Let people know what happened
Means	Explore alternatives and design your approach	Learn from what's happening

PLANNING CYCLES:
Planning and Role Setting for Public Libraries
and TELL IT!

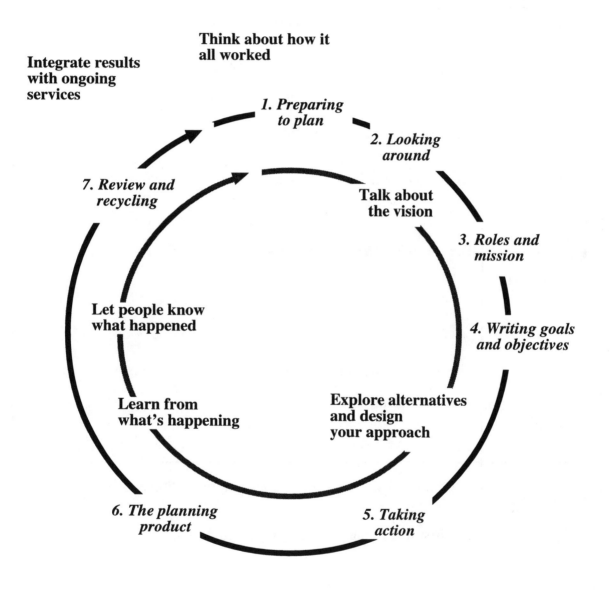

Think about how it all worked

Integrate results with ongoing services

1. Preparing to plan

2. Looking around

7. Review and recycling

Talk about the vision

3. Roles and mission

Let people know what happened

4. Writing goals and objectives

Learn from what's happening

Explore alternatives and design your approach

6. The planning product

5. Taking action

TELL IT! FRAMEWORK WORKSHEET

	AREA OF FOCUS: _____
Talk about the vision	The difference we want to make is… For these reasons…
Explore alternatives and design your approach	The best way to do this would be… For these reasons…
Learn from what's happening	The way we'll check on progress is… We can correct for problems by…
Let people know what happened	The way we'll document the difference we've made is… We'll communicate the difference by…
Integrate results with ongoing services	We'll take what we learned and relate it to the library as a whole by… The best way to integrate learnings would be…
Think about how it all worked	Improvements to be made in performance… Improvements to be made in planning…

TELL IT! WORKSHEET FOR PLANNING AND EVALUATING A WORKSHOP OR CONFERENCE

Talk about the vision	The difference I want to make with this workshop (conference) is…
Explore alternatives and design your approach	Four ways to do this are: • • • • The best way to do this would be…
Learn from what's happening	The way I'll check on progress is…
Let people know what happened	How I can document the difference my attending the workshop (conference) made: How I can communicate that difference: To whom:
Integrate results with ongoing services	The way this workshop (conference) experience will relate to my work as a whole is:
Think about how it all worked	Thoughts on how to improve this process of planning and evaluation:

EXPLORE ALTERNATIVES AND DESIGN YOUR APPROACH: AN EXERCISE IN CHOICES

1. Select someone from the group to be the group facilitator. That person's job will be to keep the discussion on track, to ensure participation by all group members, and to confirm group decisions so that the group can move on.

2. Select a second person from the group to be a recorder/reporter. That person's job will be to keep a record of decisions made by the group, to fill in the transparency chart, and to be prepared to be called on to provide a narrative for the chart.

3. The group should take about ten minutes to select an area of vision to pursue for this exercise. It will be best to keep this vision modest and as well defined as possible. It may help to think of the vision as "the difference we want to make…."

4. After the vision has been agreed upon and written down, members should individually take five minutes to think of approaches to achieving that vision. This is the time to be imaginative; later you can evaluate feasibility and acceptability to others. Each person should try to think of at least three approaches.

5. Have each person read off their list of three approaches and make a master list of all the approaches mentioned. Save any discussion of approaches until all have been listed.

6. Discuss the set of approaches and identify a set of five for further consideration. If the group can not easily reduce the alternatives, have each person list their top two choices on sheets of paper and take the five with the most votes. The discussion and selection of approaches should take about ten minutes. List the selected approaches on the chart.

7. Discuss what five criteria should be used to evaluate the selected approaches. The discussion should focus on what characteristics group members think would be most important in assessing these alternative approaches. List the selected criteria at the head of the columns of the chart.

8. Rate each of the alternative approaches against the selected criteria. Fill in the rating for each criterion as you go. After all of the approaches have been rated against each of the criteria, the group should consider the outcome and whether any changes should be made.

9. Based on the final ratings on the criteria, select an approach (or combination of approaches) to use in approaching your vision. Place a star by the approach(es) on the chart.

EXPLORE ALTERNATIVES AND DESIGN YOUR APPROACH

Use this chart to rate alternative approaches against the key criteria.

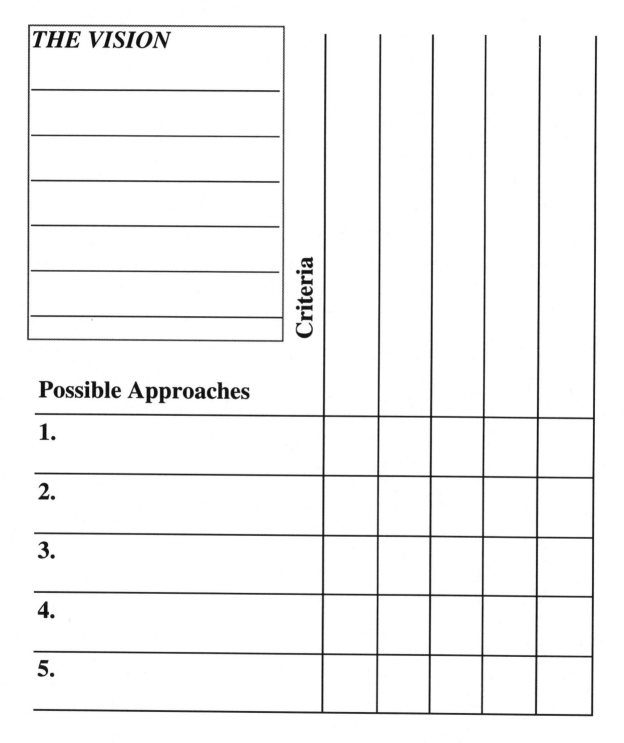

THE VISION

Criteria

Possible Approaches

1.					
2.					
3.					
4.					
5.					

PART THREE

Evaluation Methods
and Training Materials

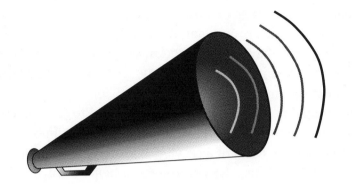

CHAPTER 12

Evaluation Methods

Debra Wilcox Johnson

Techniques for evaluation are drawn from traditional data gathering approaches used in research. Evaluators draw from a repertoire of approaches to choose a technique or combination of techniques appropriate to a given situation. This chapter provides a brief overview of the most common evaluation methods, such as questionnaires, interviews, numbers-gathering, and observation.

Another way to group evaluation methods is to consider the source of the information: self-reported, collected from others, and use of written records. These categories cross over the techniques used in this chapter.

No one method is recommended over another. Instead, an evaluation effort can include a number of techniques over the life of a service or project. All the methods are complementary.

QUESTIONNAIRES

As one of the most prevalent techniques used for data gathering, questionnaires are familiar to most librarians. Questionnaires are used to elicit either written or oral responses. In gathering questionnaire responses orally, the questions are asked in person or over the telephone, and responses are recorded by the interviewer.

The questionnaire method can be used to gather information in the three categories noted earlier: self-reported, from others, or reported from records. In one case, participants may be asked to describe their own behaviors or attitudes, while in another, the participants are asked to describe the behavior of others in the group. For the third category, the librarian uses program attendance records or circulation statistics to answer questions.

While the technique is widely used, evaluators need to take special care in deciding to use a questionnaire for evaluation. One important issue is the distribution strategy. If information is needed primarily from existing users of a service, questionnaires could be administered on-site as an entrance or exit survey. Mailing the questionnaire helps evaluators reach a broader group of people with an interest in a service, but a mailing list for the people to be surveyed is required, and additional costs are incurred for postage. A questionnaire also can be administered to groups via others, such as a social worker, senior program volunteer, PTA member, or campus group advisor. Using personal interviews to gather the information, especially by telephone, allows the library to reach groups not likely to respond in writing and, assuming a reasonably complete list of telephone numbers is available, can help assure a diverse respondent pool.

Consideration of follow-up techniques should occur prior to distribution of the survey. When, for example, the questionnaire is mailed with no way to link it to the individual respondent, anonymity is achieved. Unfortunately, for the evaluator this leaves no way to follow up with non-respondents if the response rate is too low. This is especially troubling with mail questionnaires.

The construction of the questionnaire deserves the greatest attention. The designer keeps in mind the language of respondents and attempts to develop unambiguous, jargon-free questions. Both open-ended ("What did you like most about the program?") and fixed-response (checklists, rating scales) questions are possible. If the range of responses is unknown, the open-ended question is necessary. The response rate for a given questionnaire will be affected by wording and language, as well as questionnaire length. While respondents with a strong interest in a subject will be likely to respond, caution should be taken to focus on a few important questions rather than distribute an overly long questionnaire. Tabulating results is time-consuming, especially with many open-ended questions.

A pretest is essential to the success of a questionnaire. The pretest helps assure that the wording and language is understandable to the group who will respond to the questionnaire. The pretest involves a small number of people (7 to 10) who are like those who will respond to the survey. If extensive changes are indicated after the initial pretest, another pretest is necessary. The value of the pretest in preventing unusable data cannot be overemphasized.

Ultimately, the best thing an evaluator can do when using a questionnaire is to know exactly what information is needed prior to constructing the questionnaire. This aids in keeping the questions specific to the need, rather than just collecting information "since we are at it" or because "it would be interesting to know."

Questionnaires are used to gather information on just about any subject and are especially useful for measuring attitudes. Attitude measurement determines people's opinions, notably about satisfaction with or preferences for services, processes, policies, or an institution as a whole. The questions can gather information on beliefs, feelings, and intended behaviors—the three components of attitude.

One type of questionnaire is the fast response survey. This approach is valuable for informing decisions that must be made quickly on unanticipated issues and for which no existing information is available. It involves asking a small number of questions (by mail or telephone) that do not require extraordinary effort from respondents (e.g., yes/no, multiple choice, ranking, rating scales). These approaches allow for rapid compilation of results. Exit surveys also can be this type of questionnaire.

An example of the use of questionnaires for evaluation in the library field is the reference transaction form developed by Charles Bunge and Marjorie Murfin. This is used when reference librarians want to know what proportion of their reference questions are answered satisfactorily and how they can maintain or improve question-answering success. The assessment involves question-by-question analysis of data gathered from both patrons and librarians. Since the form is machine-readable, data entry and analysis are easy. As a number of libraries use this standardized questionnaire, comparisons among the libraries can be made.

INTERVIEWING

Interviews can be categorized as individual or group and structured or unstructured. Individual, structured interviews are like questionnaires and, therefore, the same caveats apply. The structured interview is composed of specific questions and has a prescribed order. In contrast, unstructured interviews, individual or group, are more like a conversation with general categories to be covered. This feature translates into a natural flow in the interview while making sure similar kinds of information are gathered in each interview. For both types of interviews, an introduction and suggested probes make up what is known as an interview schedule or guide.

Interviewing has two key advantages over written data collection methods. The response rate tends to be better, and the primary skill needed by the respondent is the ability to speak. In addition, the interviewer can make use of probes or help explain a misunderstood question. Overall, interviewing can have a positive public relations effect since each participant receives personal attention by the library.

On the minus side, however, the interview process—especially in-person, one-on-one interviews—can be time-consuming and thus costly. An interview is not the best approach if the evaluator is interested in specific figures, since access to records would be minimal. If the evaluation focuses on sensitive issues, the participant may be reluctant to reveal opinions or information. An interviewer's personal characteristics (e.g., age, physical appearance) also can affect the respondent's answers.

Training of interviewers is a necessary step in order to help assure consistency in questioning and recording of information, although some variation will occur. A common question regarding interviewers is: "Can staff or supporters conduct the interviews?" While this is possible, careful attention needs to be paid to avoiding defense of the program during the interview and to probing equally for positive and negative information about the program. The training would include the method for recording interview data. Notes may be taken during the interview by the interviewer or a separate notetaker, and the interview can be taped.

One group interview technique that is becoming more common for evaluation is the focus group interview. This approach takes full advantage of the dynamics of the group process to elicit ideas and opinions. Some people find focus groups a more accessible means of expressing attitudes and perceptions. The method has been successful for reaching groups traditionally underserved in the community, school, or university or under-represented in other types of data collection. The approach contains four main elements:

- writing an interview guide,

- recruiting participants (8 to 12),

- conducting interviews, and

- preparing a narrative report.

A carefully prepared interview guide, combined with an effective facilitator/interviewer, is instrumental to the success of this technique. The approach can be a time and cost efficient method for gathering information not easily ascertained from surveys.

NUMBERS-GATHERING

There appears to be a strong association between evaluation and "counting up." While not the equivalent of evaluation, it is true that accurate numbers-gathering is a basic component in documenting library activities. Librarians' familiarity with recording statistics, however, may have bred contempt, resulting in criticism of the numbers-gathering approach. In reality, this method complements each of the techniques discussed in this chapter. Numbers, in particular, answer the question: "To what extent?" Over time, numbers-gathering provides for trend analysis and comparisons. Even for those desiring a more qualitative approach, numbers-gathering occurs. Tabulation of questionnaire results and reference accuracy measures are just two examples of this.

The key to using numbers-gathering as an evaluation technique is to assess the usefulness of each measure prior to collecting it. Some of the dissatisfaction with keeping statistics derives from the number of statistics currently being collected in the library that have no apparent usefulness. The process of collecting numbers contains four basic steps: determining what use the statistics will have, clearly defining what is being counted, developing a reasonable method for collecting statistics (every day or sample periods), and tabulating the counts.

The library's desired results for a given service or program help direct the numbers-gathering. Within this framework, however, the numbers-gathering tends to focus on inputs (what's available) and outputs (what's used). The library's resources—dollars, staff, volunteers, and facilities—serve as examples of inputs. The services or process of using these inputs produce certain outputs, such as circulation, program attendance, collection fill rates, and completed reference queries.

The numbers-gathering approach is limited in its ability to entirely reflect outcomes, including desired changes such as "a more literate student body" or "a community of readers." Numbers-gathering as an evaluation technique, however, provides libraries logical indicators of their movement toward their goals, mission, and vision.

Numbers-gathering can be relatively unobtrusive, requiring no additional input from the patron. Examples include reference counts tabulated by staff, programmed data collection (e.g., online circulation, count of uses of a CD-ROM database), number of items loaned to tutors, and program attendance. If the numbers-gathering requires additional patron effort or time, the evaluation is more intrusive. When determining the residence of those asking reference questions by telephone, for example, the patron is queried directly during the conversation. In contrast, residence is automatically recorded when checking out material in an automated circulation system. This is also true of collection measures. Circulation counts for segments of the collection can be gathered unobtrusively, while calculating title and author fill rates requires direct query to patrons. When characteristics of the user are of interest, such as the education level or school year of participants, it is more likely that this is asked directly.

USE OF EXISTING DATA

Associated with the numbers-gathering approach is use of existing data. In the process of "counting up," libraries and other agencies have collected numerous kinds of data. Data sources can be as comprehensive as the U.S. Census or as narrow as use of services in a single library. Existing data supply information for evaluating community or service group needs, are subject to further analysis by the library, and can be related to original data collection results.

One significant benefit of using existing data is the reduction or elimination of the amount of time required for data collection. As a result, it can reduce evaluation costs. Use of existing data is an important first step before embarking on gathering original evaluation information. Is there comparable data already collected that can answer the evaluation question? Comparison of existing data to individual library data also helps interpret evaluation results. Library standards often provide bench marks drawn from existing data sources.

For any existing data source, the evaluator seeks background information in order to determine the usefulness of the data. Among the questions to ask are:

- What was the intention or purpose of the data collection (e.g., to support a cause or primarily descriptive of a situation)?

- How were the data collected (e.g., method used, random sample or convenience sample)?

- How recent is the information?

- Are there other sources that can help verify the set of existing data?

Identification of existing sources requires the library's information services expertise. Some library sources, such as the Association of Research Libraries Statistics, the Federal-State Cooperative System (FSCS) for Public Library Data, or the Public Library Data Service (PLDS), are widely available. A search of library literature provides special topic information, such as the library buildings survey found annually in *Library Journal* or indexes of library materials prices. Sources outside the library field, such as census reports, inflation and cost indexes, and demographic databases, potentially contribute to the evaluation effort. Basically, the use of existing data for evaluation encompasses the entire range of reported surveys and research conducted within the library field.

OBSERVATION

Library staff regularly observe activities around them. This observation naturally occurs and results in anecdotal reports of library activities or patron preferences. Use of observation goes beyond this very natural skill to a more structured process that defines clearly what is to be observed and when. Structured observation allows for the study of behavior and events and includes both verbal and nonverbal behaviors. The evaluator using this method seeks to identify typical situations rather than the unusual. When conducted at a library, the observation is said to occur in a "natural setting."

Each observation can be placed on an "obtrusiveness continuum" from unobtrusive to overt. Consider, for example, an observer of children's programming. While one can attempt to be unobtrusive, the existence of a nonparticipating adult is obvious and may affect the behavior of the children. In other cases the observation is more unobtrusive, such as when the evaluator is part of the group as a participant observer. An example of this would be attendance at a library-sponsored event. Since structured observation requires note-taking, however, this in itself may set apart the observer from other participants. On the unobtrusive end of the continuum are the reference evaluation studies in which specially designed queries are asked at the reference desk by research staff posing as real users.

While observation suggests the presence of an observer, the library sometimes observes behavior automatically. Some of the numbers-gathering activities, such as circulation patterns and gate counts, are recorded daily. Online catalog transaction logs provide in-depth information on how users search the catalog.

Two activities are integral to using observation as an evaluation method. Defining the behavior to be observed is fundamental. How will the observer recognize the behavior? Agreement among observers is dependent on clear parameters established prior to the observation. These parameters also help reduce interpretation by the observers; interpretation should follow collection of the observation data. The goal is to report what is seen or heard, rather than draw inferences from what is observed. Evaluators might consider the value of disinterested observers who are not used to seeing the activity and are less likely to interpret what they are seeing.

The second basic activity is the development of a schedule for the observations, taking into account the number of observation times, the length of each observation, and selection of times. In the selection of times, choosing "typical" times relates to the desire to observe normal activities, rather than atypical behaviors. Also, observation times will be varied to allow for coverage of the range of library hours. For some evaluations, a specific event is the focus, so the schedule is more evident. Once the schedule and definitions are determined, a standard note-taking form is developed to record what the person is seeing or hearing.

Within the library field, the observation approach has been most closely linked to the evaluation of reference. In this instance, a series of questions are asked in the library. The behavior to be observed varies, from just the answer given to the interview technique used by the librarian. Observation of other librarian behaviors also deserves attention. These might include instruction in use, readers advisory techniques, and advice on information-seeking strategies. Likewise, patron behavior can be observed, such as use of library tools, including the catalog, pamphlet files, CD-ROMs, and bibliographies. Other than in reference services, direct observation is rarely reported as an evaluation technique in the library field.

OTHER SELF-REPORTING ACTIVITIES

Since library staff or evaluators cannot observe all activities, people are sometimes asked to record information that later is used for evaluation. Both questionnaires and interviews rely on individual memory to describe behaviors, but time of use reporting can be more accurate. Two techniques for collecting this "time of use" information are logs and journals.

A log usually consists of simple reports of activities and may include time of use, length of use, purpose of use, description of activity, and outcome. The log is useful for the numerous self-service activities in a library. An example of this would be log forms at the CD-ROM database stations where patrons are asked to record length of use and topic of the search. As with other self-reporting techniques, the completeness of the log is dependent on the cooperation of the user and the amount of information requested.

As a record of activities, a journal is similar to a log. The journal, however, is distinct in that it usually contains some reflection on the activity. Journals are more likely to be used to record activities during intensive programs with several sessions, such as family literacy or bibliographic instruction. Examples of the kind of entries include descriptions of family reading activities or use of new bibliographic searching skills.

CONCLUSION

We can evaluate:

> *inputs*—the resources used to provide a service,
>
> *processes*—the activities carried out to produce outputs,
>
> *outputs*—measures of the amount of services provided, and
>
> *outcomes*—how things changed for the users or the community, school, or university.

The methods introduced in this chapter can be used when evaluating any of these categories. Over the last decade, important progrress on measuring outputs has occurred. The philosophy of such an approach is that outputs are indicators of the desired outcomes—that is, that they are indirect measures of desired outcomes. Attention is now focused on more directly evaluating the impact or results from library services. Other service agencies also are struggling with the difficulties of assessing impact. Since impact occurs after use of a library service or results from a combination of library and other services, this is a difficult evaluation effort. Impact or outcomes evaluation is, at this point, dependent on the same set of evaluation approaches discussed in this chapter. Making the link between inputs, outputs, and impact requires a mix of evaluation methods and a clear vision of the desired outcomes.

REFERENCES AND FURTHER READING

Babbie, Earl. *The Practice of Social Research.* 6th ed. Belmont, Calif.: Wadsworth Publishing Company, 1992.

Bunge, Charles. "Factors Related to Output Measures for Reference Services in Public Libraries: Data From Thirty-Six Libraries." *Public Libraries* 29 (January/February 1990): 42–47.

Greenbaum, Thomas L. *The Practical Handbook and Guide to Focus Group Research.* Lexington, Mass.: D.C. Heath, 1988.

Guba, Egon G., and Yvonna S. Lincoln. *Fourth Generation Evaluation.* Newbury Park, Calif.: Sage, 1989.

Henerson, Marlene E., Lynn Lyons Morris, and Carol Taylor Fitz-Gibbon. *How to Measure Attitudes.* Newbury Park, Calif: Sage, 1987.

Johnson, Debra Wilcox. "Keeping Things in Focus: Information for Decision Making." In *Keeping the Book$: Public Library Financial Practices*, edited by Jane B. Robbins and Douglas L. Zweizig, 405–20. Fort Atkinson, Wisc.: Highsmith Press,1992.

Patton, Michael Q. *Qualitative Evaluation Methods.* Beverly Hills, Calif.: Sage, 1980.

Scriven, Michael. *Evaluation Thesaurus.* 4th ed. Newbury Park, Calif.: Sage, 1991.

Sudman, Seymour, and Norman M. Bradburn. *Asking Questions.* San Francisco: Jossey-Bass, 1983.

Van House, Nancy A., Mary Jo Lynch, Charles R. McClure, Douglas L. Zweizig, and Eleanor J. Rodger. *Output Measures for Public Libraries.* 2nd ed. Chicago: American Library Association, 1987.

Van House, Nancy A., Beth T. Weil, and Charles R. McClure. *Measuring Academic Library Performance: A Practical Approach.* Chicago: American Library Association, 1990.

COMPARISON CHART OF EVALUATION METHODS

Methods	Description	Advantages	Disadvantages
Existing Records (e.g., registration materials, financial records, usage counts)	The library staff may already be collecting information through the normal procedures of the library. By modifying current procedures or simply examining the data in a different way, the library staff may be able to answer some of the key evaluation questions.	Provides quantifiable evidence of activities and results. Requires minimum time, effort, and money.	Analysis can be complicated. Data can be misleading if originally collected for different purpose. Usually reflects quantity, not quality.
Observation (e.g., structured participation, casual conversation, counting session attendance)	The library staff or designated program participants may be able to look for specific data in a consistent way that will help to answer the evaluation questions. The observer, through informal interviews or other means, could focus on such aspects of the project as project setting, nature of interactions, program activities, library user behaviors, informal interactions, unplanned activities, and unexpected behavior.	Requires minimum interruption to program activities. Provides check on reports of staff and users. Provides context for understanding of other data.	Observer must be skilled in process observation. Observer filters data through individual perspective and values. Program participants may not be open and natural.
Individual Interviews (e.g., structured interviews with individual participants, face-to-face or by phone)	The library staff may develop structured questions for interviews with key people. The interviews with individuals should consist of a series of questions designed to provide the specific information needed. The interview can be conducted face-to-face or by telephone. Designing effective questions and conducting a good interview is not an easy task and may require an experienced interviewer.	Can probe for meaning of responses. May create participant willingness to disclose sensitive information. Can control when and how questions are asked.	Time consuming. Analysis may be difficult. Requires skilled interviewer. Some participants may feel threatened.

SOURCE: *A Stakeholder Evaluation Handbook: A Focus on Evaluation.* (Prepared and revised by Sharon Granger, Donald Leaf, and Charles Wolfe and edited by Jeff Johnson of the Library of Michigan.) Lansing, Mich.: Library of Michigan, 1993. Permission granted to reproduce.

Methods	Description	Advantages	Disadvantages
Group Interviews (e.g., focus groups, nominal groups, work groups)	The library staff may collect information from small groups of people. A focus group (8–12 persons) is used when group interaction is likely to increase the quality of the data being collected. If possible, the group should be led by a skilled group facilitator and another person should document comments of group members, the consensus of the group on specific issues, and any observations about group member interactions.	Stimulates thinking and sharing ideas. Can get different views on same subject. Can get consensus about a program.	Cannot be confidential. May be difficult to organize. Some participants may feel threatened. Requires skilled group interviewer.
Expert Opinion (e.g., panel of library directors)	The library staff may contact people who are knowledgeable because of their experience and expertise in the content or process of the project that is being evaluated. These people could be national experts, university faculty, or directors of successful programs in other libraries. Such persons can help assess the needs for new projects and programs; react to the quality of existing or planned programs; and suggest ways to improve programs. This expert opinion can be gathered through direct contacts with the individuals or through a review of reports and articles that they have written.	Is relatively simple to design and inexpensive to implement. Strengthens lines of communication between experts and participants. Brings visibility to project.	Experts may not be available for this. May be difficult to find neutral experts. Participants may not be directly familiar with program.

(continued)

123

COMPARISON CHART OF EVALUATION METHODS (continued)

Methods	Description	Advantages	Disadvantages
Journals/Logs (e.g., participants self-reports and critiques of experience)	The library staff could be asked to keep a record of anecdotes, observations, personal reactions, comments, and the frequency of specific activities relating to the project. The purpose of using this method is to understand the experience of the program from the participant's point of view. The information collected, however, will be subjective and may be difficult to analyze.	Provides record of immediate reaction to events. Provides record of change over time. Requires minimum effort to collect data. Provides record of unanticipated events.	Data is subjective and not as reliable. Can be difficult to analyze. Participants must be trained in how to record information.
Questionnaire Surveys (e.g., systematic data collection instruments: paper and pencil, telephone, computer)	The library staff can use questionnaires in obtaining information from a large number of individuals. The nature of the information to be collected should be easily categorized. Surveys may be mailed or hand-delivered, person-to-person, or telephone surveys. Questionnaires that collect accurate data are not simple to design and administer. One may wish to use an experienced individual in designing the survey. Time should be taken to obtain feedback from stakeholders and a few people in the target population should test the survey before finalizing.	Can collect data from large number of people in short time. Relatively inexpensive. Can be confidential. Provides ease of analysis and summarizing of data.	Data is restricted by the questions that are asked. Substantial planning time is required. Return rates can be quite low.

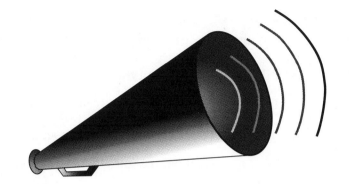

CHAPTER 13

Choosing an Evaluation Method

Debra Wilcox Johnson

The practice of evaluation is ongoing, as people are continually assessing the world around them. Scriven (1991) notes that "evaluation is a new discipline but an ancient practice" (p. 3). As the library field moves toward more systematic evaluation, it draws on a range of strategies from the discipline of evaluation. Given that choices exist, a basic query in the evaluation process is: "What method should be used?" This chapter examines this issue by asking three questions:

- How do you decide what to evaluate?

- How do you match a method to your question?

- How do you know whether you are ready to evaluate?

Within this framework, a library can consider alternative approaches in light of the specific service or program to be evaluated and the desired results.

This chapter incorporates information from a July 21, 1993 panel presentation by Debra Wilcox Johnson, Jane Robbins, and Douglas Zweizig.

HOW DO YOU DECIDE WHAT TO EVALUATE?

The most straightforward response to this question is that you can evaluate everything! Using the TELL IT! model as a framework, the range of options is evident. The library can evaluate:

- the needs, the possibilities   (**T**alk about the vision)

- the ways of responding   (**E**xplore alternatives and design your approach)

- how it is working   (**L**earn from what's happening)

- what happened   (**L**et people know what happened)

- what worked   (**I**ntegrate results with ongoing services)

- how it went   (**T**hink about how it all worked).

Since the business of a library is to provide service, not to conduct evaluations, choices of what to evaluate have to be made. One reasonable estimate is that five percent of energy and income can be spent on evaluation; the library has to be selective. Priorities need to be set to determine what to evaluate when.

A first step is to consider what the library already knows about its services and activities. One approach is to start with what has not been evaluated recently (or ever). What activities (and the outcomes from these activities) does the library know the least about? Institution-wide, an audit of evaluation activities helps to reveal areas that lack enough evaluation information to make program adjustments. While the tendency may be to focus on new services, examination of "traditional" library activities provides a fertile ground for new evaluation approaches or for examining a service from different perspectives.

The evaluation budget influences the selection of evaluation priorities. As noted earlier, only a small percentage of the library's energy and money can go toward evaluation. By concentrating on selected activities and starting with a small evaluation effort, the library increases its chances of successfully completing its evaluation priorities. These successes positively affect the organizational climate toward evaluation.

Another view of this question is to consider the different perspectives of the stakeholders in the organization. What do they want and what are their priorities? Some possible stakeholders are decision makers (board, administration), budget makers (city/county officials, foundation officers, school district administrators), users, project staff, and other agencies. Each brings a different perspective to the question of what should be evaluated. The director may be more interested in how the project helped the library achieve its goals, while the city council member or university administrator wants to know the cost-effectiveness of the program. Staff from collaborating agencies or school faculty will seek evidence that the library program complements their efforts rather than competes. Library staff outside the project might focus on the impact of the project on other library services. If consideration is given to the various stakeholders before the evaluation process is designed, this can help identify what areas to evaluate. When the library tells its story, it can use evaluation results to speak directly to the different stakeholders. The divergent views of the stakeholders provide ample ideas to focus the evaluation. Stakeholders also can provide evaluation of the reports they receive. This gives insight into the values and priorities of the various groups connected to a given service or project.

HOW DO YOU MATCH A METHOD TO YOUR QUESTION?

The criteria for choosing an evaluation method fit into two categories: meaningfulness and practicality. Meaningfulness criteria relate to usefulness of the evaluation results. These include goal-relatedness, interpretability, timeliness, comparability, and appropriateness. The category of practicality speaks to the affordability of the evaluation in terms of intrusiveness, ease, and cost.

Meaningfulness

The *goal-relatedness* criterion is connected to the question of outcomes. Does the evaluation address the important goals and desired outcomes of the project? The closer the match between the method and program priorities, the more likely the evaluation results will be used in planning and program improvement. Concentration on program goals also helps focus the evaluation on the question "What difference did the program make?"

The evaluation results need to be communicated to others, so *interpretability* is an important criterion. Can the evaluator translate the findings into a meaningful story? Given the different audiences for evaluation results, one method could be more easily interpreted than another. Making the results intelligible is basic to having the results used for program improvement. This criterion also is associated with the reduction of evaluation data into usable information for decision makers.

Timeliness relates to two factors: 1) reaching decision makers in a timely manner and 2) how long it takes to see the difference desired. In order for the evaluation information to be useful, it needs to be available when needed. A mailed questionnaire, for example, may be preferred, but when the results are needed in less than two weeks this is not an option. The other timeliness factor centers on logical increments for achievement. Given the start-up time for a new project, for example, showing progress toward desired ends may come in two or three years, rather than in twelve months. Timely evaluation uses methods that are sensitive to changes in small increments. The key question here is: "Will the change or result have occurred during the time period set?"

One use of evaluation is to compare the library's progress over time or to compare local results with those of other libraries. The *comparability* criterion speaks to these concerns. Is the method chosen likely to be easily replicated or collected periodically? Have other agencies used the same approach? Clarity of definition of what is being studied is instrumental in assuring comparability.

Appropriateness of the method is the final criterion in the meaningfulness category. This relates to the affiliated concepts of validity and reliability. Validity asks: "Does the method measure what you wanted to know?" When studying non-use, for example, a series of questions could be sent to non-registered residents or to students who have no record of borrowing materials. Since library use is broader than circulation, however, this may not be a valid way to identify non-users. Reliability, on the other hand, asks: "Is the method being used the same way by all involved?" In observation, for example, is each observer defining the behavior in the same way, such as "use of periodicals"? For one observer, this could mean picking up a periodical. For another, this could mean simply looking at the periodicals on display. This difference results in inconsistency in data collection, bringing the reliability of the results into question. Consistency is a good synonym for reliability.

Another use of the criterion appropriateness couples the method chosen to the interests of different stakeholders. The question to ask is: "Does this method have credibility with this stakeholder group?" A documented story showing impact of a program on an individual can inspire some stakeholders. For the administrator, however, the interest may be in the number of people for whom this change occurred or how long the change took. For a funder, the desire may be for information on how much the change cost per person. Reliance on only one evaluation method over time does not allow for the multiple viewpoints held by stakeholders.

Practicality

The practicality issues speak to the need to keep evaluation efforts reasonable in light of other library activities and the time of those involved in a particular service. *Intrusiveness* is concerned with how much an evaluation may interfere with the normal functioning of the library. The concern is for the distraction to people delivering a service and those using a service. When using this criterion, each method is examined for its degree of intrusiveness. Circulation counts on an automated system are basically unobtrusive for patrons and for much of the staff. In contrast, asking patrons about their use of the library upon exiting the building intrudes on the users. The time an approach takes and the amount of disruption or interference to a service or individual are the components of the criterion of intrusiveness. Obtrusive methods do not always mean they are disruptive; instead they are obvious (Scriven 1991, 368).

The criterion of *ease* of the method incorporates a number of practical concerns. Ease includes the skills needed to carry out a chosen method, the availability of potential measures or the information needed, the time it takes to carry out the method, training requirements, the number of people involved in the method (for collection and response), and the effort required to analyze results. Each method varies on the degree to which these factors are present. The ease criterion, however, needs to be considered in light of the other criteria rather than be the sole criterion driving the choice of method. For example, the number of reference questions answered is relatively easy to collect. Yet if the question of interest is the effectiveness of reference service, a more complex evaluation method will be needed, such as an accuracy study or observation of waiting time for walk-in patrons.

Ultimately, the question of choosing the method is linked to *cost*. Personnel costs make up a large percentage of any evaluation budget. These costs are affected by the use of internal or external expertise and the level of staff needed for each phase of the evaluation. Using focus group interviews as an example, the highest costs occur when the interviewer is from outside the library and is preparing the narrative report. The personnel costs for making interview arrangements and contacting participants most likely will be internal. For most evaluations there is an administrative cost, especially for sharing the results with relevant stakeholders. The basic principle is to think about whose time will be needed for the project.

Another method for determining costs involves identifying the number of steps for the evaluation method; each of these steps translates into cost components. To continue the focus group example, the steps include developing an interview guide, recruiting participants, conducting interviews, and preparing the report. Potential cost elements are personnel (internal and external), possible payment for participants, communications charges, supplies, printing, travel, and training.

It is too simplistic to state that one method, such as questionnaires, is more expensive than another, such as numbers-gathering. Within each method are a range of ways to use the technique. With questionnaires, for example, the fast response survey is quick, requiring minimal time for tabulation. Using questions from other questionnaires can save costs, although this should be done with caution and with full understanding of what the library wants to know prior to selecting specific questions. Collecting information on program impacts can involve one-on-one interviews, group interviews, or logging of all comments heard at the library at the desk or during a program. Each of these have different costs. When choosing the methods for an evaluation project, blending a more expensive approach with those requiring less staff and expertise helps keep costs reasonable. Just as with the use of library volunteers, evaluation is not free, requiring at a minimum internal staff time.

One cost element often ignored is the expense for the important stage of "making sense" of evaluation data. The person (or group) responsible for this step examines the evaluation information as a whole, interprets the results in light of the environment, and makes recommendations for program changes. Given the different stakeholders, the making sense step can be tailored to different audiences, the consequence being higher costs for this phase of the evaluation project. Without this transition from data to interpretation, all other costs can be wasted, since the results can go unused.

A less tangible, but equally important expense, is the cost to individuals involved in the evaluation effort. The respondents for any information collection technique give value to their own time. This "response burden" can hinder information gathering activities. If an individual is required to expend time and effort over and above the perceived worth of the process, an incomplete response or lack of response may be the result. A higher degree of intrusiveness translates into a higher response burden. Repeatedly asking the same people for information also reduces willingness to participate in the data collection.

Using the criterion of cost exclusive of other criteria ignores the important principle of matching the method to what services and outcomes are being studied. Using written questionnaires, for example, rather than personal interviews in evaluating a literacy program may be cheaper, but it will limit dramatically the number of usable responses. Counting circulation might be the cheapest approach for measuring collection use, but it may lack credibility with the funder who supported the purchase of a special collection. Choosing inappropriate methods, or not evaluating at all, carries a major cost, primarily for the library.

HOW DO YOU KNOW WHETHER YOU ARE READY TO EVALUATE?

Central to the question of readiness for evaluation is the current organizational climate for evaluation. There is a tendency to view evaluation as an exotic activity, occurring rarely and only when required. A certain negativism also can surround evaluation when it is linked exclusively to judgment, criticism, or punishment. On the extreme edge is a condition Scriven (1991) calls "valuephobia" or the "irrational fear of evaluation, often manifested in unreasonably strong dislike of—or opposition to—evaluation" (p. 375). While some anxiety is present in conducting and using evaluation, an openness to the value of evaluation and the usefulness of the results is a necessary condition for asking the questions of what and how to evaluate a given library program. As is implicit in the stakeholder model, different constituencies have a "share" in the evaluation outcomes. For each of the stakeholders, clear understanding of the purposes of evaluation and how the results will be used begin to overcome a resistance to evaluation efforts. Creating an environment where evaluation occurs naturally begins prior to selecting an evaluation approach. That environment is influenced by how actual evaluations are conducted and how the results are incorporated into the library's operations. Showing that evaluation is not just an administrative task also helps to create a positive climate for evaluation efforts.

Readiness for evaluation is strongly tied to the level of expertise available to conduct the evaluation. This expertise may be external or internal. Outside expertise can be found in one readily obtainable source—the literature. People make their living studying evaluation methods and share that expertise in articles and books. Mining the literature for expert advice is a logical first step for any evaluation venture.

Hiring outside evaluators has the advantage of bringing in, when necessary, the expertise needed to use a new method. Prior to using the outside expert, however, the library determines what it wants to evaluate and identifies important outcomes for the service. Abdicating responsibility for evaluation to outside consultants does not take into account internal expertise and knowledge of individual library conditions. Negotiating the relationship with consultants means clarifying the criteria the library will use to evaluate the product from the consultant. The library can use its internal expertise to carry out much of the evaluation; the consultant can be used for only selected evaluation activities. Part of the consultant contract can include training for the staff to build internal expertise for future evaluation efforts. If evaluation is to become part of the fabric of the institution, internal expertise must be present and used. Staff development opportunities can build staff skills in evaluation, and practice in evaluation strengthens these skills. A library, or group of libraries, can identify a "pool" of staff interested in evaluation and holding special skills such as interviewing or questionnaire design. Project staff can draw on this pool for needed advice. An exchange system among libraries of evaluation expertise would result in trading expertise to help each of the libraries in the pool.

The development and use of an evaluation pool is well illustrated by the peer evaluation approach. Peer evaluation is a process which involves colleagues, community members, or other individuals who have a stake in the project or service being evaluated. An individual or panel of representatives conducts a formal evaluation culminating in a final report which is submitted to the administrators of the project or service being evaluated. This report may serve various purposes:

- as a formal evaluation of a project or service to fulfill a reporting requirement of the funding authority;

- as a mechanism for justifying additional or continued support for a project or service;

- as an internal method for improving management of a project or service; or,

- as a method for evaluating a trial or prototype project or service that may be of interest to other libraries or information services.

A good example of the peer evaluation process was developed by the Oregon State Library. In Oregon, the peer review process is used to evaluate Library Services and Construction Act (LSCA) grants and draws its evaluators from the practitioners in the state. The peer review approach builds a cadre of evaluators within a state or region. The advantage of this approach is not only the expertise available, but the practical experience of the evaluators with similar problems, contexts, and settings. Practitioners who participate in the peer review process also increase their understanding of library services and evaluation. A complete set of sample documents from the Oregon peer evaluation process can be found appended to this chapter.

OTHER FACTORS TO CONSIDER

As discussed earlier, creating a supportive climate for evaluation is a necessary precondition for using evaluation regularly. Failure to do evaluation, however, may also come from a fear of the answer or a "bad" evaluation. Evaluation results should help improve services; this implies changes in design and cost and requires new energy from program organizers. This can be daunting for program personnel, especially those who may not have wanted to hear the answers to the evaluation questions.

Another barrier to evaluation may be the perception that it is too costly in terms of energy and dollars. Normally, evaluation has to be reasonable, in proportion to the scope of the service being evaluated. Starting small and demonstrating the usefulness of evaluation helps to incorporate the process into normal library operations. Building on information gathered over time can provide a fuller picture of the effect of a program. Given the cyclical nature of a model such as TELL IT!, the evaluation process improves over time and builds on previously collected information.

Every method has flaws, and trade-offs occur when one technique is chosen over another. The moral of this is to use a mix of approaches over and over. It also means there is not one perfect evaluation method for a given evaluation situation. In truth, it is a matter of seeking an optimal method or combination of methods, rather than the one best approach.

It is necessary to recognize up-front that evaluation is politically charged. Questions abound regarding the proper relationship between evaluators, policy analyzers, decision makers, and the organization, services, and people being evaluated. Recognizing the political climate surrounding evaluation efforts, including the potentially divergent views of different stakeholders, places the evaluation efforts into a larger context than just a given service or program.

Finally, choosing an evaluation method is strongly linked to knowing what questions the library wants answered in the evaluation process. The more specifically the desired outcomes or impacts of the service are articulated, the more consensus will exist regarding the appropriate methods for evaluation. The clarity of vision about what difference the library can make guides the design of evaluation strategies. Clarity in the objectives to be met supports targeted evaluations of measurable outcomes.

REFERENCES AND FURTHER READING

Guba, Egon G., and Yvonna S. Lincoln. *Fourth Generation Evaluation*. Newbury Park, Calif.: Sage, 1989.

Hernon, Peter, and Charles R. McClure. *Evaluation and Library Decision Making*. Norwood, N.J.: Ablex, 1990.

Scriven, Michael. *Evaluation Thesaurus*. 4th ed. Newbury Park, Calif.: Sage, 1991.

A Stakeholder Evaluation Handbook: A Focus on Evaluation. (Prepared and revised by Sharon Granger, Donald Leaf, and Charles Wolfe and edited by Jeff Johnson of the Library of Michigan.) Lansing, Mich.: Library of Michigan, [1993].

Zweizig, Douglas L. "Tailoring Measures to Fit Your Service: A Guide for the Manager of Reference Services." *The Reference Librarian* 11 (Fall/Winter 1984) 53–61.

FACTORS TO CONSIDER WHEN CHOOSING AN EVALUATION METHOD

What do you need to know from the evaluation?

- What questions need to be addressed in the evaluation? These are linked to the desired outcomes.

- In light of these questions, what would be possible method(s) to use?

Is the method appropriate for the type of information you need?

- Will it speak to the various stakeholders' concerns?

- What are the advantages and disadvantages of the method(s) you are considering?

- Will the method gather the information you need to answer your evaluation questions? Does the method measure what you want to know? (Validity)

- Are the people involved in your project likely to participate if you use the method(s)?

Will the method gather information in a timely manner?

- Will the information be available when needed?

    How long does it take to organize the data collection?
    How long will it take to gather the information?
    How long will it take to analyze or "make sense" of the results?

- Have you allowed enough time for the desired outcome(s) to happen?

Do you and/or your staff have the expertise needed to carry out the method?

- What do you need to know in order to use the method?

- What sources of expertise can you draw upon when using the technique?

- Will the method be used the same way by all involved? (Reliability)

What are the costs associated with the method(s) chosen?

- What personnel are needed to carry out the method(s), e.g., existing staff, outside consultants, volunteers?

- What direct costs are associated with the method(s), e.g., mailing, printing, long-distance telephone calls, refreshments?

Developed by Debra Wilcox Johnson, Johnson & Johnson Consulting, 1015 Holiday Drive, Waunakee, WI 53597. (608) 849-7286.

DEVELOPING AN EVALUATION PLAN

The purpose of this exercise is to develop your skills in designing evaluation strategies for your library. Keep in mind that the results are of interest to many stakeholders, so a variety of approaches are needed. Consider the basic options: counting up, questionnaires, interviews (individual and group), observation, and logs and journals.

1. Choose one of the scenarios below for this exercise. You may further refine these to match your group's interests.

2. Select a recorder/reporter for your group. This person will share the results of your work with the large group.

3. Brainstorm ideas on the following questions: What results or changes do you expect? What difference will the service or changes make for users, the community, and the library?

4. How can you collect the information needed to document results and to communicate with stakeholders?

Scenario One: The library is revisiting the way in which its materials budget is being spent. The increase in publishing and variety of formats, combined with increased demand, means that the materials budget has not been adequate. This lead to changes in the buying patterns for the library.

Scenario Two: Sometimes the library feels like it is on the "information dirt road." In order to access the information superhighway, the library would like to provide Internet services to its staff and public as well as introduce electronic reference tools.

Scenario Three: The library has tried to refocus its attention on its older users. This effort has touched collections, facilities, programming and services. Before institutionalizing these changes, the library is interested in the effect of these changes and the needs not currently being met with the existing services.

Scenario Four: A growing number of youth are in child care during the work day. In order to reach out to these children and the adult caregivers, the library is planning to work with child care centers to improve programming, book collections, and reading activities in the centers.

Developed by Debra Wilcox Johnson, Johnson & Johnson Consulting, 1015 Holiday Drive, Waunakee, WI 53597. (608) 849-7286.

Oregon State Library

SPECIFICATIONS FOR LSCA GRANT PROJECT EVALUATIONS

Purpose

The purpose of the LSCA Grant Project Evaluations is to provide the State Library, the State Advisory Council on Libraries, and the library community in Oregon with a thorough, objective assessment of the results of each LSCA grant project funded by the State Library. It is hoped that these reports will be a valuable resource for Oregon libraries, and especially for libraries where an attempt might be made to replicate or adapt a given project to meet local needs. For projects which are continuing, with or without LSCA assistance, it is hoped that the project participants will obtain suggestions for strengthening the project as a result of the evaluation.

Method

Project evaluators will be assigned by the State Library to each project from a pool of library professionals who have indicated their interest in serving as evaluators. Every effort will be made to match the knowledge and experience of the potential evaluator to a given project. Once the evaluator has accepted his/her assignment, the State Library will provide their name and phone number to the grant project manager who will be asked to contact the evaluator about arranging for a site visit. The project manager will also be asked to send a Memorandum of Understanding to the evaluator to formalize the arrangements for the evaluation. Site visits are to last a minimum of one day (including travel time). They are to be conducted in the last month of the project grant year (usually December) on a date to be mutually agreed upon by the evaluator and the grant project manager. Following the site visit, the evaluator will write a narrative report presenting his/her findings. A copy of the completed report will be sent to the State Library (Attn: Mary Ginnane) and to the project manager. The report must be mailed to the project manager no later than the last day of the project grant year. An invoice dated no later than the last day of the grant period, in the amount of $300, should accompany the report. Once the report is received, the project manager will take steps necessary to pay to the evaluator a stipend of $300, charged against the grant, which is intended to cover all costs of the evaluation.

Evaluation Report

The evaluation report may not exceed 15 double-spaced typewritten pages in length. It should contain a "Summary of Evaluation" which presents a summary of the entire contents of the evaluation report. This summary should be no longer than one or two pages in length. The report should cover the following areas:

- *Project objectives*—What was the project trying to accomplish?

These examples of materials used in the peer evaluation process were provided by Mary Ginnane, Library Development Administrator, Oregon State Library.

- *Project method*—Briefly describe how the project set about to accomplish its objectives. What staff resources or other resources were employed? What plans or timelines were adopted to accomplish the project objectives?

- *Project results*—What concrete results did the project generate during the grant period? How do these compare with the original objectives of the project? What additional results (if any) are likely to be seen in the future?

- *Project impact*—How do you assess the long-term significance of this project, both locally (i.e., at the project site, if applicable) and statewide? What can be learned from the results of this project?

- *Suggestions for improvement*—In retrospect, what (if anything) would have made this a stronger project (e.g., better management, more resources, more participation, more publicity, etc.)? If the project will be continuing, what (if anything) would make this a stronger project in the future?

Oregon State Library

MEMORANDUM

TO: Oregon Library Professionals   DATE:

FROM: Library Development Administrator

SUBJECT: Recruitment for Library Services and Construction Act Grant Project
         Evaluators

Beginning this year, the State Library is establishing a program of independent evaluations for LSCA grant projects. This is being done at the suggestion of the State Advisory Council on Libraries in hopes that these evaluations and their dissemination will allow more libraries to learn from the results of these projects. LSCA grant project managers will continue to be required to file progress reports, but it is hoped that the independent evaluations will provide, in addition, a very useful, objective analysis of the results of each project.

Each evaluator will receive a stipend of $300 to cover all costs in performing the evaluation, including travel costs. The State Library plans to establish a list of qualified evaluators and to match persons on the list with relevant knowledge and experience to the various projects. Detailed specifications for the evaluations will be established by the State Library. These will include the following:

- Evaluators must agree to spend a minimum of one day at the project site on a date to be agreed upon with the grant project manager.

- Evaluators must agree to submit a written evaluation report, not to exceed 15 pages in length, to the State Library and to the project manager on a date to be specified by the State Library.

Once an evaluator has been selected by the State Library, the project manager will be notified and a Letter of Agreement between the evaluator and the fiscal agent for the grant will be executed. Payment of the stipend will be made by the fiscal agent following receipt of the evaluation report.

To be placed on the list of potential evaluators at the State Library, please fill out the attached Recruitment Form and return it to the State Library by June 15, 19__. A total of 18 evaluators will be needed in 19__. Most of the evaluations will be scheduled for September, though several may also be scheduled for later in the year. Submitting your name for inclusion on the list will not obligate you in any way. If you are selected by the State Library as an evaluator for a particular project in 19__, you will be contacted in July and given the opportunity to accept or decline the assignment. Your name will stay on the list for three years, unless you request that it be removed.

If you have other professionals on your staff who might be interested in serving as LSCA grant project evaluators, I hope you will share this information with them. Please make copies of the attached Recruitment Form if necessary.

Oregon State Library

RECRUITMENT FORM

Library Services and Construction Act Grant Project Evaluators

To be placed on the list of potential evaluators for Library Services and Construction Act projects, please complete the information below and mail the completed form to: Library Development Services, Oregon State Library, State Library Building, Salem, Oregon 97310, Attention: Val Vogt. In order to be placed on the list, the form must be received by [date].

1. Name:_____

2. Address:_____

3. Daytime phone number:_____

4. Current employer:_____

5. Current position:_____

6. Other professional employment in the past ten years:

    _____   _____
    (Employer)   (Position)

    _____   _____
    (Employer)   (Position)

    _____   _____
    (Employer)   (Position)

    _____   _____
    (Employer)   (Position)

7. Do you have experience and/or knowledge in any of these areas?
    (Check all that apply)

❏ Library automation	❏ Service to business	❏ Library resource sharing
❏ Technical services	❏ Library programming	❏ Limited English-speaking
❏ Children's services	❏ Service to elderly	❏ Information and referral
❏ Reference services	❏ Service to disadvantaged	❏ Continuing education
❏ Outreach services	❏ Adult literacy services	❏ Audiovisual services
❏ Collection development	❏ Service to disabled	❏ Planning and management

8. Please list below other areas of experience and/or knowledge not listed under line 7 above (if any):

9. Are there areas of the state to which you would *not* be willing to travel to visit a project site? (Check all that apply)

❑ North Coast   ❑ Willamette Valley   ❑ Southern Oregon

❑ Portland Metro   ❑ South Coast   ❑ Central Oregon

❑ Columbia Gorge   ❑ Northeastern Oregon   ❑ Southeastern Oregon

10. Are there any other factors which would limit your ability to serve as a project evaluator? (Please describe)

11. Thank you for your interest! Please sign and date this form below:

_____   _____
            Signature   Date

Oregon State Library

MEMORANDUM OF UNDERSTANDING

TO: [LSCA Grant Project Evaluator]   DATE:

FROM: [LSCA Grantee]

SUBJECT: Terms and Conditions of LSCA Grant Project Evaluation

The undersigned LSCA Grant Project Evaluator (henceforth, "Evaluator") and the LSCA Grantee (henceforth, "Grantee") do hereby agree to the following terms and conditions for the evaluation of the Grantee's LSCA grant project:

1. The evaluation will be conducted by the Evaluator in accordance with the Oregon State Library's "Specifications for LSCA Grant Project Evaluations" (henceforth, "Specifications").

2. The Evaluator will conduct whatever investigations are necessary to produce an evaluation report in accordance with the Oregon State Library's "Specifications," including at least one visit to the project site on a date to be mutually agreed upon by the Grantee and the Evaluator. This date should fall within the last months of the grant period as stipulated in the grant agreement between the Grantee and the Oregon State Library, and any amendments to the grant agreement.

3. The Evaluator will mail to the Grantee an evaluation report meeting the "Specifications." The report will be mailed no later than the last day of the grant period as stipulated in the grant agreement between the Grantee and the Oregon State Library, and any amendments to the grant agreement.

4. The Evaluator will mail, along with the report, an invoice for all services rendered and all expenses incurred in the amount of $300.00. The invoice will be dated no later than the last day of the grant period and will be paid promptly by the Grantee from grant funds.

5. The Evaluator will also mail a copy of the evaluation report to the Library Development Services Division, Oregon State Library, Salem, Oregon 97310, Attn: Mary Ginnane.

6. The evaluation report will become the joint property of the Evaluator, the Grantee, and the Oregon State Library and may be reproduced, in whole or in part, by any of these parties without permission.

_____   _____
        Grantee Signature   Evaluator Signature

_____   _____
        Date   Date

Oregon State Library

MEMORANDUM

TO: [LSCA Grant Project Evaluator]   DATE:

FROM: [Library Development Administrator]

SUBJECT: Assignment of LSCA Project Evaluators for 19__ Grant Projects

I am pleased to announce that for the fifth year we will be asking library professionals in Oregon to assist the State Library in conducting evaluations of Library Services and Construction Act grant projects. We will use the same pool of evaluators that we have used in previous years. I would like to request that you tentatively agree to be assigned to evaluate the following project:

Project name:	Senior Outreach/Online Link
Project site:	Salem Public Library
Project manager:	Cliff Smith

The evaluation of this project will need to take place during the month of [month, year] (including one visit to the project site on a date to be arranged with the project manager). The evaluation report should be submitted to the State Library and the project manager no later than [date]. Payment of a $300 stipend will be made by the project fiscal agent upon receipt of the evaluation report.

Attached to this letter is a brief description of the project copied from the State Library's *LSCA Annual Program for [year].* Also attached is a copy of our "Specifications for LSCA Project Evaluations." I hope this information is sufficient for you to decide whether to accept this assignment. If you would like more information, please feel free to contact me at [phone].

To indicate whether you would be willing to accept this assignment please return the form below. If you agree, we will forward your name, address, and phone number to the project manager, who will be contacting you about scheduling a site visit. You will also be sent a Memorandum of Understanding by the project manager, which will formalize the arrangements for the evaluation.

I will appreciate your returning the response form to me by [date]. I thank you again for your interest in serving as a project evaluator.

- -

LSCA PROJECT EVALUATOR RESPONSE FORM

❑ Yes, I am willing to serve as LSCA project evaluator for the project you have assigned to me.

❑ No, I am not able to accept this assignment at this time.

Comments:

_____   _____
                Signature   Date

Oregon State Library

MEMORANDUM

To: [Grantee Project Director]   Date:
           [Grantee Institution]

From: [Library Development Administrator]

Subject: LSCA Grant Project Evaluation

The following peer evaluator has been assigned to conduct the evaluation of your FY [year] LSCA grant project, "Senior Outreach/Online Link." All evaluators have already indicated that they are able to accept the assignment.

> *Evaluator:*   [evaluator name]
>   [evaluator institution]
>
> *Library phone:*   [phone]

You should contact the evaluator promptly to schedule their site visit. Their site visit should take place in the last month of the grant period. Their report needs to be finished, and a copy submitted to both you and me, by the end of the grant project period. In most cases, the evaluation completion date will be [date], unless you are requesting a modification to the grant extending the grant period.

I've enclosed a sample "Memorandum of Understanding," which your local government may want to use in contracting with the evaluator. Some sort of "Memorandum of Understanding," "Letter of Agreement," or other contract is advised, to set forth the terms and conditions of the evaluation. I've also enclosed the "Specifications for LSCA Grant Project Evaluations" with which all evaluators have been provided. The "Specifications" describe the evaluation process and the requirements of the final report. Be sure to check with your evaluator where they want to receive mail. The evaluators are working as private contractors, not as library employees, and may want to have communications sent to their home address.

Please call me if you have any questions about the LSCA grant project evaluation process. I can be reached at [phone].

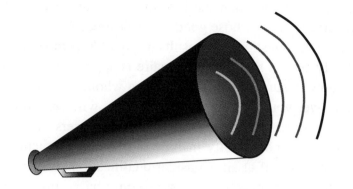

CHAPTER 14

Questionnaires

Keith Curry Lance and Debra Wilcox Johnson

Surveys help to establish baseline data on a new program or service, to gather facts or tap beliefs or attitudes about a program or service during its formative stage, or otherwise to inform decisions for which existing data are not available. Surveys usually gather information to be generalized to a larger group than the sample actually participating as respondents. The specific techniques for gathering information include face-to-face interviews, telephone interviews, and mailed questionnaires. This chapter provides instruction and direction on questionnaires as an instrument used to gather data.

DESCRIPTION OF TECHNIQUE

Before designing a questionnaire, it is critical to clarify the issues on which information will be gathered. Consulting with library staff, board members and other interested parties generates several issues. These will need to be prioritized, so only the information needed is collected, rather than everything that is "just interesting." This will help keep the questionnaire focused and of a reasonable length. This process also helps to clarify questions and whether they might be answered with existing data. Reviewing local records and consulting state and national sources of available information will help prevent collecting information easily found elsewhere and will keep evaluation efforts efficient. (See the bibliography "Available Data for Library Managers," page 200.) Conducting a survey when the information is already available wastes money and time and risks aggravating people whose goodwill is desired. Available data, at a minimum, provide a useful context for the questionnaire results or possible comparisons.

When absolutely certain that a questionnaire is appropriate, the next step is to determine whom to survey and how to survey them. In deciding whom to survey consider what group is in the best position to answer your questions. For example, will randomly selected library patrons entering the library be best? Or are the questions really for users of a particular service? Or perhaps the group of interest is community members, students, or faculty who may not currently come to the library frequently, if at all. Consider qualifications of respondents as well as appropriateness. If employing this approach on a fast response basis (that is, attempting to obtain data needed for a decision quickly), it is important to call upon the smallest number of respondents from whom meaningful data can be gathered.

Who is being surveyed, as well as the issues behind the survey, will affect how to survey respondents. Direct mail, fax, and e-mail are cheaper and faster options, but provide little opportunity for in-depth questions or followup. Telephone and face-to-face interviews using a questionnaire are more expensive and more time-consuming, but provide more opportunity for in-depth questioning or followup as needed. This chapter focuses on mailed questionnaires.

Questionnaire Design

Whether a questionnaire is to be sent out in the mail or used as an interview guide, it is important to consider four issues.

General format—Be brief; do not crowd the page. Use the flexibility of word processing software to design an attractive questionnaire that makes it easy to respond.

Item formats—Opt for structured responses whenever possible. Structured response formats include: yes/no or true/false, multiple choice, check off or ranking lists, Likert or semantic differential scales, and matrix items. Be sure structured response sets are standardized, comprehensive, and mutually exclusive. People may have some resistance to forced answer choices; making the choices clear, making sure they cover possible answers thoroughly ("none of the above" and "other" offer respondents a choice if they have a different answer in mind, but you should try to anticipate the most likely answers), and making sure answers do not overlap will reduce resistance and confusion. Remember that open-ended questions (those to which respondents answer in their own words) are easy to ask and can provide rich data, but are more time-consuming and difficult for respondents to answer and for evaluators to analyze.

Wording items—Use neutral terms that do not direct the respondent toward one response. Be clear and brief. Do not ask compound questions (those that address two items at once). Avoid redundancy, except when you have a compelling reason to be checking the reliability of respondents' answers.

Ordering items—Arrange items in a logical or time sequence. Remember that early questions will inevitably become part of the context for later questions. Controversial items are best placed in the middle of a questionnaire where their controversial nature will not be underscored by the prominence of first or last question placement.

When deciding on questions to be asked and format to be used, think ahead to how analysis will be done before finalizing the questionnaire. Use questions that collect the level of data appropriate to planned statistical tests (see Chapter 17, "Gathering Numbers for Evaluation," for an explanation of levels of data). And make sure that questions get at the variables of interest in a clear manner. For example, if an "average" or "score" is desired for satisfaction with library services, a range of answers (poor to excellent) or scale (1–5) are needed instead of a yes-no combination that answers "were you satisfied?" If comparisons are desired, appropriate screening questions are needed. To compare responses of urban versus rural users, for example, a question on residence is needed to separate the two groups of answers.

Pretesting

If there is a "golden rule" in questionnaire design it might be: "Always pretest a questionnaire." However well it may have been designed and however quickly it may need to be completed, it will benefit from the input of potential respondents. That question which seems obvious may prove to be confusing. Or perhaps, there is another question that should be asked which was overlooked. If possible, call a number of people in your potential respondent pool (how many will depend on money, time, and how large the survey is to be; 3 to 12 should be adequate) and ask if you can send them a draft copy of a questionnaire to respond to and comment on. Send the draft copy with a cover letter reiterating your phone conversation and clearly indicating a date by which you need the response. Choose representative pretesters, but if there are respondents that are important to have answer the questionnaire as part of the data set, save them for the finished questionnaire. In addition to improving the questions, the pretesters can provide an estimate of the time it takes to fill out the questionnaire.

Fostering a High Response Rate

Getting a good response rate is the result of good design of the questionnaire, or the instrument, combined with "sales" of the process. Good design of the questionnaire refers to format issues. Keeping the questionnaire as brief as possible is key to a good response rate. While people like to be asked their opinions, they have many demands on their time and a long questionnaire is likely to land in a "do it later" (i.e., often never) pile. It is a good idea to include a time estimate of how long it will take to complete the questionnaire in a cover letter or instructions; the fore-warning respects busy schedules and increases the chance that someone will allow enough time when starting so as not to get half-way done and never return to it. As a part of paying attention to time and difficulty for respondents, minimize open-ended questions. Make sure a date for response is prominent on the form and reasonable in terms of length of time allowed (i.e., neither too short to get done nor too long and easily forgotten). And be sure to make it easy to return the completed questionnaire; include a self-addressed stamped envelope and a fax number (at least for shorter questionnaires), or design a back page so it is obvious how to fold for return mail. Also, let respondents know whom to contact should they wish to ask questions about the questionnaire.

The other part of good design has to do with the survey more generally. What's being asked and who is asked? Are the questions obviously pertinent? Are they meaningful and potentially important to respondents? Were the respondents picked for particular expertise? It may be worth pointing out why respondents have been chosen and how the survey is important. Share the purpose of the survey and how respondents will impact decisions. This begins to get to the "sales" aspect of getting people to become respondents. While the evaluator may be the most interested party in the responses, establishing a "common good" or public benefit and valuing the individual will help raise the response rate.

Explaining how the findings will be used also helps convince people to participate. Let respondents know how they can be notified when a report is available—and how it will be made available (for example: a report free for the asking, or for sale; an executive summary for an outside agency; a display at the library). Also be sure to explain anonymity or confidentiality procedures when appropriate. Anonymity only truly exists if there is no identification, including no demographic information that would point to a particular individual or institution, on the returned questionnaire. However, if identification is needed for follow-up procedures, you can still assure confidentiality. That is, let respondents know that no individual or agency will be identified in any information reported.

These latter methods of fostering a high response rate may be considered common courtesy as much as "sales." But as retailers know, common courtesy goes a long way in creating a profitable relationship. In this case, the profit of interest is a good response rate. Additional persuasion to respond can take the form of a concrete incentive. Consider including a small reward or entering respondents in a drawing. While the intangible incentives of affecting decision-making, or getting "listened to," or doing one's professional or civic duty may be the strongest for creating a response, a drawing among the first fifty (or 100) respondents may help get the questionnaire immediate attention.

When the questionnaire has been mailed, keep a copy handy in case respondents do contact you. Staff should be aware of the questionnaire and its purposes so they are not caught by surprise with questions from the public. As the questionnaires are returned, keep track of who responds and when. (This requires that some kind of code has been placed on each questionnaire so you can tell from whom it is being returned.) This information will be needed if a second mailing or other follow-up is done. Time is usually of the essence. Be prepared to encourage slow respondents with a postcard or phone call. Also be prepared to close-out returns. Decide ahead of time how long after the announced due date returns will be accepted.

Be aware that while the answer to "what's a good response rate?" most commonly is "it depends," a response rate below fifty percent limits statistical analysis; a seventy-five percent or greater response rate is most desirable. This means be prepared to "remind," "plead with," or "badger" (politely, of course) the potential respondents. It may mean that a due date gets pushed beyond what was planned. For results from the survey sample to be generalizable, they must be representative. A low response rate compromises that representativeness. A good general principle to use with response rates is that the higher the response rate, the more confident you can be about your results; combining these results with other evaluation information can help fill out the picture indicated in the survey results.

Analyzing Data

As the questionnaires come in, check off the respondents and note on the questionnaires the date received. Review and mark responses to identify problem responses and clarify any ambiguous ones before someone enters the data. Code open-ended question responses (see Chapter 20, "Making Sense of Narrative Responses"). Underlining or circling responses in a bright color as they are reviewed will speed up data entry and provide an obvious check that the responses have been reviewed.

If there are a lot of respondents or a lot of questions, use a spreadsheet or database software. You may wish to find an experienced data entry operator, as the quality of the data may depend on this person's skills. Often, however, in-house support staff can do the data entry with simple software, or just a word processing program. Regardless of who does data entry, make sure quality checks are built into the process. This may include defining fields in a database such that only appropriate numbers or symbols will be accepted and periodically rechecking the data entered, i.e., on every tenth questionnaire or the first fifty.

When near close-out time, the demographics (or other descriptors) of who responded need to be checked to see if the returns have skewed the sample. How representative are the respondents of the population under study? Are more responses needed? If it is possible to collect more data, focus on those underrepresented in the returns. If it is impossible to collect more data, clarify what population is actually represented by the data received.

The results of a questionnaire may be explained in many ways. Remember it is best to decide on how the data will be analyzed before the questionnaire is put in final form. Consider the following analytical techniques:

> *Frequencies and percentages*—The simplest descriptive explanation is to report how many and what percentage of respondents gave different answers.

> *Compare responses from group to group*—A breakdown and comparison of questionnaire results by different groups of respondents can be very revealing. For instance, public librarians, older library users, and working

parents might offer very different responses to a questionnaire about latch-key children.

Cross tabulate items—A table which creates a matrix between variables can identify relationships between responses. For example, whether a library has bilingual staff could be matched against library size. SPSS, SAS, or another statistical software package will generate such tables very rapidly for larger samples. For smaller samples, such tables may be produced using word processing software and a calculator.

Correlate items—Correlation analysis indicates if something varies in relationship to something else. That is, a positive correlation exists when an increase in something is accompanied by an increase in something else. A negative correlation exists when an increase in something is associated with a decrease in the other. For example, the results might show that satisfaction with the online catalog is related to a person's experience with computers, or a willingness to support a bond issue is related to length of residence in the community. Correlation can help to confirm that relationships exist between one response and another or between certain responses and certain respondent characteristics. Remember that correlation does not mean causation, only that things tend to occur together. Also, care should be exercised in discussing the significance of the correlation. Statistical significance does not automatically translate to significance in the world.

Analyze trends from survey to survey—A fast response survey may be a good option for collecting follow-up data on a particularly useful question from an earlier, perhaps more in-depth questionnaire. Of course, doing this depends on asking some of the same questions the same way from one questionnaire to the next. A library that makes improvements in a service or area of the collection as a result of earlier questionnaire results can repeat the question that elicited the information that led to the change.

After data has been processed, generate and display findings. At the very least, summarize findings on the questionnaire or in a similar format. Charts and maps should also be considered. Most spreadsheet and database software have adequate graphics capabilities. Finally, draw conclusions from the displayed findings. The data provides information; the information must still be interpreted to provide answers for decision-making. Extracting key findings or themes makes the results more useful as an aid to decision-making.

USE OF RESULTS

Results from a questionnaire may be reported to any number of stakeholders. Consider the audience for any particular report and emphasize those things of special interest for that stakeholder group. Make the report as readable and quotable as possible. Selected tables and graphics are almost always helpful in communicating findings. Regardless of which parts of the questionnaire findings are to be highlighted, the narrative should include a clear overview of the issues, a description of the sample, and an explanation of the methods used.

When a report is produced, disseminate it directly to known appropriate parties and consider a press release to let others know summary results and how they may get more detailed information. Be prepared to make presentations based on the report. In fact, do not count on others to read the report for themselves; design a presentation and actively seek opportunities to share the information gathered. See that the questionnaire results are fed back into the decision-making process responsible for them in the first place.

There are many other ways to ensure that your project makes a contribution outside of your library. Writing articles for state or national publications and submitting a copy of the report to the Educational Research Information Clearinghouse (ERIC) helps disseminate not only the results but information on using questionnaires in evaluation. Contributing sessions at state and national conferences and sharing the questionnaire and report with others embarking on similar projects are additional dissemination activities.

EXAMPLE OF USE OF THE TECHNIQUE

In 1992, the Colorado Council for Library Development (CCLD) began developing a long-range plan for library service to ethnic minority populations. In February 1993, a questionnaire was deemed necessary to establish baseline data on five issues identified by that plan. The need to provide data to guide the planning effort required a fast response survey approach. Because Colorado's ethnic populations are concentrated in the state's metropolitan areas, libraries with budgets over $675,000 received the questionnaire. Following are the five questions posed in the instrument and some of the issues which arose in their development. (See the copy of the questionnaire used at the end of this chapter for suggested format.)

- Does the library employ any staff serving the public who can communicate in Spanish or another language other than English?

- Does the library employ any staff serving the public who attended training designed to promote multicultural awareness?

- Does the library have any materials in Spanish or another language other than English?

- Does the library provide library maps, reading lists, signs, or other user information in Spanish or another language other than English?

- Does the library offer reading lists, exhibits, events or other activities to acknowledge holidays or special dates associated with minority racial/ethnic heritage?

Notably, these are essentially yes/no questions. Early drafts of these questions asked for counts of staff, materials, or events—counts that were not very likely to be readily available. These five questions also include several combinations of earlier questions, such as the fourth question, which combines several earlier questions about different types of user information.

Responses to these questions are presented in case-by-case tables and illustrated with pie charts, all of which were shared with responding libraries in April 1993. This report was published as "Cultural Diversity at Selected Colorado Public Libraries" (FAST FACTS: Recent Statistics from the Library Research Service, No. 70, May 21, 1993). The baseline data also were incorporated in the CCLD plan issued in July 1993. The results of this fast response survey are reported when presentations on this plan are made by Colorado State Library staff or CCLD members. Individual libraries are encouraged to set objectives based on each of the five questions and to monitor their progress toward those objectives. This fast response survey will be repeated annually for at least five years, so that state trends can be monitored.

EXAMPLES OF TRAINING ON THE TECHNIQUE

A good way to train evaluation participants who have not designed questionnaires before is to:

- introduce them to the basic concepts and steps;

- present several scenarios in which questionnaires would be appropriate;

- have participants meet in small groups to draft questionnaires that address those scenarios. (See sample scenarios at the end of this chapter.)

This training model requires at least two hours and enough space for breakout groups to meet comfortably. It is also helpful to select breakout group leaders in advance, review the basic concepts and steps with them, and introduce them to the scenarios. Another person for each group can act as recorder, so the group leader can focus on encouraging and guiding participation in this exercise. After the breakout group exercise, it is desirable to hold a debriefing general session in which group representatives report and everyone has a chance to ask questions.

When students of evaluation are not able to meet together for a large group event, such as a conference session or workshop, an alternative is to duplicate as much of the experience as possible using an audio- or videotaped presentation and handouts. Evaluation students may use these materials individually or in small groups. In such cases, it may be helpful to increase the number of model questionnaires.

Another training approach involves the participants as respondents. Design a questionnaire that illustrates both good and bad techniques in question construction and graphic design. Have participants fill out the questionnaire and then debrief the group on the various strengths and weaknesses of the instrument. This debriefing can first be done in small groups to encourage fuller discussion.

This approach also can be used to simulate a pretest. By providing both the questionnaire and a form for evaluating the instrument, workshop participants potentially see the benefits of the pretest step. Among the specific questions used on such a pretest form are those relating to wording, question order, and length.

REFERENCES AND FURTHER READING

Babbie, Earl. *The Practice of Social Research*, 6th ed. Belmont, Calif.: Wadsworth Publishing Company, 1992.

Leedy, Paul D. *Practical Research: Planning and Design*, 5th ed. New York: Macmillan, 1993.

Swisher, Robert, and Charles McClure. *Research for Decision Making: Methods for Librarians*. Chicago: American Library Association, 1984.

TRAINING CHECKLIST FOR QUESTIONNAIRES

Purpose: The recommended training activities are designed to:

- introduce prospective evaluators to the basic principles of using questionnaires,

- give participants an opportunity to apply those principles in designing a questionnaire, and

- provide an opportunity to give and receive constructive feedback regarding questionnaire design.

Rationale: A hands-on approach to training is recommended to ensure these purposes are fulfilled. Giving prospective evaluators opportunities to apply questionnaire design principles immediately and to provide constructive feedback encourages real-life applications of this evaluation technique.

Number of participants: There is no practical limitation on the overall number of trainees for the proposed training activities. For breakout groups, however, a limit of eight to ten is recommended. When such groups exceed this size, it is very difficult for all group members to participate actively. The overall limit on participants in such training activities is driven by the number of breakout groups for which trainers can obtain spaces, facilitators, and recorders.

Estimated time for activity: Trainees can be introduced to questionnaires in as little as 30 minutes. But, a longer "lecture" period permits the use of more examples. At least 45 minutes should be scheduled for breakout groups to meet. Inevitably, such groups take a few minutes to gather and, later, to return to the larger group, leaving 30 minutes for actual breakout group work. A maximum of 30 minutes is recommended for the debriefing session. While this activity is valuable, there is a limit on most people's patience with it. It is important for training organizers to ensure that breakout group facilitators are individuals who can report back to the larger group concisely and can field questions raised by other participants.

Instructional approach: The recommended training activities include lecture, small group discussion, and large group discussion.

Room arrangement: For large group activities, a "wide-and-shallow" room arrangement is recommended to promote fuller participation. For break-out groups, smaller, separate rooms are preferable. When such arrangements cannot be made, a single room should be large enough to space breakout groups so that they can do their work comfortably, with minimal distractions from other groups.

Special supplies needed: The lecture portion of this training will be more effective for most participants if the presenter uses some type of visual aids (e.g., overhead transparencies, projected computer graphics). Each breakout group should be equipped with basic writing supplies for each member as well as a flip chart, blank overhead transparencies and masking tape.

Advance preparation: Handouts summarizing basic principles of questionnaire design and including model questions are recommended. Trainees should be pre-assigned to equal-sized breakout groups in a readily understandable way (e.g., name tag color, state, evaluation topic). Training staff should verify the breakout groups have needed supplies and be available—and able—to obtain any missing or additional supplies. During the debriefing session, an easel or wall for displaying flip charts and an overhead projector for displaying transparencies should be ready. It is also helpful if someone is available to post flip charts or change transparencies, so that the breakout group reporters do not have to fidget over these tasks.

Directions:

1. Introduce the participants to the basic concepts and steps of questionnaire design.

2. Present several scenarios in which questionnaires would be appropriate.

3. Have participants meet in small groups to draft questionnaires that address those scenarios.

4. Have recorders from small groups report results in a large group session.

The effectiveness of this training may be assessed on the spot by querying as to what was learned or what further information is needed. After the event, training organizers may wish to have any evaluation questionnaire resulting from the training submitted for review and potential use as models for future training events.

TELL IT! Tip Sheet

FAST RESPONSE SURVEYS

Purpose and Logic Behind Use of This Technique

To inform decisions on unanticipated issues that must be made quickly and cannot be addressed with available data or wait for regular survey

Type(s) of Situation(s) for Which Technique Is Used

Any time sufficient data may be obtained from a small sample or universe by asking a few simple questions (yes/no, multiple choice, ranking, rating, Likert scales)

Components of Technique

- Check for available data
- Determine whom to survey and how to survey them
- Conduct a mini-test
- Administer survey
- Tabulate responses
- Analyze data

Supplies Needed

- To administer survey: telephone and/or fax and/or word processing capability
- To tabulate results: spreadsheet software useful
- If you offer prizes you may increase response rate

Personnel Needed

- Individuals to create survey, conduct survey and analyze responses and results

Time Factors

- Time varies with how you collect data (phone, fax, mail)
- Purpose is to operate in a short time span (day, week, month)

Cost Factors

- Varies, but can be done very inexpensively

Further Reading on This Technique

No books or articles exist on fast response survey per se. A good introductory textbook on social science research methods such as the following is recommended: Earl Babbie. *The Practice of Social Research*, 6th ed. Belmont, Calif.: Wadsworth, 1992.

SURVEY PROCESS

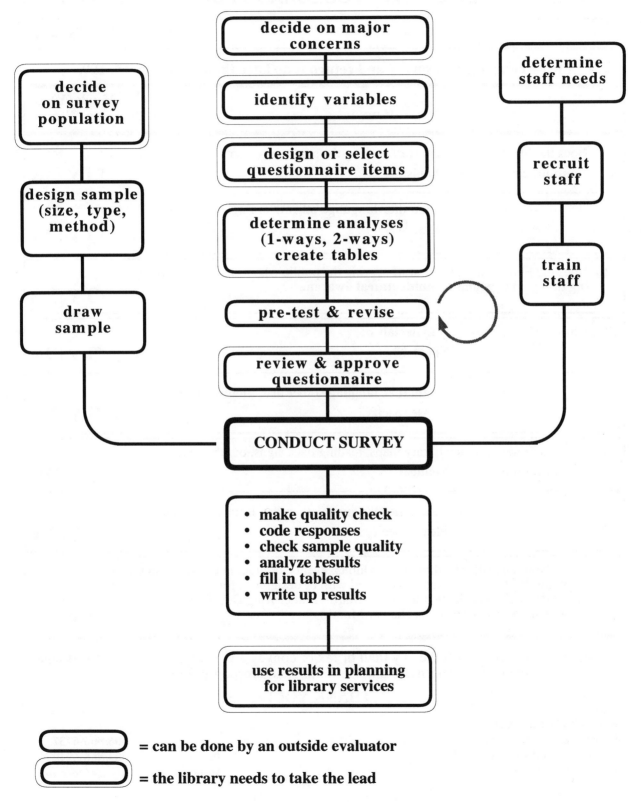

- = can be done by an outside evaluator
- = the library needs to take the lead

CULTURAL DIVERSITY IN COLORADO PUBLIC LIBRARIES

A FAST FACTS Survey

☞ **Please complete this survey and return it no later than February 15, 1993**

Item	Mark (Y)es or (N)o
1. Does the library employ any **staff** serving the public who can **communicate in** a. **Spanish?**	☐ Y ☐ N
b. **... another language** other than English or Spanish? Please specify	☐ Y ☐ N
2 Does the library employ any **staff** serving the public who have attended **training** designed to **promote multicultural awareness?**	☐ Y ☐ N
3. Does the library have any **materials in** a. **Spanish?**	☐ Y ☐ N
b. **... another language** other than English or Spanish? Please specify	☐ Y ☐ N
4. Does the library provide library maps, reading lists, signs, or other **user information in** a. **Spanish?**	☐ Y ☐ N
b. **... another language** other than English or Spanish? Please specify	☐ Y ☐ N
5. Does the library offer reading lists, exhibits, events, or other **activities to acknowledge** holidays or special dates associated with or designated for the celebration of **minority racial/ethnic heritage** (e.g., Martin Luther King Day, Cinco de Mayo, Hanukkah, African-American History Month)	☐ Y ☐ N

Return this completed survey by mail or fax or convey a voice-mail or Internet message containing your name and the number and response for each item.

THANK YOU!

Keith Curry Lance, Director
Library Research Service
201 E. Colfax Ave., Room 309
Denver, CO 80203-1799

voice	**306/866-6737**
fax	**303/866-6940**
Internet	**klance@csn.net**

POINTERS FOR DESIGNING QUESTIONNAIRES

1. What Questions to Ask
- Competence of respondent
- Privacy of respondent
- Relevance to issue
- Needing vs. wanting to know
- Survey as educational tool

2. General Format
- Length
- White space on page
- Columns, back of page
- Defining sections, spaces; emphasizing key items (lines, boxes, shading, placement)

3. Item Formats
- Open-ended questions
- Structured responses:

Yes/no, true/false	Ranking lists
Multiple choice	Likert scales
Check-off lists	Matrix items

4. Structured Responses
- Standardize ranges
- Comprehensive, exhaustive
- Mutually exclusive

5. Wording Items
- Neutrality, balanced viewpoints
- Clear, brief items
- Simple items (no compounds)
- Redundant items (testing reliability)

6. Ordering of Items
- Logical sequence
- Time sequence
- Controversial items
- Halo effect, response sets
- Alternating item format

7. Maximizing Usable Returns
- Keep it short, keep it short.
- "Bribery" to respond (reward, prizes)
- Easing return (SASE, fold/refold)
- Organizing to receive returns (addressee i.d., storage)
- Follow-up mailings, calls

8. Format for Data Entry
- Numbering cases
- Numbering items
- Placing item numbers
- Spacing responses
- Using column, matrix items
- Alternating item formats
- Capturing numeric responses (check, circle; line, spaces, boxes)

9. Data Entry and Analysis
- Coding alpha, string responses (converting words to numbers)
- Missing responses, pages
- Unclear, illegible, inaccurate, or multiple responses
- Numbering cases
- Spreadsheet, database, data entry/ statistical software

Source: Keith Curry Lance, Library Research Service, Denver, Colo.

Scenario 1

EVALUATING PROGRAMS

Your library has recently established full-text document delivery services. A month of publicity has won over a variety of professionals, business people, and educators who are able to take advantage of these new services remotely. Despite this success, these services are threatened by constraints on next year's city budget. The library's supporters on the city council have recommended that the reference staff conduct a small study to ascertain the valuable outcomes resulting from this innovation. Notably, these supporters do not believe it will be helpful to document the volume of service being provided or the end-users' satisfaction with it.

After some discussion, you (the staff) have agreed that the only way to gather this information efficiently before the next council meeting is a fast response survey of frequent new clients. Some preliminary brainstorming has produced the following list of potential outcomes to document:

- How much more quickly clients received needed information,

- the currency of documents delivered,

- the appropriateness of such documents,

- the perceived value the information obtained from the documents, and

- specific consequences (i.e., in terms of professional practice, sales, savings, learning, etc.) which end-users attribute to these services.

Produce a first draft of this fast response survey.

Source: Keith Curry Lance, Library Research Service, Denver, Colo.

Scenario 2

MAKING MID-COURSE CORRECTIONS

You are the state LSCA advisory committee's subcommittee for Title II construction projects. Your state is almost one year into three years of giving LSCA priority to Americans with Disabilities Act (ADA) compliance projects. Nine months ago, potential project directors participated in a two-day workshop that was intended to prepare them to lead such projects. In the evaluation of the workshop during the closing session, participants indicated that they felt prepared adequately to serve as project directors.

Now—with the first year almost at an end—the state's first major ADA court case has resulted in a more complicated—indeed, stricter—interpretation of "reasonable accommodation" than that shared at your original event. (Example: Carrying people up the Carnegie library's front steps is no longer acceptable under any circumstances.) This news had been publicized in the general and library press. Still, most of you believe that the legal position of older, and only partially accessible libraries in the state is not much weaker.

There are some Title II funds remaining which could be used to support expansion of some of the current projects, but it is left over and must be expended before the end of the fiscal year. The committee is agreed that it would be inappropriate to simply announce this fact as so little additional funding is available. Instead, most believe it would be a good idea to do a questionnaire to identify the likely best sites for these additional grants.

Produce a first draft of this questionnaire.

Source: Keith Curry Lance, Library Research Service, Denver, Colo.

FAST RESPONSE QUESTIONNAIRES

The purpose of this exercise is to develop your skills in designing a succinct and focused questionnaire. A user friendly questionnaire (i.e., short and with well-crafted questions) can help improve response rates and make this an efficient evaluation tool.

1. Choose <u>one</u> of the scenarios below for this exercise.

2. Choose a recorder/reporter for your group. The reporter will share the group's work with other workshop participants.

3. Decide who should be surveyed. How will the questionnaire be distributed?

4. Design the questionnaire. This would include five to eight questions with instructions. Create closed-ended questions whenever possible.

5. If time permits, consider what other evaluation information you would need for your scenario.

Scenario One: The library has recently begun offering electronic information directly to patrons via CD-ROM. Before approving an increase in funding to continue and expand this service, decision makers want to know more about the use and effect of the electronic databases.

Scenario Two: Your library has been redesigned to include a popular reading room that features a renewed emphasis on readers advisory. This project was funded by a government grant. For the final evaluation report, more information on the effect of the center is needed.

Scenario Three: Recently, the library staff had an in-service program on customer service. As a result, staff would like to know more about how the patrons rate the library's customer service.

Scenario Four: The library has had its current online catalog for six years. As part of the process to upgrade the system, the library needs to know more about users' impressions and desired changes for the online catalog.

Developed by Debra Wilcox Johnson, Johnson & Johnson Consulting, 1015 Holiday Drive, Waunakee, WI 53597. (608) 849-7286.

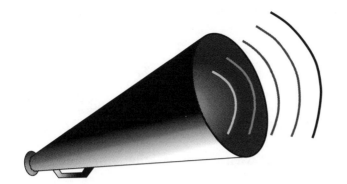

CHAPTER 15

Interviewing

Jane Robbins

For the evaluator who enjoys listening to, observing and "getting to the heart of" the perspectives of library users, the interview may well be the method of choice for gathering evaluative information. A questionnaire administered over the telephone is one type of interviewing and some discussion of telephone interviews is included here; however, for the purposes of this chapter the emphasis will be on person-to-person(s) interviewing. Such interviewing entails a structured time during which the evaluator can sit down with either individual users or one or more groups of users, to have a "conversation." The interview is, though, a special type of conversation because the interviewer must do very little of the talking. In the press of everyday library activities it is rarely possible to take time out, to concentrate on hearing users' voices; interviewing allows for that time-out and most types of interviewing allow for establishing a special relationship with a set of users that can be maintained long past the "official" evaluation activity.

ELEMENTS OF INTERVIEWING

Interviewing is best described as orally asking people questions; yet, this simple description belies that there are many different *types* of interviews: person-to-person interviews with either individuals or groups, including focus groups; elite (e.g., political figures, chief executive officers, media personages) and key informant interviews (e.g., person responsible for success of library fund-raising activity, person responsible for organizing a "save the library" campaign); and telephone interviews. The key components of the interview are good questions and good listening skills.

Good Questions

The guidelines for the development of questionnaires tend to be the same as those for the development of interview schedules for structured interviews. In brief these admonitions are:

- Be crystal clear about what you are asking.

- Ask only the most important and necessary questions.

- Use language that *really will* be understood by your interviewees.

- Favor specific over general questions.

- Favor fact over attitude questions.

- When asking respondents to choose, use lists with no more than seven (7) choices per list—lists of four or five (4 or 5) are preferable.

- Avoid the hypothetical.

- Ask about only one fact, idea or concept in each question.

- Favor questions about the present rather than the past.

- Pretest, *pretest, PRETEST* all questions!

Good Listening Skills

It is essential in interviewing to remember that the goal is to understand what the respondent is saying, not to agree with or evaluate the quality of the answers given. The environment in which the interview takes place must be conducive to good conversation. Interviewers must be genuine, accepting, and empathetic toward those being interviewed. Interviewers also need to be comfortable with people; their posture, gestures and eye contact should invite people to communicate. Guidelines for effective listening are:

- Keep an open mind.

- Create a supportive atmosphere.

- Take note of cues, gestures, tone of voice, body positions, eye movements, breathing and similar body language.

- Listen for feelings as well as words.

- Occasionally check for understanding by paraphrasing what the interviewee stated.

- Demonstrate acceptance and understanding, both verbally and nonverbally.

- Concentrate attention on the interviewee.

- Listen for ideas as well as information.

- Listen optimistically.

While it was pointed out above that a key element of interviews is good questions, there is a type of interviewing, variously called non-standardized or non-structured, used predominately in key informant or elite interviewing, in which there is often only one question, usually framed as "Tell me about...." When interviewing a mayor, principal, or university president about her/his understanding of the library's contribution, the question could be "Tell me about how you see the library contributing to the community, school, or university." Another type of unstructured interview is used with consumers/users of services. An example to be used with a known frequent library user might be: "Tell me about the last time you used the library." This type of interviewing stresses the interviewee's definition of the "situation" of interest; it allows the interviewee to introduce what is relevant. In essence, the interviewee teaches the interviewer what is important. It is a common type of response from interviewers in the unstructured interview to comment that they learned the answers to questions they would not even have had the presence to ask.

Interviewers

The interviewer's roles are to ask well-crafted questions, to probe for clarification or elaboration, to listen, and to observe. Interviewers should like people and should like to listen; they should be as similar in appearance and demeanor to those being interviewed as is possible. It is best if the interviewer's age, race, and social circumstances are similar to the interviewee's; where an interviewee speaks a language other than English as their primary language, interviewing in the interviewee's language, including black vernacular, is wise. When utilizing several interviewers, it is crucial to provide them with training in the interview process as well as in the purposes for the specific interviewing being undertaken. Consistency among interviews is needed.

Interviewees

While most people selected to be interviewees are fine participants in the evaluation process, the analysis of vast amounts of interview data and studies of interviewers have identified common problematic "types" of interviewees. On the grounds that being forewarned can aid an interviewer in getting useful results even though the interviewee is somewhat difficult, the types of problem respondents are here listed: ax grinders; self-styled experts; single topic respondents; special cases; "yes/no" or brief mumble only respondents; and, the helpful or "what do you want me to say" respondents. In group interviews, respondents can also be identified who are non-participants or advisors, i.e., respondents who want to rephrase what the other respondents "really meant" to say.

This list of types of interviewees describes adults, and it is usually adults who are interviewed in library evaluation activities; however, the interview is an excellent and rewarding, if challenging, means to gather information from children. The critical elements for interviewing children are the same as those for adults: warmth, genuineness, and empathy. Interviewing children does, though, require special considerations. Some of these considerations are:

> Children younger than eight generally understand twice as much language as they are able to express. They do understand; they just have limited abilities in articulation.

> Use simple, direct words. Avoid pronouns, double negatives, if/then constructions, and complex sentences.

> Children are egocentric. Provide plenty of time to listen to their responses, understand that they include themselves in each happening, and that the only experience important to them is their personal experience.

> Make sure the environment in which the interview takes place is child-friendly. Toys, color, meeting eye to eye at the child's level, and making sure your nonverbal messages are welcoming are particularly important.

> Be patient. The child does not particularly want to be interviewed; the interview is scheduled to meet your needs, not the child's. Give the child equal time; for however long the interview will take, the child gets that amount of time for their agenda.

> Kids like to: play, guess things, show adults that they are wrong, repeat, be powerful, take turns, be active, know what is going on, and leave a place with something in their hands (McDonald and Willett, 1990).

Telephone Interviews

Many libraries have undertaken telephone interviews to assess the perceived impact of their services on both their user and non-user communities. All the recommendations regarding other types of interviews, except those related to the environment of the interview location, apply. In telephone interviews the interviewer can control the place from which the telephone calls are made. The location should be quiet and comfortable with a telephone instrument that is comfortable to use and allows for free hands to fill in the interview schedule. At the other end of the telephone connection, the interviewer, as well as the interviewee, are at the mercy of the location of the phone answered and any activities that may be going on at that location such as television, stereo, or children playing. Also, in telephone interviewing the demeanor of the interviewer does not carry such a high level of importance, but listening ability and tone of voice are equally, if not more, important.

The relatively recent advent of the low-cost, widely used telephone answering machine has caused concern among some users of the telephone interview that response rates to telephone surveys may be reduced due to these devices. A 1990 California based random-digit dialing survey that generated about 330,000 calls and completed interviews at over 24,000 households confirmed that 31 percent of the households had operating answering machines. It is important to note that many other of the called households could have had machines that were not in use when the interviewer called (Piazza, 1993). Recent telecommunications industry estimates (1991) suggest that over 43% of U.S. households have telephone answering machines (Xu, Bates, and Schweitzer, 1993).

One telephone interview study found that households where answering machines were encountered on the initial call attempt were more likely eventually to complete the survey than households where no answer or a busy signal was encountered. In another study it was found that answering machine households were more likely to be contacted, more likely to complete an interview, and less likely to refuse to participate. These and similar results suggest that answering machines, rather than inhibiting telephone interview success, actually aid in facilitating communications between interviewers and respondents. It has been hypothesized that although it is undoubtedly true that some people use answering machines to weed out unwanted calls, many owners use the machines as a way of maximizing their accessibility (Piazza, 1993).

AN EXAMPLE OF THE USE OF THE INTERVIEW TECHNIQUE

As part of an evaluation of bookmobile service it has been decided that it is important to capture the behaviors and perspectives of bookmobile users. Decisions have been made regarding:

which routes and which stops will be included in the study; what days and times the interviews will take place;

that the interviews will take place in the bookmobile rather than via telephone;

the selection method of the interviewees from among those using the bookmobile during the interview time;

the total number of interviews needed; and

the number of individuals conducting the interviewing (in order to determine interviewer training requirements).

An interview schedule that has been prepared to guide the interview follows.

BOOKMOBILE EVALUATION USER INTERVIEW SCHEDULE

Bookmobile route:

Location of stop:

Date: _____ _____ _____
                  day of week   month   date

Approximate age of user: _____ _____ _____ _____
                           under 10   11–20   21–65   66 or older

First name of user: _____

1. What do you "get out" of using the bookmobile?

       a. materials
       b. talking with the librarian/driver
       c. talking with other users
       d. something to look forward to
       e. other

2. Of the items/things you mentioned, which are most important to you?

3. If you couldn't come to the bookmobile, what would you miss the most?

4. Other comments?

USE OF RESULTS

Upon completion of each interviewing session the interviewer needs to analyze the interviews by searching for themes and extracting useful quotes, i.e., the voices of the users. When all the interviews are completed, the interviewing session themes that have been identified should be analyzed to determine whether there are important characteristics that apply to specific groups of interviewees or other variables being analyzed. In the bookmobile evaluation example given above, it would be important to analyze responses by route, stop location, age of user, and perhaps, day, time, and date of stop. The analysis needs to keep in mind what would be meaningful to each of the stakeholder groups—librarians, users, taxpayers, funders—that have an interest in the evaluation being undertaken. It may be useful to prepare a set of executive summary sheets for each stakeholder group to attach to the final report of the interview section of the evaluation report.

REFERENCES AND FURTHER READING

Garrett, Annette. *Interviewing: Its Principles and Methods*. 3rd rev. ed. Edited by Margaret Mangold and Eleanor Zaki. New York: Family Service Association of America, 1982.

McDonald, Lynn, and Holly Willet. "Interviewing Young Children." In *Evaluating Strategies and Techniques for Public Library Children's Services: A Sourcebook.*, ed. Jane Robbins, et al., 115–30. Madison, Wisc.: University of Wisconsin, School of Library and Information Studies, 1990.

Piazza, Thomas. "Meeting the Challenge of Answering Machines." *Public Opinion Quarterly* 57 (Summer 1993): 219–31.

Richetto, Gary M., and Joseph P. Zima. *Interviewing*. Chicago: Science Research Associates, 1981.

Seidman, I. E. *Interviewing as Qualitative Research: A Guide for Researchers in Education and the Social Sciences*. New York: Teachers College, 1991.

Xu, Minghua, Benjamin J. Bates, and John C. Schweitzer. "The Impact of Messages on Survey Participation in Answering Machine Households." *Public Opinion Quarterly* 57 (Summer 1993): 232–37.

SUGGESTION FOR TRAINING: INTERVIEWING A YOUNG CHILD

This training example is designed to provide experience in interviewing a child under eight years of age. While truly *effective* interviewing of young children requires a thorough understanding of the social, psychological, and cognitive development of young children, working through this exercise will be valuable for potential interviewers of any age interviewee. This exercise can be set up as a *role-play* in which one participant agrees to portray the child being interviewed and another the librarian-interviewer, while other participants are active observers of the interview. A perhaps better alternative is to have an actual child and children's librarian pair perform a *demonstration* of an interview and have all participants in the training be active observers. This exercise requires that a *storyteller* tell a short (no more than five minute) story or read a brief book as the first part of the actual training session. This will be necessary whether the session is set up as a role-play or a demonstration. It is useful to have a children's librarian aid in making the selection of the story or book. Other personnel will be the *child* (or someone playing the role of a child) and the *librarian-interviewer* (or role-player). All other participants act as observers. An explanation of the interview session is given on the next page.

SESSION ON INTERVIEWING A CHILD

Storyteller: You are to tell a story or read a book suitable for children ages 5 to 8. The story will be read to all the participants in this training session.

Child (age 6 or 7): You have just attended story hour at the library. The librarian has asked to talk with you about the last story you heard and you have agreed. You have been to a story hour several times before; however, this is the first time you've heard this story.

Librarian: You are a children's librarian familiar with storytelling techniques and with the story told. In this case, you have determined that the story was told well and you "like" the story.

You are trying to determine two things through your interview with the child:

1. Did the child like this story enough to want to hear
    a. this story again
    b. stories similar to this story

2. Anything additional the child may want to tell you related to either
    a. this story
    b. story hour
        i. this specific story hour
        ii. story hours at the library in general

You are to begin the interview by showing the child an object and asking the child to comment on how this object reminds her/him of the story.

Observers: All observers are to observe the interview without participating either orally or with body language. At the close of the interview each observer is to complete an Observer Answer Sheet.

Trainer: As trainer you are responsible for seeing that an appropriate story or book is selected. You are to determine whether the session will be a role-play or a demonstration and further you are to see that all supplies and answer forms are prepared and available in sufficient quantity. You are the timekeeper and the discussion leader. The discussion can follow the order of the Observer Answer Sheet questions.

OBSERVER ANSWER SHEET

Please respond to these questions individually before discussing them with other participants.

1. How comfortable would you say the child was with the librarian?

    Very comfortable_____
    Somewhat comfortable_____
    Somewhat uncomfortable_____
    Very uncomfortable_____

2. How comfortable would you say the librarian was with the child?

    Very comfortable_____
    Somewhat comfortable_____
    Somewhat uncomfortable_____
    Very uncomfortable_____

3. How mature did the librarian consider the child to be?

    Very mature_____
    Somewhat mature_____
    Somewhat immature_____
    Very immature_____

4. How mature did you judge the child to be?

    Very mature_____
    Somewhat mature_____
    Somewhat immature_____
    Very immature_____

5. At the end of the interview, would you say this interview came to a successful close?

    Successful close _____
    Partially successful close_____
    Unsuccessful close _____

6. Overall, would you say that the librarian helped the child in her/his attempts to express her/himself?

    No   (go to 6.a.)
    Yes   (go to 6.b.)

    a. At what points in the interview would you say the librarian was not helpful? What happened? How wasn't it helpful? What happened next?

    b. At what points in the interview would you say the librarian was helpful? What happened? How was it helpful? What happened next?

7. Did you observe any communications accidents/failures during the interview?

    No   (go to 8)
    Yes   How might each have been averted?

8. Was there anything said or heard during the interview that surprised you? If so, could any of that surprise be attributed to the way the interview was conducted?

9. What events occurred during the interview that could be used as measures of the quality of the interview? Which elements of a librarian/child interview should be tracked as measures of progress in such an interview?

SUGGESTION FOR TRAINING: LISTENING

The Process

1. Have two volunteers leave the room.

2. Have one more person sit at the front of the room.

3. Read the story below slowly and distinctly to the person sitting at the front of the room.

4. Call in one of the people who left and have the person at the front tell her/him the story as best as s/he can remember.

5. Call the other person who left the room back and have the person who last heard the story repeat it to her/him as best as possible.

6. Ask questions of the entire group.

   - What time of day was it?
   - What season of the year was it?
   - What happened?
   - Why did the driver feel as he did at the end?

7. After all questions have been "answered," lead a discussion focused on the following:

   There are no answers to the questions; what assumptions were made? Why?

The Story

(Read slowly and distinctly)

It was dark and the streets were slippery. The driver was tired and eager to get home to his family. As he rounded the curve, he did not see the frail figure standing by the side of the road. Only when he felt the truck skid and heard the impact did he realize what had happened. For one brief minute he wanted to keep going, but he managed to pull over and stop. He jumped out and hurried back. As he approached the scene he felt a strange sense of relief.

TRAINING CHECKLIST FOR INTERVIEWING

Purpose: To provide an opportunity to observe an interview between a young child and a librarian in order to reinforce instruction regarding key elements of interviewing.

Rationale for approach: Regardless of whether the role play or demonstration version is used, this approach allows persons unfamiliar with the interviewing process, and especially that process involving young children, to observe the process in action. The approach allows participants to gain familiarity with the process without actually being an interviewer and provides an opportunity to analyze a live interview.

Number of participants: No limitations, except those dictated by the size of the training facility.

Time required:		
	Telling the story	7 minutes
	(The story itself must be no more than 5 minutes)	
	Child/Librarian interview	5 to 8 minutes
	Completing observation forms	5 minutes
	Discussion	10 minutes
	Total time (approximately)	30 minutes

Instructional approach: Lecture on the interview method, application and observation (combined), and discussion based on application and observation (reflection).

Room arrangement: Lecture style. Room needs enough space and good sight lines so that the storyteller and the child and children's librarian interview can be easily observed by all in the room.

TRAINING CHECKLIST FOR LISTENING

Purpose: To demonstrate:

- It is difficult to listen completely.

- People bring to human interactions their unique histories and thus all people hear what is said filtered through their own experience.

Rationale for approach: This approach allows participants to experience how a group of people, all listening to the same information at the same time, can understand what is heard differently. It further allows them to listen to how two people interpret the story—noting especially the person who hears the story only through the words of someone who did not experience the original telling of the story. Participants also get to experience their own "hearing" of the story and to compare their hearing with others' understandings, thus pointing out the effect of life history on hearing.

Number of participants: No limitations, except those dictated by the size of the training facility. It is also possible to have breakout groups of approximately 10 each do the exercise. One person then needs to be assigned the responsibilities of the trainer.

Time required: Approximately 20 to 30 minutes.

Instructional approach: Lecture on listening skills, application and observation (combined), and discussion based on application and observation (reflection).

Room arrangement: Lecture style. Can utilize breakout rooms and have the three volunteers sit in a chair in the middle of a circle made up of the other members of the breakout group.

Special supplies: None required.

Advance preparation: Make up a "generic" story and questions about it (or use the exercise on page 172).

Directions: No special directions are required as this training activity is without complication.

1. Have two people leave the room.

2. Read a story.

3. Have someone retell the story to one person who left the room and have that person retell it to the second person who left the room.

4. Ask questions about the story.

5. Discuss "answers."

TELL IT! Tip Sheet
INTERVIEWING

Purpose and Logic Behind Use of This Technique

- To understand individuals' experiences and their meanings for them
- To make one-to-one contact between individuals and the interviewer
- To hear the voices of those interviewed

Type(s) of Situation(s) for Which Technique Is Used

- When person-to-person interaction is desired
- When information in more depth than questionnaires can accommodate is needed
- When interviewees know more about the question(s) to be asked than the framer of the question(s)

Components of Technique

- Determine the question(s) to be asked
- Determine whom to ask
- Determine how (person-to-person, telephone) to ask them
- Prepare interview schedule
- Decide on method to capture interview data (notes, tape recording)
- Administer interviews making sure that permission is granted for use of information
- Analyze notes or tapes
- Prepare report

Supplies Needed

- Comfortable and quiet room if person-to-person interviewing
- Quiet space with comfortable desk chair, telephone equipment, and writing space
- Interview schedules or tape recorder
- Writing instruments

Personnel Needed

- One or more interviewers depending upon the number of interviews to be undertaken

Time Factors

- Will vary depending upon number and complexity of interviews

Cost Factors

- Relatively high cost if interviewing large numbers
- Training interviewers is an important part of costing

Further Reading on This Technique

Annette Garrett. *Interviewing: Its Principles and Methods.* 3rd rev. ed. Edited by Margaret Mangold and Eleanor Zaki. New York: Family Service Association of America, 1982.

I. E. Seidman. *Interviewing as Qualitative Research: A Guide for Researchers in Education and the Social Sciences.* New York: Teachers College, 1991.

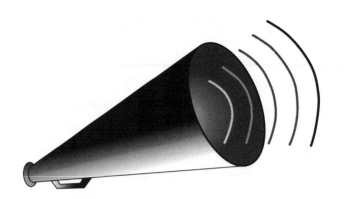

CHAPTER 16

Focus Groups

Debra Wilcox Johnson

Focus groups offer information agencies a personalized approach for gathering evaluation and needs assessment information. The service professions, in particular, are drawn to this technique developed in the marketing field. The reasons for this lie in the dynamics of the group process and the usefulness of the technique for reaching people not traditionally represented in other approaches, such as questionnaires. Focus groups are useful when evaluators are seeking innovative or creative solutions and are particularly suited for collecting information not easily obtained in other ways.

A focus group is an in-depth, face-to-face interview of a group of eight to twelve people representing some target group and centered on a single topic. The method is useful for explaining reasons behind interviewees' attitudes, feelings, and behaviors. The results provide a range of responses about a certain service or issue. Generally, consensus is not the aim of focus groups, although a uniformity in some responses may result. Likewise, the intent is not to quantify the extent to which opinions are held in the group. Instead, the process generates information that increases the library's understanding of complex issues from multiple perspectives. The method also has the advantage of being able to be used with all age groups.

The assumption underlying the technique is that the energy generated by the group process results in greater diversity and depth of responses. This means that the combined group effort produces more (and richer) information than the sum of individual responses. This is sometimes compared to snowballing, when one person's response triggers another. The interviewer can build follow-up questions based on one response, or contrast different points of view in order to promote discussion.

The focus group approach often is contrasted to the questionnaire as a data-gathering technique. The group interview process tends to elicit more complete answers, since the interviewer can probe for further explanation or clarify misunderstood questions. This technique is especially useful for working with those who are not inclined to respond to written questionnaires. These people can include those who have been over-surveyed or who cannot fill out the written survey due to skill level or disability. In libraries, the technique has been successful for reaching those not usually represented in data gathering, such as young people, or those under-served by the library.

Sometimes the focus group is a replacement for the written questionnaire, but it works well in conjunction with the survey method. Once questionnaire results have been collected, the interview process can be used to help explain in more depth the reasons behind the responses or to explore the implications of the questionnaire responses. Focus groups conducted prior to the design of a questionnaire aid in the construction of the instrument. This is true in two areas: how to communicate with the group (language, jargon) and how much is known about the topic of interest by the group (never used a service or library, minimal exposure to concepts).

There are, of course, limits to the use of focus groups. Other approaches can gather data from a systematically drawn sample of the population of interest. In contrast, the focus group uses a "purposive" sample, i.e., those that fit the purposes of the study and are selected by the evaluator because of their ability to speak to the questions of interest. Given this type of sampling, the evaluator uses caution when generalizing the results to everyone who might use the service or desire a service.

The results of a focus group are illustrative and give a range of ideas in relation to the topic of interest. As noted earlier, the technique is not designed to get at the "extent" questions. One example relates to a public library bond issue. If the library desires to know the likelihood of passage, a telephone interview of randomly selected citizens is the desired approach to gain an estimate of the percentage of votes in favor. The focus group, on the other hand, would be useful for identifying possible media messages, barriers to passage, and potential supporters for the bond issue. The focus group also could be used after an unsuccessful bond vote to broaden understanding of the results and provide insights into changes for future efforts.

ELEMENTS OF THE METHOD

Prior to choosing the method, the evaluator needs to carefully consider what the library wants and needs to know about a given topic. As is the case with choosing any evaluation approach, the first question is: "What do you want to know?" Once this is known, the evaluator can determine if the focus group is the appropriate technique for what the library is seeking.

Once this basic step occurs, the process includes four key elements: preparing an interview guide, recruiting participants, conducting the sessions, and writing a report on the results. In all cases, the library may use its own staff to carry out the activities or use outside expertise. If using outside assistance, it is most likely the library would use an outside interviewer for two of the steps: to conduct the sessions and to prepare a report.

The purpose of *preparing an interview guide* is to clearly state the objectives of the interview and to develop questions focused on these objectives. The objectives are stated in terms of what is desired from the interviews. What information is needed? This could be new information, clarification of anticipated perspectives, opinions about a specific service (or lack of service), and confirmation of "the blinding flash of the obvious" (e.g., widely held views).

Once the objectives are set, three to five questions are written. The questions start with a warm-up query to get people talking; they then move from the general to the more specific. The structure of the questions is similar to a funnel, where each one feeds into the next, more specific question. The questions are supported with probes to be used by the interviewer to elicit a good range of responses and to address different aspects of a question. Generally the interviewer will follow the order of the questions, although not to the degree of preventing discussion of issues that may naturally occur earlier in the interview. (See two sample interview guides on pp. 181 and 182.)

Recruitment of participants is affected by the objectives of the focus group. What participants are most likely to be able to speak to the outcomes specified in the objectives? Who can best answer the questions in the interview guide?

Eight to twelve people are selected because of homogeneity of characteristics related to the subject of the interview. A simple example of this is the user-nonuser split. If the library desires to know why a particular service is not used, the participants need to come from the non-user group. Sometimes, representatives from other agencies in the community or other departments in the school may speak about their agencies' constituencies from their experience with the client group. A few simple screening questions often are used to help select participants.

Candidates for participation can be contacted in person or in writing. In either approach, potential participants are told that they are part of a pool and may or may not be chosen. Confirmation of participation usually is sent in writing, and telephone reminders are made 24 to 48 hours prior to the interview.

Two issues come up in this stage of the process. First is size of the group. Groups in the eight to twelve range are considered necessary to the group dynamic. A smaller number can reduce the likelihood of diversity of views, and too large a group makes it difficult for full participation. Usually two extra people are invited to allow for last minute drop-outs.

The second issue is compensation for participants. Reports by libraries about use of the method show that cash payment is not always used, although some "thank you" gift might be given, such as gift certificates to local businesses or for the library book sale. While the "payment for participation" model seems necessary for the marketing field, within the service professions it has not been critical to attendance in many cases. At a minimum, participants are offered refreshments and transportation reimbursement if needed.

The *conducting the session* stage is the most simply described. The session lasts from one-and-a-half hours to two. The moderator orients the group to the process by briefly stating the purpose of the interview (i.e., to learn more about...), setting ground rules for the session (e.g., one person speaking at a time), and explaining his or her role in the process. With the interview guide as the structure, the moderator uses the warm-up question as a rapport-building device; it helps orient the group to the process. Throughout the interview, the moderator makes opportunities for all to participate and uses the probes to provide in-depth responses. In closing the session, the interviewer gives respondents time for any additional comments, briefly explains how the results will be used, and thanks the group for participation on behalf of the library.

The key to the success of the interview is the moderator. Care in the selection and, if necessary, training of the interviewer is essential to assuring useful results. Since the focus group method can often translate into positive public relations for the library, the interpersonal dynamics carry much importance.

Supporting the work of the interviewer is a note-taker. Working with the interview guide, the note-taker identifies speakers and records key points made by participants. This note-taking can be supported by taping (audio or video) that would allow for transcripts, if desired.

While the "rich" data that comes from the interviews is an advantage of the process, it does present some challenges for *writing up results*. The interview guide can serve as a structure to the report, although the discussion may not have followed the questions neatly. The objectives for the evaluation may be a better way of organizing, allowing the writer to draw from responses to each of the questions as they relate to the objectives.

Within the broad framework chosen, the writer seeks to identify categories of responses in order to group the results in a meaningful way. What themes emerged? Individual quotations can be used to support the overall summary in each of the categories or themes. A short introductory summary of key findings is very useful for orienting the reader to the fuller report.

EXAMPLES OF USING THE TECHNIQUE

The focus group technique is very versatile, allowing the library to use it for a wide range of services and to reach a variety of people. The interview can elicit information to evaluate any aspect of library service or the library as a whole. Evaluation of library processes (e.g., circulation) and products (e.g., community service directory) can occur with the method. It has been used to reach nonusers, children and young adults, undergraduates, new faculty, and other groups traditionally underrepresented in evaluation data collection efforts. The process also can be used to evaluate the library's public relations efforts, including testing the efficacy of library media messages. If the library engages in collaborative ventures, the technique can bring different partners together to assess the library's contribution to the total effort. Finally, the focus group is an effective management tool to assess staff perceptions and analyze work and library processes.

Two sample interview guides pertaining to public libraries are presented here to illustrate some ways in which the method can be applied in a library setting (see pp. 181 and 182). The first centers on a major library product—the online catalog. Participants would need to be screened for use of the catalog. The second addresses the collaborative role of the library in local literacy efforts. In this case, participants are from the literacy agencies or volunteer tutors.

USE OF RESULTS

Clarity of objectives at the beginning of the focus group process is the key to producing usable results. Keeping in mind the different stakeholders for any project, do the objectives for the interviews speak to more than one stakeholder? Program organizers, for example, may be most interested in information that may lead to program changes. The library administrator may be interested in community awareness of the service or support of a given service or product. A board member might be interested in impact stories that emerge from the interview. While not every stakeholder's concern will be addressed, the method can speak to many at one time within the framework established by the interview guide.

No matter what method is chosen for evaluation, someone can question the results or method used. As noted earlier, the approach has limits, and users of the technique have to guard against an overzealous acceptance of the results. Instead, reporting the results in terms of indicators of the type of responses to a service or as a range of possible explanations keeps the results in perspective. When there is virtual consensus across different groups being interviewed, this lends more credibility to stronger claims about the results in relation to the program being evaluated.

Paring down the results into usable pieces is another strategy for making the results meaningful. While the staff of a project might desire the fuller report, a fact sheet highlighting key findings helps to translate the findings to a more diverse, and possibly tangential, audience.

The best use of evaluation results is to blend the findings from the focus group with other information gathered in relation to a specific service. Service statistics, exit surveys, anecdotal reports, and observations by staff can be combined with the results from the focus group. As results from different data sources converge, program evaluators can tell a more complete and accurate story about the service to a variety of stakeholders.

Sample Interview Guide
EVALUATION OF CATALOG

Objectives: To increase the library's understanding of the reasons for and characteristics of use of the library catalog. To assess public perceptions about the quality and usefulness of the library's catalog. To identify needed improvements in the existing catalog.

Questions:

1. Briefly describe what library catalogs you have used and how often you use them.
   [Warm-up Question]
   [*Probes*: Online? Card? As student? During every library visit?]

2. For what purposes do you use the library catalog?
   [*Probes*: Identify specific title? Information on a subject of interest? For work information? For school? Finding something good to read?]

3. What features of this library's online catalog do you find useful?
   [*Probes* (based on features of the library's catalog): Help screens? Documentation for use? Signage?]

4. Which features of our online catalog cause you difficulty or are lacking altogether?
   [*Probes* (based on features of the library's catalog): Help screens? Documentation for use? Signage?]

5. What characteristics do you think are the most important in an online catalog?
   [*Probes*: Staff assistance? Remote access? Speed? Accuracy? All library materials? Terminals in stacks? Cross references? Forgiving commands? Menu?]

Sample Interview Guide
EVALUATION OF COLLABORATIVE LITERACY EFFORTS

Objectives: To describe the information seeking behavior of literacy providers. To understand the role of the library in the delivery of literacy instruction. To learn what factors contribute to increased use of library resources by literacy providers. To assess awareness of library services in support of literacy education.

Questions:

1. Most of you have been involved in literacy education for more than a year.
   Can you share one story from your experiences? (Warm-up question)
   [*Probes*: Unique experiences? Success stories? Several examples from tutoring or teaching over time?]

2. When you are tutoring or teaching, what types of questions arise?
   [*Probes*: Your own or students' questions. Related to preparing lesson? Resources to supplement learning? Personal needs of students? About their children? Employment?]

3. Where do you find the information or materials you need?
   [*Probes*: Colleagues? Own library? Agency collection?]

4. What resources and services are available from the public library to support your work and the local literacy effort?
   [*Probes*: Range of services from materials to space. Involvement of library in area literacy consortium?]

5. What would make your use of library services as a tutor or teacher more convenient?
   [*Probes*: Publicity? Specific types of materials? Display of collections? Aids for students? Procedures and rules? Contact person?]

TRAINING ON THE METHOD

Training on use of focus groups, patterned on the following three components, offers an effective instructional framework. The three elements are:

- presentation on the rationale and four stages of the focus group technique,

- application of some aspect of the focus group process, and

- discussion of application in light of information covered during the presentation.

Following an outline similar to the one used in this chapter, the trainer reviews the rationale and purposes of the focus group technique. Description of the four stages of the process can be enlarged to discuss the pros and cons of different approaches to each stage (e.g., taping the session or not; hiring an outside interviewer vs. use of staff person). A sample interview guide linked to a topic familiar to the audience can be used as an example throughout the presentation.

During the second part of the training, one of two activities can be used. The first module would result in sample written interview guides. With this tactic, the workshop participants are split into groups of approximately eight people. Several scenarios are developed by the trainer, but each scenario is related to a common topic. An example of this would be a set of scenarios that addresses different aspects of children's services, circulation services, or reference services. The number of scenarios used is dependent on the number of groups, but each scenario would be used by at least two groups for comparison purposes. Workshop participants can embellish or refine the scenarios as desired. Based on the scenario, the group details the objectives of the interviews and prepares questions (three to five) with probes. Additionally, the group can describe logical interviewee groups and methods of recruitment.

Following the group exercise, the trainer asks groups to share some portion of their work with the group as a whole. This might be a sample objective, a warm-up question, or final question. The trainer can point to effective strategies from the examples, and participants can be asked for further suggestions on approaches for a given scenario. Observations about the process of developing an interview guide can be elicited from the group as a summary to the discussion. The trainer concludes with observations about what was learned and entertains other questions about the process.

In the second training module, more preparation is required. Prior to the training, the trainer recruits interviewers from participants to conduct a focus group interview with those attending the training. Individuals are preassigned to groups of eight to twelve, and a note-taker is designated. In this case, the trainer develops an interview guide. This can be a library-related topic or a "neutral" non-library topic, such as dining out or travel. Since the interest is in observing the method rather than the content of the interview, there is some advantage to avoiding library topics for the demonstration. Each interviewer would be oriented prior to the training, as a group or individually over the telephone.

Workshop attendees are asked to participate in a focus group interview and to observe the nature of the group dynamics, effectiveness of the questions and probes, and techniques used by the interviewer. The note-takers will be able to make observations about the process of note-taking during an interview.

Upon completion of the interviews, the group reconvenes for discussion of the process. Observations about the process are elicited from the group by the trainer, taking one aspect of the interview at a time (e.g., questions used, group dynamics). The trainer concludes with observations about what was learned and entertains other questions about the process.

REFERENCES AND FURTHER READING

Greenbaum, Thomas L. *The Practical Handbook and Guide to Focus Group Research.* Lexington, Mass.: D.C. Heath, 1988.

Hutton, Bruce, and Suzanne Walters. "Focus Groups: Linkages to the Community." *Public Libraries* 27 (Fall 1988): 149–52.

Johnson, Debra Wilcox. "Keeping Things in Focus: Information for Decision Making." In *Keeping the Book$: Public Library Financial Practices*, ed. Jane B. Robbins and Douglas L. Zweizig, 405–19. Fort Atkinson, Wisc.: Highsmith Press, 1992.

Krueger, Richard A. *Focus Groups*. Newbury Park, Calif.: Sage, 1988.

Widdow, Richard, et al. "The Focus Group Interview: A Method for Assessing Users' Evaluation of Library Service." *College and Research Libraries* 52 (July 1991): 352–59.

TRAINING CHECKLIST FOR FOCUS GROUPS

Purpose: To review the elements of the focus group process and the rationale for use of the technique and to put this method in the context of other evaluation approaches.

Rationale for approach: Depending on which training module is used, the design blends several ways of learning: listening, writing, observing, hands-on, and reflection. This variety helps assure the training will fit the diversity of learning styles present in the group, and each approach reinforces the other.

Number of participants: No limitations, except those dictated by the size of the training facility.

Time required: The training as described takes approximately two and one-half hours. While the first module may be done in less time, the second module involving the demonstration of the focus groups needs the full two and one-half hours.

Instructional approach: The two modules described use lecture, application and observation (combined), and discussion based on application and observation (reflection).

Room arrangement: Lecture hall or tables of eight to ten. For the first training module, participants can do the exercise in logical groupings where they are already seated. For the demonstration, groups will need to be dispersed to other rooms, although up to two demonstrations could be done in the same room if it is large enough to accommodate the simultaneous conversations of each group.

Special supplies: For the first module, a scenario and outline of an interview guide is prepared for each group. A sample interview guide can be attached for reference. For the demonstration module, a list of groups is distributed and a guide for the notetakers (questions for the interview dispersed over several pages of paper) is produced.

Advance preparation for participants: A reading distributed prior to the training can help orient participants to the topic. A query about the prior experience of participants with focus groups, either as participant and/or interviewer, can be helpful to the trainer.

Directions: Instructions for each of the modules can be given orally at the end of the presentation. In addition, written directions for the process in the first module can be included with the interview guide outline distributed to each participant. In the second module, the interviewers are oriented about the process prior to doing the demonstration.

FOCUS GROUP INTERVIEWS

The purpose of this exercise is to learn more about designing an interview guide for a focus group interview. The interview guide is essential to a successful group interview and helps assure that the needed information is collected.

1. Choose <u>one</u> of the scenarios below for this exercise.

2. Choose a recorder/reporter for your group. The reporter will share the group's work with other workshop participants.

3. Decide who should be interviewed. What are important screening questions?

4. Design an interview guide. This would include a warm-up question and up to five other questions, moving from the general to the specific. Add probes to aid the interviewer.

5. If time permits, consider what other information you would need for your scenario in addition to focus group results.

Scenario One: The library needs more information from its *nonusers*. The library lacks information on how nonusers perceive the library and how the library can reach out to nonusers.

Scenario Two: The library has introduced a limited number of CD-ROM databases and reference tools to the reference department. Before adding additional resources, the library needs to know more about users' impressions of the tools, their ways of using the sources, and need for the electronic information.

Scenario Three: The library has never evaluated its services from the perspective of its younger patrons—children or young adults (choose one). How would they evaluate library services?

Scenario Four: Recently, the library staff had an inservice program on customer service. As a result, staff would like to know more about how the patrons rate the library's customer service.

Developed by Debra Wilcox Johnson, Johnson & Johnson Consulting, 1015 Holiday Drive, Waunakee, WI 53597. (608) 849-7286.

TELL IT! Tip Sheet
FOCUS GROUPS

Purpose and Logic Behind Use of This Technique
- Takes full advantage of group process
- Gets information and ideas from an identified segment of the population
- Provides excellent public relations with participants
- Cost and time efficient
- Can get at information often unavailable from surveys or individual interviews

Type(s) of Situation(s) for Which Technique Is Used
- Useful to access the needs of groups traditionally under-served in the community or underrepresented in other types of data collection efforts
- Some group respondents find the format a more comfortable way to express attitudes, perceptions and opinions
- Can be used for needs assessment for target groups, evaluation of library or pretesting of media messages or programs

Components of Technique
- Determine the role of the focus group study in the overall assessment or evaluation
- Determine the target group
- Identify pool of potential participants
- Select a facilitator
- Develop an interview guide
- Recruit participants (8–12 is best)
- Conduct interviews
- Prepare the report from notes and tape, if used

Supplies Needed
- Comfortable and quiet room
- Newsprint pads and easels (sometimes useful)
- Recording equipment, if taped

Personnel Needed
- Interviewer/facilitator and note-taker for each focus group
- Staff for recruiting participants

Time Factors
- Most time needed for recruitment and confirmation of participants
- Time for actual focus groups usually 1.5–2.5 hours
- Transcription of tape, if used, 3–6 hours

Cost Factors
From essentially free to more than $500 depending on if participants are paid, a professional facilitator hired, or a room needs to be rented

Further Reading on This Technique
Debra Wilcox Johnson. "Keeping Things in Focus: Information for Decision Making." In *Keeping the Book$: Public Library Financial Practices*, ed. Jane Robbins and Douglas Zweizig for the Urban Libraries Council, 405–19. Fort Atkinson, Wisc.: Highsmith, 1993.

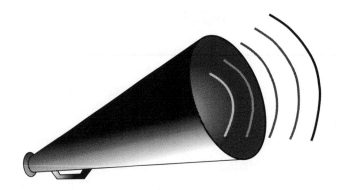

CHAPTER 17

Gathering Numbers for Evaluation

Douglas Zweizig

TAKING THE MEASURE

Numbers seem to be a necessary part of making systematic observations. Mao Tse-Tung pointed out their importance to his followers:

> We must attend to the quantitative aspect of a situation or problem and make a basic quantitative analysis. Every quality manifests itself in a certain quantity, and without quantity there can be no quality. To this day many of our comrades still do not understand that they must attend to the quantitative aspect of things—the basic statistics, the main percentages and the quantitative limits that determine the qualities of things. They have no figures in their heads and as a result cannot help making mistakes.[1]

While this quotation has historical charm, its frustration with vague expression is found today when public officials hear such evaluation statements as:

"Many people seemed to like the program."

"We're losing a lot of books this year."

"Users seem much more pleased with the service this year."

Statements like these cry out for quantification: just how many people was that?; how many books were lost? compared to what?; how much has the service improved? at what cost?

Managers, public officials, school boards, university administrators, and other stakeholders need information that allows them to determine just how much benefit a program or service has provided and to assess whether that benefit was worth the cost. Therefore, numbers are often used for evaluation because they are concise and relatively unambiguous, but the evaluator needs to determine which numbers to use and how to interpret them. A library swarms with numbers that could be used to inform evaluations:

- routinely collected statistics on circulation of materials, services offered, and number of visits;

- periodic surveys showing the number of users or satisfaction with library services, with the results reported in numbers;

- an automated circulation system providing unrequested quantities of data;

- regular statistical reports required by the state or by the library system;

- a study of the community the library serves resulting in numbers about demographic characteristics.

Numbers on which to base evaluations are plentiful, but the meaning of the numbers is often unclear, and identifying the ones on which to focus is complicated. It also is possible that none of the data presently available address the evaluation question of the moment.

This chapter provides some ways of thinking about numbers that will aid in determining which number(s) to use to speak to your evaluation question. In talking about numbers used for evaluation, the term "measure" will be used. Measure means a specific number used to describe some particular attribute of a service or the community, such as the number of people attending library programs or the percentage of residents with a high school education. Some measures have been characterized as input or resource measures. These are used to describe characteristics of the resources that go into a library to support services, such as the number of items held, the income for staff, or the square feet of the building. Other measures have been labeled output or performance measures. These describe the products of the library, such as the number of books circulated, the number of reference questions answered, the percentage of items successfully found by patrons. In between input and output measures are process measures that describe library activities that make the outputs possible. Examples would be number of books processed, number of staff trained, percentage of tasks performed on schedule, and so on. There has been much recent interest in what are termed outcome measures—measures that describe what the impacts of library services were on users or the population served. The National Education Goals state desired outcomes that could be measured in individual communities. Other kinds of outcome measures might be numbers of adults who obtained employment as a result of library assistance, number of new adult readers resulting from library programs, number of General Equivalency Diplomas obtained as a result of library services, increase in number of graduates, or increase in achievement scores.

Many kinds of library measures have already been defined. Sources of data for library managers and evaluators have been identified by the Library Research Service of the Colorado Department of Education, and the most current version of their report is appended to this chapter. It includes data relating to type of library and to topics such as automation or finances. Reports of library statistics are included as well as data collection handbooks such as *Measuring Academic Library Performance: A Practical Approach*. The chances are good that the kind of data desired by an evaluator has already been collected or defined in one of the sources listed here.

The task, therefore, is to select from the many possibilities available the single measure or set of measures that will best provide the evaluation information you need. This chapter will distinguish among different kinds of numbers and will present criteria that can be used to assess the degree to which a candidate measure will be suitable for your purpose.

DIFFERENT KINDS OF NUMBERS

Gregory Bateson has defined information as "a difference that makes a difference." In making sense of numerical information, that definition is a useful reminder that the meaning in numerical data is determined as much by the viewer's response as by the numbers themselves.

Numbers are symbols that encode meaning in a variety of ways, and their interpretation requires an understanding of how they have been used. The number "12" could mean the number of people attending a program, someone's shoe size, the degree of difficulty achieved on a scale of 15, or the twelfth seat in a theater row. The different ways in which numbers can code information are referred to as "levels" of data. The four levels of data—nominal, ordinal, interval, and ratio—are distinguished in terms of the amount of information contained in the data and in terms of the appropriate summary statistics used to describe them.

The most basic level of data is *nominal*, that is, the number is just used as a name for a category. Data at this level are simply indicators of the classes into which items fall. For example, data describing the colors of cars, the gender of respondents to a survey, or the service desk used at a library would be nominal. Numbers would be arbitrarily assigned as codes to indicate different colors, genders, or service desks. The appropriate summary statistic indicates the category into which most cases fall. The statistic, known as the mode, would tell what was the most popular color of car, which gender occurred more frequently among the respondents, or which service desk was most used. Chapter 20 shows how to assign numerical codes to verbal responses. The numbers assigned through such coding are most often nominal level data (see Chapter 20, "Making Sense of Narrative Responses").

While nominal categories are organized in no particular order, the next level of data, *ordinal*, refers to data that, in addition to discriminating between cases in terms of some characteristic, also implies an order. An example would be sizes of cars: sub-compact, compact, intermediate, full-size. The code of 1 would be assigned to the smallest size, sub-compact; 2 to the next size; and so on. Therefore, a value of 2 for car size would indicate a car larger than a car with a value of 1 and smaller than a car with a value of 3. An ordinal level of data implies order only; it does not indicate how much larger or smaller one car is from another.

Many survey questions produce data of this nature: data ranking preferences for service, or data reflecting knowledge of library services. The appropriate summary statistic indicates how many cases fell above or below a particular value. For example, the median indicates how many cases fall above or below the mid-point of the considered scores. A percentile score indicates what percentage of scores fell below the percentile score.

The next level of data, *interval* data, not only implies an order, but also has equal intervals between successive values. For example, on the Fahrenheit scale, a degree interval has been defined so that each degree measures the same amount of temperature change. Thus, the difference between 30° F and 31° F is the same as the difference between 209° F and 210° F. The appropriate summary statistic indicates the score produced by dividing the sum of the scores by the number of scores summed, i. e., the common average or arithmetic mean.

The highest level of data, *ratio* data, has the quality of interval data with the additional characteristic of having a true value of zero. Examples are data relating to weight, distance, or money. That is, it is possible to have zero weight, zero distance, or zero money. Therefore, in addition to being able to add and subtract ratio data (to say that one weight is a specific amount greater or less than another), it is also possible to multiply or divide ratio data. It is sensible to say one object weighs twice as much as another; it is not sensible to say that it is twice as hot today as it was yesterday. Ratio data are found in library studies when absolute counts are used: counts of users of items, and so on. A full range of arithmetic and statistical calculations are legitimate with ratio data.

Since measures at a higher level of data contain more information and can be analyzed in more complex ways, in considering what measure to use, it is good to measure at the highest level possible. Conversely, it is important not to use summary statistics that are not appropriate for the level measured, for example, computing averages for ordinal data.

CRITERIA FOR SELECTING A MEASURE[2]

It is useful to think of measures as having two main aspects: the conceptual and the operational. The conceptual aspect concerns the meaning of the measure. The operational aspect relates to how the measure is obtained or just what operations are used to determine a number. The first five criteria are concerned with the conceptual aspect of a measure and the second five with the operational.

Conceptual Criteria

Validity or Appropriateness

How close is the measure to measuring what the library *really* wants to know? Is the proposed measure appropriate for measuring what we want to measure? It's possible to be measuring something other than what was intended. For example, early studies of voter behavior would conduct door-to-door surveys and would ask, "For whom did you vote in the last election?" When the researchers tallied their results, their data showed that many more people said that they had voted than had actually been recorded at the polls. The problem was that people were reluctant to admit to the interviewer that they had not voted. So the question was not measuring voter behavior; it was measuring people's desire to be seen as good citizens. When the surveyors used a screening question: "A lot of people weren't able to get to the polls for the last election. Were you able to get to the polls?" Those who answered "yes" could then be asked about their choices in the voting booth, and the results more closely reflected actual voting behavior. Asking residents of the community in a telephone survey whether they use the public library can obtain the same kind of "courtesy bias" since most people think that using the library is a good thing to do. Telling the respondents that the survey is being conducted by the library would increase this lack of validity.

When a waiter comes by your table and asks, "Is everything satisfactory with your meal?" your response is probably not a good measure of the quality of the meal. Your quick, kind words about the dinner are more likely a measure of your reluctance to interrupt your meal at that moment. Similarly, our measures of user satisfaction can fail to measure the quality of our service and tap instead the politeness of our users. A more valid measure would ask, "In what way did the service help you?" Or the measure would focus more on behavior than on attitude: "How were the results of our service used?"

Establishing the validity of a measure is complex—recall the controversy over the validity of I.Q. testing. For evaluation purposes, it is enough to be able to speak to the question: Are you confident that the measure you are using measures what you think it does?

Interpretability

At some point, the results of measurement will need to be communicated to others. Some data may be of interest to the staff but may not speak to the interests of those who provide the funds for the program. For example, how meaningful would the results be to public officials? This need to be able to quickly communicate the results of measurement relates to earlier observations about the expectations of stakeholders; the variety of groups with an interest in the library will want to be quickly informed about its performance in terms they will easily understand. A test of a proposed measure is whether the results can be communicated in a sentence to staff or funders.

Ohio State University Libraries were able to gain support for an automated circulation system in the mid-1960s by explaining: "We can save a quarter million user hours a year with the proposed system." The *Output Measures for Public Libraries*' Reference Completion Rate allows the library to say: "We are presently able to complete ___% of our reference transactions by the end of the business day."

Controllability

To what degree can the library control the outcome for the measure? Some of the library's impact can be controlled by the library; some of the impact is primarily in the user's control. There seems to be an inevitable tension between the aspects of service of most interest and the aspects over which the library has control. The library intends that its materials will help readers better understand themselves and the world around them, but the library staff have virtually no control over the uses made of the library's materials. On the other hand, the library has a large amount of control over which materials are owned. In between these extremes, the library shares control with the user: the library can control to some extent which materials circulate, the user controls whether material that is circulated is read. The most satisfactory output measures are those that point toward desired impacts of service and that also can be affected by management decision-making—measures in the middle range, such as circulation or demand for service.

Comparability

Some measures are of local interest only; some are more useful when the results can be compared with those from other libraries. Some measures are related to special projects; some are intended to be collected periodically over time. If comparisons with other libraries or over time are intended, then the measure needs to include definitions that are shared among libraries and needs to assess aspects of the service that are relatively unchanging. The sources of available data for library managers listed at the end of this chapter depend on data being collected in comparable ways by large numbers of libraries.

Informativeness

This criterion tests whether the proposed measure will give the manager information on which to base decisions. A way to test a measure for informativeness is to ask: what decisions would be made if the result of measurement produced a high score? a low score? a moderate score? One public library administrator asked in a community survey whether respondents wanted the library to purchase more duplicate copies of popular items or to reduce duplication and purchase more unique titles. He intended to base the library's collection policy on the community's preference. The results of the survey were that 49% of the community wanted more duplicate copies and 51% wanted more unique titles. This unexpected result did not allow him to resolve the conflict within his library's collection development policy. In order to reduce the amount of unused data in the library, it is useful to pretest how the results of the measurement will result in better decisions.

The above five criteria (validity or appropriateness, interpretability, controllability, comparability, and informativeness) test proposed measures in terms of what will be measured, the concept. They provide tests which help clarify the thinking behind a proposed measure and help ensure that a measure will produce useful information for decision making. The next criteria focus on how well the proposed measure will work in practice, how well the measure can be put into operation. The criteria move beyond considerations of the concept of the measure to addressing concerns with the design of the measure.

Operational Criteria

Practicality

This criterion asks whether the proposed measure is affordable in terms of time, money, and effort required to produce the results. In assessing reference service, many have argued that unobtrusive testing of accuracy of responses to proxy-administered questions is the most valid measure. But libraries may question this methodology in terms of the expense involved. So validity is traded off against costs. Explicitly addressing this issue may bring to mind ways of making desired measures affordable. For example, measuring an aspect of library service periodically will be less expensive than measuring it every day the library is open. Sampling will be less expensive (and more accurate) than attempting to count every instance.

A related question is, how easy would it be to obtain this measure? Some data are already available or are easy to collect; others require special studies. Where choice is possible, the easier measure is to be preferred, not only because it is less costly, but also because it is more likely to be collected frequently and be useful as a management tool.

A further concern for libraries: How intrusive would data collection be? Some data can be collected without the users' or clients' awareness; others can only be collected with the cooperation of the user or will cause a disruption in the service.

Test questions to be asked under this criterion are: Does the proposed method of measurement make maximum use of already collected data? Does it avoid duplication with already collected data? How can this measure be made less expensive? How would the measure be designed if money were no object?

Timeliness of Feedback

This criterion relates to the timing of the measurement. Results that arrive too late to affect decisions can be avoided by explicitly addressing this criterion. If the data are needed in time for the annual budget request, the design needs to take that schedule into account. Progress measures may be required to provide information prior to the end of a cycle or a project. A further consideration of timeliness is how long it will take for a change in practice to affect results. For example, if document availability is the aspect being measured, how long will it take for a change in interlibrary loan or ordering practice to show up in increased document availability?

Reliability and Accuracy

This criterion deals with the trustworthiness of the data produced. A reliable measure is one that produces consistent results. To what degree are different staff likely to collect data in the same way? The understanding of some measures will differ from one staff member to another, while other measures will be easier for staff to understand and to record accurately.

A measure can be tested for reliability by inquiring where mistakes are likely to occur and can be increased in reliability by pre-testing the measurement process. Sampling produces more accurate data than counting everything because there is less fatigue and boredom with the measure.

Representativeness

In selecting periods for measurement, the issue of representativeness needs to be taken into account. Some time periods are fairly typical, others are not. In public libraries, for example, the months of April and October seem representative of the school-year months. In academic or secondary school libraries, use of services will be strongly affected by the school calendar. Days of the week probably differ in their use patterns. If the aspect being measured is affected by the calendar or the clock, then the sample design needs to include periods to represent proportionally the entire year or periods of different levels of use.

Precision Required

A final practical consideration is the precision that is required in the results. Precision refers to how close an estimate obtained through a study will be to the actual value. Metaphorically, the issue of precision refers to the fineness of mesh used in a sifting screen, or the resolution of a picture. With increased precision, you can make finer discrimination, but precision is costly, and fine discriminations may not be needed. Because increases in precision involve increased cost, the issue here is a managerial one. It is wasteful to buy more precision than necessary, so the manager or evaluator needs to decide how much precision is needed.

For example, the precision of estimates obtained by sampling is directly linked to the size of the sample.[3] Generally, a sample size of 100 will produce an estimate that has a 95% chance of being within ±10% of the value for the entire population. A result of 40% produced from a sample of 100 gives a 95% chance of the "true" value being between 30% and 50%. In order to increase the precision to ±5%, the sample size would have to be quadrupled to 400. When national polls are conducted, generally samples of about 1500 people are used to estimate national characteristics. These estimates are found to be within 2% of the national figure (95% of the time).

Since increased precision involves an escalation in the sample size, and therefore in expense, the manager needs to determine how much precision is required. For many library decisions, small differences are not of interest. If the library has introduced a service innovation, a five percent increase in usage is not sufficiently different from no change. A five percent decline in materials availability will probably not cause a manager to redesign ordering practices. For most areas of service, managers are only concerned with differences of ten percent or more. Therefore, in most cases, evaluators are better off with smaller, less precise measures that are affordable and can be applied regularly.

The table on page 197 recapitulates these criteria on a single sheet as a reminder or for use in training. While it is useful to test a specific measure against each of the criteria in turn, it is important to recognize that these criteria interact and that there is no perfect measure. To illustrate, one of the things that helps a sailor navigate is a buoy. An object that floats is anchored over a particular spot, and the sailor steers by it; it's a reference point. A *valid* buoy is one that is anchored directly over the desired point or over the hazard. A buoy will lack validity to the degree that it is not indicating the underwater condition it is supposed to mark. *Reliability* deals with the length or elasticity of the line connecting the buoy to the anchor. If the line is too long or too springy, the buoy is able to move around on the surface and will be an unreliable indicator, changing its location based on the winds and tides. With a shorter line, the location of the buoy will be fairly stable and will be a more reliable indicator.

A point to be made here is that the validity or reliability of a given measure are not absolute; they are variable. It is not meaningful to say a measure is not valid or not reliable. The question is "*How* valid is it? *How* reliable is it?" And these questions are relevant to the library manager because the validity and reliability of a measure are directly related to cost. A researcher can determine how much reliability or validity a measure has, but it is the manager who needs to decide how much of each to buy, how much is necessary for the evaluation decisions the manager needs to make. Personal interviews cost at least ten times more than mail surveys. Are they worth it? Our estimate from a sample can be twice as accurate if we quadruple the sample size. How good an estimate do we need? These are the type of questions that the evaluator needs to address when making decisions about what measure to use in evaluating library programs and services.

CONCLUSION

While numbers provide an opportunity for conciseness and precision, it is also important to view them realistically, as was done by an English judge when commenting on statistics reported from India:

> The government are very keen on amassing statistics. They collect them, add them, raise them to the nth power, take the cube root, and prepare wonderful diagrams. But you must never forget that every one of these figures comes in the first instance from the village watchman, who just puts down what he damn pleases.

NOTES

1. From "Methods of Work of Party Committees," March 13, 1949.

2. The application of criteria to measures that is formalized here has been aided by Richard H. Orr, "Measuring the Goodness of Library Services: A General Framework for Considering Quantitative Measures," *Journal of Documentation*, Vol. 29, no. 3 (September 1973), 315–32 and Harry P. Hatry et al., *How Effective are Your Community Services? Procedures for Monitoring the Effectiveness of Municipal Services*, Washington, D.C.: The Urban Institute and the International City Management Association, 1977.

3. The exception to this is when the population being sampled is small—below 2,000. While almost all library data are from larger populations, for special projects, the number of people being served or other aspects may well involve populations of less than 2,000. With small populations, either the entire population should be studied or an appropriate sample size can be calculated (formulas are available in statistics texts).

CRITERIA FOR THE EVALUATION
OF A MEASURE OF LIBRARY ACTIVITY

Criteria for WHAT You Measure

Validity or Appropriateness Is this the right measure for this desired area of improvement?

Interpretability Will the measure provide results able to be expressed in one sentence to the funders?

Controllability Is the aspect measured one over which the library has at least partial control?

Comparability Will this measure be comparable across time? across different libraries?

Informativeness Will this measure tell what we need to know to make a decision?

Criteria for HOW You Measure

Practicality Is the method affordable in terms of time, money, and effort required? Does the method of measurement make maximum use of already collected data, avoid duplication with already collected data?

Timeliness of Feedback Will this method of measurement produce results in time to affect needed decisions? Will it allow enough time for results to show up?

Reliability or Accuracy Will this method of measurement produce data that can be trusted? Would different persons collecting data get the same results?

Representativeness Have the effects of non-typical time periods been accounted for?

Precision Required Will this method of measurement produce data sensitive enough to guide management decisions in this area of concern?

EXAMPLE OF A TRAINING SESSION

Participants can apply the criteria presented in this chapter to library measures in a variety of ways. In the simplest form, participants could be introduced to the criteria by having them read the chapter on gathering measures or by presenting the content of the chapter in a mini-lecture. Then participants can be formed into small groups. Each group is given a library measure to assess against the criteria. Example measures that can be used for this purpose would be annual circulation, annual number of reference transactions, in-library materials use, or any of the measures contained in such sources as *Output Measures for Public Libraries* (2nd edition), *Measuring Academic Library Performance: A Practical Approach*, or others listed in the attached list of available data for library managers. The group task, after rating the measure against each of the ten criteria, is to make a recommendation about whether, on balance, the measure can be used to provide information useful for decision making.

Variations on this training session would be to

Give each small group a different measure to evaluate and to report their recommendation to the large group.

Give two small groups the same measure, asking one small group to make a case for not using the measure as designed and the second group to make a case for using the measure as is. Each group would present its recommendation and the large group would discuss whether to use the measure or not.

Give groups a set of measures intended to produce comparable information. Examples would be:

- measures of use, such as circulation, number of visits, and in–library materials use;
- measures of financial support, such as income from local sources, total income, and per capita income;
- measures of quality of reference service, such as reference completion rate from *Output Measures for Public Libraries* (2nd ed.) and reference accuracy measured unobtrusively using proxy reference users (see Chapter 18).

The group task is to assess each of the measures against the criteria and to recommend which measure of the set should be used.

TRAINING CHECKLIST FOR EVALUATING A MEASURE

Purpose: To enable the participants to:

- assess measures of library service or activity in terms of their meaningfulness and utility, and

- make a recommendation of what measure to use for a given purpose.

Rationale for approach: Most library employees have not been asked to consider what measures should be used to reflect the services or activities of the library. Their involvement in measurement is limited to the collection of data that they may not use themselves in making decisions. Discussion of the characteristics of a measure and assessment of the qualities of a given measure will strengthen the employees' capability to select the appropriate measure to use for a particular purpose or to understand the qualities of the measures now being used.

Number of participants: The number is limited only by the number of small groups that can be handled. For a very large group, only selected groups may report.

Estimated time for activity: Forty-five minutes for the lecture/discussion on criteria for evaluation of measures, one hour for small group assessment of a measure, ten minutes per group for reporting back.

Instructional approach: A combination of lecture, small group work, and large group discussion.

Room arrangement: A flexible room with chairs and small tables that can be arranged for a single lecturer as well as for small group activities. If only chairs are provided, they need to have arms for writing.

Special supplies needed: Pencils, notepads, chalkboard or newsprint pad and easel, overhead transparencies and projector, screen, marking pens, and handouts.

Advance preparation: Prepare lecture notes and handouts; assemble supplies.

Directions:

1. Introductions of instructor and participants.

2. Overview of instructional objectives and timetable.

3. Lecture/discussion criteria for evaluating measures, with plentiful examples of measures in use in libraries.

4. Small group assessment of a measure.

5. Small group reports to large group.

6. Final comments by instructor and participants.

AVAILABLE DATA FOR LIBRARY MANAGERS

Prepared by the
Library Research Service
Colorado Department of Education

Introduction

There is a wealth of data available for library managers. For most types of libraries, there are annual reports of general input and output statistics. There are several annual statistical reports on topics that cut across library type. And, data on topics of special interest to public libraries alone are also available.

Keeping track of the many sources of available data can be a challenging and onerous task for library managers who must wear many other hats as well and whose first priority is providing quality service to their users. For those reasons, the Library Research Service maintains a bibliography of available data sources by library type and topic. This bibliography, previously updated annually, will now be updated quarterly.

While our aim is to make this bibliography as comprehensive as possible, we feel certain that it does not presently list all sources. So, if you know of any sources of available data not listed herein, please share their citations with us so we can include them in subsequent editions. Your contributions will be credited gratefully.

Keith Curry Lance
Director, Library Research Service

Contact Information
LIBRARY RESEARCH SERVICE
State Library & Adult Education Office
COLORADO DEPARTMENT OF EDUCATION
201 East Colfax Avenue, Room 309
Denver, Colorado 80203-1799

Keith Curry Lance • Director
Voice 303/866–6737 • Internet klance@csn.net

CONTENTS

By Library Type

ACADEMIC LIBRARIES

PUBLIC LIBRARIES
    American Library Association Office for Research and Statistics
    Federal–State Cooperative System for Public Library Data
    Public Library Association
    Public Opinion Polls
    Children's Services
    Referenda

SCHOOL LIBRARY MEDIA CENTERS

SPECIAL LIBRARIES

By Topic

AUTOMATED SYSTEMS AND NETWORKS
    For all types of libraries.

BUILDINGS
    Public and academic library buildings only.

FISCAL INDEXES
    For all types of libraries.

LIBRARY-RELATED STATISTICS

STAFFING AND SALARIES
    Includes data for all types of libraries.

ACADEMIC LIBRARIES

Annual   *ARL Statistics.* Washington, D.C.: Association of Research Libraries. [Note: Available in machine-readable form.]

Biennial   *ACRL University Library Statistics.* Chicago: Association of College and Research Libraries. [Note: Available in machine-readable form.]

1990   Van House, Nancy, Beth Weil, and Charles R. McClure. *Measuring Academic Library Performance: A Practical Approach.* Chicago and London: American Library Association.

1991   Lynch, Mary Jo. *Alternative Sources of Revenue in Academic Libraries.* Chicago: American Library Association.

PUBLIC LIBRARIES

American Library Association
Office for Research and Statistics

1988   Lynch, Mary Jo. *Sources of Non-Tax Revenue for Public Libraries.* Chicago: American Library Association.

Federal–State Cooperative System (FSCS)
for Public Library Data

1988   *An Action Plan for a Federal-State Cooperative System for Public Library Data.* Washington, D.C.: U.S. Government Printing Office.

1989   *Public Libraries in Forty-Four States and the District of Columbia: 1988: An NCES Working Paper.* Washington, D.C.: National Center for Education Statistics.

1991   Lynch, Mary Jo. "New, National, and Ready to Fly: The Federal–State Cooperative System (FSCS) for Public Library Data." *Public Libraries*, November 1, p. 358.

    Public Libraries in the 50 States and the District of Columbia, 1989. Washington, D.C.: U.S. Government Printing Office.

Annual   *Public Libraries in the U.S., [year].* Washington, D.C.: U.S. Government Printing Office. [Annual from 1992. Also available on diskette.]

Public Library Association

1987   McClure, Charles, Amy Owen, Douglas Zweizig, Mary Jo Lynch, and Nancy Van House. *Planning and Role-Setting for Public Libraries: A Manual of Options and Procedures.* Chicago and London: American Library Association.

Van House, Nancy, Mary Jo Lynch, Charles McClure, Douglas Zweizig, and Eleanor Jo Rodger. *Output Measures for Public Libraries: A Manual of Standardized Procedures* (second edition). Chicago and London: American Library Association.

1988–   *Public Library Data Service Statistical Report.* Chicago: Public Library Association. From 1990, includes special reports on the following topics:

1990   Literacy, Economic Development, and Local Government Services
1991   Children's Services
1992   Technology
1993   Finance
1994   Children's Services
1995   Technology

Public Opinion Polls

1991   Miller, Thomas I., and Michelle A. Miller. "Standards of Excellence: U. S. Residents' Evaluations of Local Government Services." *Public Administration Review*, November/December, p. 503 ff.

Westin, Alan F., and Anne L. Finger. *Using the Public Library in the Computer Age. Present Patterns, Future Possibilities.* [Equifax-Harris poll] Chicago: American Library Association.

1992   Estabrook, Leigh, and Chris Horak. "Public vs. Professional Opinion on Libraries: The Great Divide?" [Library Research Center poll] *Library Journal*, April 1, pp. 52–55.

National Center for Education Statistics. *National Household Education Survey.* Washington, D.C.: U. S. Government Printing Office.

1993   Childers, Thomas. *What's Good?: Describing Your Public Library's Effectiveness.* Chicago: American Library Association.

D'Elia, George. *The Roles of the Public Library in Society: The Complete Report.* Chicago: American Library Association.

Van House, Nancy, and Thomas Childers. *The Public Library Effectiveness Study: The Complete Report.* Chicago: American Library Association.

1994   D'Elia, George, and Eleanor Jo Rodger. "Public Opinion about the Roles of the Public Library in the Community: The Results of a Recent Gallup Poll." *Public Libraries*, January/February, p. 23 ff.

            Scheppke, Jim. "Who's Using the Public Library? Good News and Bad News from the National Household Education Survey." *Library Journal*, October 15, pp. 35–37.

1995   D'Elia, George, and Eleanor Jo Rodger. "The Roles of the Public Library in the Community: Results of a Gallop Poll." *Public Libraries*, March/April, pp. 94–101.

Children's Services

1990   Immroth, Barbara. "How Is the Next Generation of Library Users Being Raised? The First National Survey on Services and Resources for Children in Public Libraries." *Public Libraries*, November/December, p. 339.

1992   Garland, Kathleen. "Children's Services Statistics: A Study of State Agency and Individual Library Activity." *Public Libraries*, November/December, pp. 351–55.

            Walter, Virginia A. *Output Measures for Public Library Services to Children: A Manual of Standardized Procedures*. Chicago: American Library Association.

1993   Zweizig, Douglas L. "The Children's Services Story." [PLDS data] *Public Libraries*, January/February, pp. 26–28.

Referenda

1991   Hall, Richard B. "Public Library Referenda 1990: Still a Boom for Bonds?" *Library Journal*, June 15, p. 48 ff.

1992   Hall, Richard B. "Public Library Referenda 1991: 85 Percent Approved." *Library Journal*, June 15, p. 36 ff.

1993   Hall, Richard B. "Public Library Referenda 1992: Library Buildings Slump at the Polls." *Library Journal*, June 15, p. 34 ff.

1994   Hall, Richard B. "Public Library Referenda 1993: Referenda Set A Record," *Library Journal*, June 15, 1994, p. 35 ff.

SCHOOL LIBRARY MEDIA CENTERS

Annual
Estimates of School Statistics. Washington, D.C.: National Education Association.

1988
Information Power: Guidelines for School Library Media Programs. Chicago and London: American Library Association. Washington, D.C.: Association for Educational Communications and Technology.

National Center for Education Statistics. *Statistics of Public and Private School Library Media Centers, 1985–86.* Washington, D.C.: U.S. Government Printing Office.

1989
Miller, Marilyn L., and Marilyn L. Shontz. "Expenditures for Resources in School Library Media Centers, FY '88–'89." *School Library Journal,* June 1989, p. 31 ff.

1991
Miller, Marilyn L., and Marilyn L. Shontz. "Expenditures for Resources in School Library Media Centers, FY 1990–91." *School Library Journal,* August 1991, p. 32 ff.

1993
Garland, Kathleen. "An Analysis of School Library Media Center Statistics Collected By State Agencies and Individual Library Media Specialists." *School Library Media Quarterly,* Winter, pp. 106–11.

Miller, Marilyn L., and Marilyn L. Shontz. "Expenditures for Resources in School Library Media Centers, FY 1991–92." *School Library Journal,* August 1991, p. 26 ff.

1994
Miller, Marilyn L., and Marilyn L. Shontz. "Inside High-Tech School Library Media Centers: Problems and Possibilities." *School Library Journal,* April, p. 24 ff.

SPECIAL LIBRARIES

Law Libraries

Annual
Statistical Survey of Law School Libraries and Librarians. Office of Consultant on Legal Education, American Bar Association.

Survey of Private Law Libraries. Chicago: American Association of Law Librarians.

Medical Libraries

Annual   *Annual Statistics of Medical School Libraries in the United States and Canada.* Houston, Tex.: Association of Academic Health Sciences Library Directors.

AUTOMATED SYSTEMS AND NETWORKS

1990   Walton, Robert A., and Frank R. Bridge. "Automated System Marketplace '90: Focusing on Software Sales and Joint Ventures." *Library Journal*, April 1, p. 55 ff.

1991   Bridge, Frank R. "Automated System Marketplace '91: Redefining System Frontiers." *Library Journal*, April 1, p. 50 ff.

1992   Bridge, Frank R. "Automated System Marketplace '92: Redefining the Market Itself." *Library Journal*, April 1, p. 58 ff.

1993   Bridge, Frank R. "Automated System Marketplace '93. Part I: Focus on Minicomputers." *Library Journal*, April 1, p. 52 ff.

Bridge, Frank R. "Automated System Marketplace '93. Part II: Focus on Microcomputers." *Library Journal*, April 15, p. 50 ff.

"LJ's Statewide Networks Survey." *Library Journal*, October 1, pp. 45–46.

1994   Griffiths, Jose-Marie, and Kimberly Kertis. "Automated System Marketplace '94: A New Take on Who's Buying, What's Selling." *Library Journal*, April 1, pp. 50–59.

BUILDINGS

1990   Fox, Bette-Lee, and Michael Rogers. "Library Buildings 1990: Service to the People." *Library Journal*, December, p. 56 ff.

1991   Fox, Bette-Lee, Michael Rogers, and Ann Burns. "Library Buildings 1991: Between a Recession and a Hard Place." *Library Journal*, December, p. 58 ff.

1992   Bobinski, George. "Carnegie Libraries: Their Current and Future Status—The Results of a Survey." *Public Libraries*, January/February, pp. 18–22.

Fox, Bette-Lee, Ann Burns, Michael Rogers, and Louisa Weber. "Library Buildings 1992: Building a Brighter Tomorrow." *Library Journal*, December, pp. 50–81.

1993   Fox, Bette-Lee, and Corinne O. Nelson. "Library Buildings 1993: Library Construction Hits the Ceiling." *Library Journal*, December, pp. 53–72.

1994   Fox, Bette-Lee, and Corinne O. Nelson. "Library Buildings 1994: Renovations—And Additions—On the Rise." *Library Journal*, December, pp. 41–52.

FISCAL INDEXES

American Library Index of Circulation and Expenditures (ALICE) [includes an index of public library expenditures]

1990   Sherlock, Katy. "Annual Statistics Show Circulation and Expenditures Edging Upward." *American Libraries*, September, p. 740.

1991   Palmer, Carole. "Public Library Circ Static, Spending Up 11.5%." *American Libraries*, July, p. 659.

1992   Palmer, Carole. "Public Library Circ Leaps, While Inflation Outstrips Spending." *American Libraries*, July, pp. 596–97.

1993   Hamilton, Lynn. "Public Library Circ Stats." *American Libraries*, September, p. 713.

1994   Wright, Lisa A. "As Public Library Circ Declines, Spending Continues to Top Inflation." *American Libraries*, October, p. 884 ff.

Cost of Living Index

Quarterly.   *Cost of Living Index*. Washington, D.C.: American Chamber of Commerce Researchers Association.

1992   *Wages, Amenities, and Cost of Living: Theory and Measurement of Geographic Differentials, 1990 Data*. Washington, D.C.: Research Associates of Washington.

Inflation Index

Monthly   *The Consumer Price Index.* Washington, D.C.: Bureau of Labor Statistics.

Library Materials Price Indexes

Annual   *Bowker Annual.* New York: R. R. Bowker Co.

Annual   *Inflation Measures for Schools and Colleges.* Washington, D.C.: Research Associates of Washington.

1992   Carpenter, Katherine Hammell, and Adrian W. Alexander. "Price Index for U. S. Periodicals 1992." *Library Journal*, April 15, pp. 55–62.

Grannis, C. B. "Output Levels Off, Prices Inch Upward." *Publishers Weekly*, April 6, pp. 532–35.

1993   Alexander, Adrian W., and Katherine Hammell Carpenter. "Periodicals Price Index for 1993." *American Libraries*, May, pp. 390–438.

Grannis, Chandler B. "Moving On Up? Titles Show Second Consecutive Gain; Prices Modestly Up." [book price index] *Publisher's Weekly*, March 1, pp. S32–S35.

Mason, Pamela R. "Price Indexes for the New Media A CD-ROM Case History." *Library Acquisitions: Practice & Theory*, v. 17, pp. 239–48.

1994   Carpenter, Kathryn Hammell, and Adrian W. Alexander. "U.S. Periodical Price Index for 1994." *American Libraries*, May, p. 450 ff.

Ink, Gary. "Inching Ahead: The year's title output and average book prices both advanced, but more slowly than in the past." *Publisher's Weekly*, March 7, p. S28 ff.

Ketcham, Lee, and Kathleen Born. "Projecting Serials Costs: Banking on the Past To Buy for the Future." [34th Annual Report Periodical Price Survey], *Library Journal*, April 15, p. 44 ff.

Rowley, Jennifer, and David Butcher. "A Comparison of Pricing Strategies for Bibliographic Databases on CD-ROM and Equivalent Printed Products." *The Electronic Library* v. 12, n. 3, June, pp. 169–75.

1995   Alexander, Adrian W., and Kathryn Hammell Carpenter. "U.S. Periodical Price-Index for 1995." *American Libraries*, May, pp. 446–55.

Chaffin, Nancy J. "U.S. Serial Services Price Index for 1995." *American Libraries*, May, pp. 456–57.

Ink, Gary. "Ups & Downs: While title output continued to slowly rise, hardcover dropped off dramatically." [The Red & The Black: Output & Prices] *Publishers Weekly*, March 20, pp. S29–S31.

Ketcham, Lee, and Kathleen Born. "Serials vs. the Dollar Dilemma: Currency Swings and Rising Costs Play Havoc With Prices." [35th Annual Report, Periodical Price Survey 1995] *Library Journal*, April 15, pp. 43–49.

Library Price Indexes

Annual   *Inflation Measures for Schools, Colleges & Libraries* [formerly *Inflation Measures for Schools & Colleges*] Washington, D.C.: Research Associates of Washington.

Includes Academic Library Price Index, Public Library Price Index, and School Price Index with sub-indexes for librarians and library clerks as well as elementary and secondary library materials by format.

Local Financial Effort Index

Annual   *Utah Public Library Service* (includes index of local financial effort). Salt Lake City: Utah State Library Division, Department of Community and Economic Development.

LIBRARY-RELATED STATISTICS

Annual   *Library and Information Science Education Statistical Report.* Sarasota, Fla,: Association for Library and Information Science Education.

State Library Agencies Financial Survey. Lexington, Ky.: Council of State Governments.

1993   Kellerstrass, Amy Louise Sutton. *The State Library Agencies 1991.* Tenth edition. Chicago: Association of Specialized and Cooperative Library Agencies.

STAFFING AND SALARIES

Annual   *Administrative Compensation Survey.* Washington, D.C.: College and University Personnel Association.

ALA Survey of Librarian Salaries. Chicago and London: American Library Association.

ARL Annual Salary Survey. Washington, D.C.: Association of Research Libraries.

Lynch, Mary Jo. "Salaries of Library Directors: Data from the Municipal Year Book." *Public Libraries*, July.

MLA Salary Survey. Chicago: Medical Library Association.

National Survey of Salaries and Wages in Public Schools. Arlington, Va.: Educational Research Service.

Biennial   Bureau of Labor Statistics. *Occupational Outlook Handbook.* Washington, D.C.: U.S. Government Printing Office.

1990   Brimsek, Tobi A. "SLA Biennial Salary Survey Report." *Special Libraries*, Fall, pp. 338–40.

Learmont, Carol, and Stephen Van Houten. "Placements & Salaries 1989: Steady On." *Library Journal*, October 15, p. 46 ff.

Martinez, E. B., and R. G. Roney. "Library Support Staff Salary Survey 1990." *Library Mosaics*, July/August, pp. 8–12.

1991   Lynch, Mary Jo. "Good News About Salaries? Librarians' salaries increased an average of 7.6% for 1991, says Mary Jo Lynch, but staff cutbacks are the flip side of the glad stats." *American Libraries*, November, p. 976.

Thompson, A. "1991 [SLA] Salary Survey Update." *Special Libraries*, Fall, pp. 295–97.

Zipkowitz, Fay. "Placements & Salaries 1990: Losing Ground in the Recession." *Library Journal*, November 1, p. 44 ff.

1992   "ARL Releases 1991 Salary Stats." *Library Journal*, March 1, p. 25.

Lynch, Mary Jo. "Librarians' Salaries: Small Increases Like Everyone Else [1992 ALA Salary Survey]." *American Libraries*, October, p. 784 ff.

Zipkowitz, Fay. "Placements & Salaries 1991: Jobs Tight Salaries Holding. Little Gain Made in Our 41st Annual Survey." *Library Journal*, October 15, p. 30 ff.

1993   Lynch, Mary Jo. "Increasing at a Decreasing Rate." [1993 ALA Salary Survey] *American Libraries*, November, p. 945 ff.

Sadowski, Michael, and Randy Meyer. "States of Inequality: School Library Staffing Survey 1993." *School Library Journal*, June, p. 34 ff.

Zipkowitz, Fay. "Placements & Salaries 1992: Fewer Graduates but Salaries Climb." *Library Journal*, October 15, p. 30 ff.

1994   Lynch, Mary Jo. "Librarians' Salaries: Moving Upward at a Higher Rate." *American Libraries*, November, pp. 954–56.

Martinez, Ed, and Raymond Roney. "1993 Library Support Staff Salary Survey," *Library Mosaics*, May 1, p. 6 ff.

Sadowski, Michael, and Randy Meyer. "Staffing for Success: School Library Staffing Survey 1994." *School Library Journal*, p. 29 ff.

St. Lifer, Evan. "Are You Happy in Your Job? LJ's Exclusive Report." [LJ Career Survey, Part 2: Job Satisfaction] *Library Journal*, November 1, pp. 44–49.

Williams, Wilda W. "You Can Take Your MLS Out of the Library." [LJ Career Survey, Part 3: Alternative Careers] *Library Journal*, November 15, pp. 43–46.

Zipkowski, Fay. "1993 Placements Up, but Full-Time Jobs Are Scarce." [LJ Career Survey, Part 1: Placements & Salaries] *Library Journal*, October 15, pp. 26–32.

TELL IT! Tip Sheet

USING EXISTING DATA

Purpose and Logic Behind Use of This Technique

To use statistics and other published information to demonstrate impact of library services and programs

Type(s) of Situation(s) for Which Technique Is Used

When analysis of existing data can provide meaningful information about the impact of a service or program.

Components of Technique

- Be familiar with existing statistics and other sources of information.

- Analyze collection of local library statistics to ensure you're getting what you need.

- Select data that relates to impact of objective/project being evaluated.

- Select data that speaks to the values of intended audiences.

Supplies Needed

- Access to existing data.

- Microcomputer with spreadsheet, database, and/or statistical analysis software.

Personnel Needed

- Staff with access to existing data and experience in applying basic research skills for evaluation purposes.

Time Factors

Can be done with minimal effort.

Cost Factors

Inexpensive; some staff time and computer capability required.

Further Reading on This Technique

Robert Swisher and Charles R. McClure. *Research for decision making; methods for librarians*. Chicago: American Library Association, 1984.

Fitz-Gibbon, Carol Taylor, and Lynn Lyons Morris. *How to Analyze Data*. Newbury Park, Calif.: Sage, 1987.

Text for this tip sheet came from Sandra Nelson, Tennessee State Library and Archives.

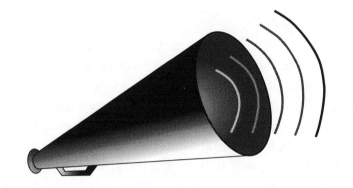

CHAPTER 18

Observation

Douglas Zweizig and Debra Wilcox Johnson

"You can observe a lot just by watching."
Yogi Berra

Observing events and people is a natural activity—we learn by watching. When being used as an evaluation technique, a more systematic approach to observation is needed. Defining what behavior is to be studied and standardizing the process used to observe will help an evaluator produce credible evidence of the effectiveness of a library service or process.

Observational techniques can be used in a variety of situations (behavior of users at the online catalog, use of the reading tables, use of the vertical files). In libraries, much of the "counting up" or recording of activity levels is a simplified form of observation. While most literature on the use of observation focuses on the study of reference services, observation can also be used in small scale studies in a library to address management questions inexpensively.

This chapter examines the key components of the observation method and discusses some issues related to this technique. The focus is on applying unobtrusive observation, that is, observing without alerting the people being observed.

OVERVIEW

When people know that they are being observed, they are likely to behave differently than they would without that awareness. The act of observation may change what you hope to observe. For example, people want to appear polite, informed, cooperative, and so on. When people are asked their opinion, they may attempt to give an answer that they believe will be acceptable to the person asking the question. When we ask library users whether they were satisfied with the library service today, they are likely to say that they were, even if they were frustrated in obtaining what they came for. A user coming to the library to take a nap is likely to respond on a survey that the reason for using the library today was to borrow a book, a more acceptable answer.

This phenomenon—when people behave differently than they would otherwise as a reaction to being observed—is called reactivity. If we are interested in what people *really* think or what they *really* do, we must consider how observation will affect their responses and behavior.

In general, the questions to ask are: Will people respond differently from their actual opinion or feeling if we ask them directly? Will they behave differently if they know they are being observed? If the answer to either question is yes, it would be useful to think of how the observations could be made unobtrusively. Unobtrusive observation—observing behavior without the awareness of the people being observed—avoids reactivity.

In the library setting, circulation figures can generally be thought of as data collected in an unobtrusive manner. (Some users are aware that circulation data are collected, however. One patron was known to check out regularly the titles of lesser known American poets so that their works would survive weeding based on circulation.) Turnstiles are another example; they are so commonplace that their counting of persons entering or leaving the library is virtually unobtrusive.

Other observations also may indicate use. Some online catalogs produce a record of use and logs of user behavior (transaction logs). The number of handouts picked up at a program may be an indicator of interest in the topic. The number of books left in the book drop may reflect the effect of a change in library hours open. To determine traffic patterns in a library, staff could study patterns of wear in the carpet. In a children's museum, display cases were cleaned each night and noseprints on the glass were counted each day to identify the most compelling exhibits.

A related form of observation is participant observation. It contrasts with the distant or remote observer who studies the log of online catalog usage or views the service desk from an inconspicuous vantage point. Participant observers partake of the activity that they are observing; they are unobtrusive in that they are probably not suspected to be conducting an observation, but they themselves are also the object of their evaluation. Similar principles guide participant observation and unobtrusive observation (clarifying the purpose of the observation, recording observations systematically, and so on), but the participant observers have additional issues of their relationship with those being observed and their own experience. ("Guidelines for Participant Observers" are provided at the end of this chapter as an example of instructions given to observers of a staff development activity.)

As can be seen, observation principles can be applied directly to a variety of library activities such as service at the circulation desk, users' success or frustration with the online catalog, book sales, or responses to a library program. Therefore, observation can be a useful, and often inexpensive, evaluation tool.

DESCRIPTION OF THE TECHNIQUE

The checklist below illustrates the key elements of the process, including defining the behavior to be observed, a timeline for information gathering, a method for recording observations, and making sense of the results.

In conducting an evaluation by observation, it is important to determine:

1. ***What you are trying to learn.*** In other words, just what will be studied and why is it important? The "Things to Observe..." sheet at the end of this chapter suggests aspects of library service for which observation may be an appropriate evaluation approach. Sharply defining what will be studied and how results will be used will increase the chances of collecting interpretable and useful data.

2. ***Where you are going to make the observations.*** Observations could be made at a specific service desk, at all of the online catalog terminals, at each department library, or other defined locations. Explicitly defining the locations at which to make observations helps in knowing where results could be applied.

3. ***When the observations will occur.*** Library use differs by time of day, day of the lending period, season of the year, and so on. By making observations at selected times, we are in effect sampling from the entire time possible for study. The main concern with sampling is representativeness: are the times selected for study representative of the overall use of the library in the aspect being studied? *Output Measures for Public Libraries* (2d ed.) has suggestions for determining a schedule for collecting data to represent the range of library usage.

4. ***Who will make the observations.*** In order that comparable observations can be made across a number of locations or times, you will need to recruit a set of observers and provide training in how to conduct the evaluation. The kind and number of observers will be determined by the study's characteristics. In order to remain unobtrusive, observers should be selected and dressed in ways that will not attract notice. An observer reading at one of the library's tables while observing users of the consumer information shelf should appear to belong

there; a participant observer of a library program should be perceived to be a natural member of the audience.

Sources of observers are library staff from another department, library staff from another library in the system, and volunteers such as members of the Friends of the Library, of an advisory committee, or of a local service club. The observers will need to know what is being studied and how to record observations in a standardized manner. Training should involve practice and checking the effectiveness of the instruction by having more than one observer observe the same phenomenon independently and comparing results. Some suggestions for the general training of observers are appended to this chapter.

5. ***How the observations will be made.*** The persons responsible for conducting an observation study should make test observations to determine how observations will be made and to learn how well procedures work. The resulting methods should be written out to support the training of the observers and to include in the report of the results of the observation.

6. ***How the observations will be recorded.*** Comparability of observations requires that they are recorded in a standardized form. Evaluation designers should create and test a form that will include the needed information, such as who made the observation, when it occurred, where, what was observed, and so on. Observations should be recorded in a manner that is not obtrusive and that will not require the observer to trust too much to memory. While participant observers cannot take notes continually if it would be unnatural to do so, they should be instructed to record their observations at their first opportunity after gathering them. You will find it helpful to have written explanation of how the observation recording form is to be used.

7. ***How the results will be analyzed.*** A plan for analyzing the results should be in place before data collection has begun. How to analyze the data will be guided by thinking about the kinds of statements you intend to make in the conclusions. For example, if you want to be able to discuss how long users spend at the electronic periodical index stations, then the observation form must have a place for noting the times a given user arrives at and leaves from the station. The analysis will involve making a calculation of the time spent by subtracting the time of arrival from the time of leaving. The report will need to summarize the observed times so that a reader can see their range and pattern. If you want to make a statement such as, "Half of our users spend less than ____ minutes at an electronic periodical index station," then your results will have to be ar-

ranged in order of time spent so that it is possible to identify the middle score (the median).

8. ***How to report the results.*** From the beginning, it is well to think about the report of findings. In general, the task of the report is to explain the data presented and to interpret it in terms of the reasons for the study. (Return to point 1, What you are trying to learn.) In order to communicate the richness of the observations made, it is likely that the report will contain a mix of numerical data and narrative description: "Over half of the brochures were picked up at the end of the program. One person called out to her companions, 'Look there are other programs coming up!'"

Thinking about the stakeholders for the service examined will give some guidance about who needs to know the evaluation's results. Somewhat different forms of report may be appropriate for readers with different levels of interest in the service. Early consideration of such questions will increase the chance that the desired forms of report will be possible at the end of the evaluation.

Uses of the Findings within Libraries

The use to be made of an observation-based evaluation relates directly to its purpose. If the evaluation was conducted to understand user behavior at work stations in the library, then the use of the findings may be to relocate some work stations to allow more privacy. If the purpose was to observe user reactions at the circulation desk, then the findings may be used in staff development or training of new staff. Even though the specific use of the findings is determined by the purpose of the evaluation, it is important that some use be made of the findings. Library staff will be more willing to participate in evaluation studies if they believe that their efforts will result in decisions that improve services.

Strengths and Weaknesses

It is important to acknowledge that unobtrusive observation has limitations. It allows study of what can be directly observed, but does not gain access to feelings or opinions, or to behaviors that take place beyond the observation point. Observation can address the question: "Are the materials of the business reference collection used in the library?" Observation can not determine why those materials were used or whether they provided the needed information; questions such as these require questionnaires or interviews.

Persons intending to conduct an unobtrusive observation will want to consider some ethical questions raised by this approach. Is it ethical to observe people's behavior when they are unaware that they are being observed? Is it ethical to pose as a member of a group in order to conduct a participant observation? Is it right to have an observer ask a reference librarian to answer an artificial reference question for the purpose of checking the accuracy of an answer you already know? While one could argue that responsibility to the users requires rigorous evaluation of actual quality of service provided, it is also possible to see that there are issues that could be sensitive and interests that need to be balanced. One solution that has been used for the observation of staff performance is to notify the staff that an evaluation will take place at some time in the future, but not to announce just when the study is being conducted. Such an approach has commonly been used in evaluations of the accuracy of reference services.

Nonreactivity was given as the primary reason for considering use of observation, but there are other benefits as well. Observation studies have relatively low cost in terms of time and materials, although reference accuracy studies are more complex and require additional resources. Further, the involvement of staff in designing and conducting observations of library services provides important managerial training.

TRAINING ON THE METHOD

Training will be required for the observers any time more than one observer will be conducting an observation study. In addition, general training on the evaluation technique of observation may be used to explain to staff the nature and purpose of an observation study being planned or to acquaint staff with this evaluation approach so that they can consider its use in evaluating services.

This chapter may serve as an outline for such training: overview and purpose, description of the technique, and discussion of issues. It also will be useful to provide an experiential exercise to allow the practice of observation.

An exercise that can be used in a day-long workshop is the observation of lunch. Participants are told to "observe lunch" and to be ready to share their observations in the afternoon. The discussion after lunch can illustrate the variety of things chosen for observation since the trainer did not specify what to observe, making the point of the importance of carefully defining the aspect to be observed. Questions that might guide the discussion are

What were the results of not being clear?

- focussed on very different things

- observations would not be comparable

What would be an example of clear instructions on what to observe?

- how many people at your table were left-handed?

- how long did it take for all people at your table to be served?

- how clean were the plates when they were removed?

218

What are the benefits of clear specification of what is to be observed?

- observers will be more secure about the task

- comparable, interpretable results

Other discussion topics could include

- the degree of obtrusiveness of different observation methods (noting which people ate dessert would be unobtrusive; peering intently into a person's salad plate to determine ingredients would be much more obtrusive)

- the role of participant observer: the "Guidelines for Participant Observers" could be introduced at this point

- how the experience of observing lunch would relate to making observations in the library, such as reference service or circulation

- aspects of library service in the individual library that could usefully be observed (see "Things to Observe...").

In another food-related example, one of the state library agencies instructed their staff in evaluation by having them evaluate the carrot cakes offered by restaurants in the state capital on successive weeks as they went to lunch as a group. Over the weeks, the discussions became more sophisticated on evaluation as staff discussed the qualities of a good carrot cake, the ways used to score each example, how to communicate the results, and so on. The instruction was memorable and enjoyable.

The training checklist that follows describes an exercise on observation in which the observing is done in advance of the training event. Participants, who may or may not have been given prior information on observation, are given instructions for designing their own observation and making some sample observations. The training event then makes use of this experience to address the points to be considered when designing an observation-based evaluation.

REFERENCES AND FURTHER READING

Childers, Thomas. "Scouting the Perimeters of Unobtrusive Study of Reference." In *Evaluation of Public Services and Public Services Personnel*, ed. Bryce Allen, 27–42. Champaign, Ill.: University of Illinois, Graduate School of Library and Information Science, 1991.

Hernon, Peter and Charles R. McClure. *Unobtrusive Testing and Library Reference Services.* Norwood, N.J.: Ablex, 1987.

Webb, Eugene J., et al. *Nonreactive Measures in the Social Sciences.* 2nd ed. Boston: Houghton, Mifflin, 1981.

TRAINING CHECKLIST FOR UNOBTRUSIVE OBSERVATION

Purpose: To provide experience with the complexities and possibilities in collecting data through direct observation.

Rationale for approach: As opposed to reading or being told about issues in data collection, participants have direct experience in making observations and in instructing others in observation.

Number of participants: Can be any size group. Limited only by logistics needed to handle discussion of the experience.

Time required: One hour for making observations (done as an individual exercise in advance of the training session). 30 minutes for discussion. Another hour and a half for observation and discussion if second observations are made.

Instructional approach: Hands-on exercise, discussion, mini-lecture

Room arrangement: Suitable for a large group discussion.

Special supplies: Handouts distributed in advance. Newsprint or transparency material for recording discussion.

Advance preparation: Preparation and distribution of the handout to participants in advance of the training. (As alternatives, observations could take place during a lengthy workshop at previously identified locations where observations could be conducted conveniently or observations could be done at home between sessions of a continuing workshop.)

Directions: Participants are sent the "Reflection on Observation" sheet in advance of the workshop so that they can design, carry out, and write up a simple observation before coming.

Discussion at the workshop can address such questions as:

- How confident do you feel that another person would have obtained the same results?

- What did you do to increase the quality of your observations?

- Would you be willing to act on data produced through this kind of study? Why or why not?

- What kind of data would you want to supplement this kind?

Participants can then exchange instructions and carry out observations following the received instructions.

Discussion can center on principles to follow when providing instructions to others for collecting observations.

To conclude, a mini-lecture can be given by the leader on issues to address when collecting information through observation.

REFLECTIONS ON OBSERVATION

The purpose of this exercise is to give you experience in making observations in order to identify some of the complexities in data gathering. The observations are to be made unobtrusively. That is, the people being observed should not be aware of the observation. Therefore, surveys or interviews should not be used for this exercise.

Follow these steps:

1. Identify a question about how people actually behave in a library. It should be something simple for this exercise: how many people who come into the library are carrying books or how many people at any time are asleep? Try to isolate the key elements of the question and develop clear definitions for them. For example, what will you consider carrying books to be? Does a book bag count, even if you can't see in it? How will you decide if a person is asleep or not? Write the rules for these decisions down so that you will be able to reconsider them later.

2. Develop a method for making observations about the key terms of your question.

3. Observe at least 7 to 10 individuals or instances in terms of your question.

4. Make some notes about the results and the conclusions about your question that might be drawn from them.

5. Reflect on the process of making observations. What are the sources of confusion or error? What changes in the method you used might reduce problems in making observations?

6. A way of testing soundness of evaluation is if two observers of the same thing reach similar conclusions. Bring instructions for making your observations with you to the training so that another person can test them for clarity to more than one person.

TELL IT! Tip Sheet

UNOBTRUSIVE OBSERVATION

Purpose and Logic Behind Use of This Technique
- To achieve a non-reactive view of services
- Can give one a client-based view of services
- If done cooperatively in a library system, the observers can be staff and learn from each other

Type(s) of Situation(s) for Which Technique Is Used
- Traditionally, for observing services interactions, especially the reference transaction
- Useful in any setting where behaviors or records of behaviors (i.e., OPAC transaction logs, circulation records, in-house use) can be systematically observed

Components of Technique
- Observation training
- Observations at service point
- Write-up of observations
- Sharing of notes on observations with service point staff

Personnel Needed
- Individual to train observers
- Observers
- Individual(s) to facilitate discussion of findings with service point staff

Time Factors
- Can be organized quickly if needed
- Observer training time
- Actual time for observations varies widely, depending on service and plan. Observations should be made multiple times and over a period of time that is representative of the activity level for a given service
- For a single event, observation may occur only once, but could be repeated at similar programs

Supplies Needed
- Procedures for observers
- Forms for recording observations

Cost Factors
- Tends to be low cost; time of staff or volunteers required
- Reference accuracy studies would require the most resources

Further Reading on This Technique
Peter Hernon and Charles R. McClure. *Unobtrusive Testing and Library Reference Services.* Norwood, N.J.: Ablex, 1987.

Eleanor Jo Rodger and Jane Goodwin. "To See Ourselves as Others See Us: A Cooperative, Do-It-Yourself Reference Accuracy Study." *Reference Librarian* 18 (Summer 1987): 135–147.

Eugene J. Webb, et al. *Nonreactive Measures in the Social Sciences.* 2nd ed. Boston: Houghton, Mifflin, 1981.

THINGS TO OBSERVE . . .

1. Staff behavior at service desks

2. Instruction in use of library resources

3. Readers advisory service

4. Online, CD, database searches

5. Internet searches

6. Reference queries

7. Card or online catalog behavior

8. In-house use of special collections, e.g., reference, business, consumer resources, and vertical files

9. Monitoring use of

    - Community calender

    - Community resource directory

    - Use of bibliographies

    - Brochures

    - Displays and exhibits.

10. Queueing behavior, e.g., wait times at service desks

11. Facilities use, e.g., occupancy of seating

12. Programs

13. Special services, e.g., literacy services

GUIDELINES FOR PARTICIPANT OBSERVERS

"You can observe a lot just by watching."
Yogi Berra

The purpose of these guidelines is to remind participant observers of the goals of participant observation and to provide some techniques for enhancing the process. These are equally applicable to observing library processes and activities as well as observing educational activities. A participant observer is examining activities as they actually occur. The motivation for attending an activity or using a service is observing the process; use of the service is secondary.

During the observation, the participant observer has several responsibilities:

1. Listen carefully and attempt to blend in with group members or users while always remaining neutral.

2. Watch closely the interactions of group members.

3. Informal conversations and casual questioning can be used to elicit insights. This would be natural interaction as part of the group, but not used when observing individuals using a service.

4. Note discreetly what is happening within the group.

5. Participate in any debriefing/reporting sessions.

As with all evaluation techniques, the first and foremost responsibility is to determine why the observations are being made. Whether the observation is to take place over a lengthy period of time (periodic or multiple days) or on a one-time basis, a plan is necessary. It is advisable for organizers and observers to agree ahead of time on the following:

1. What should be observed, while still remaining open to the unexpected.

2. How observations will be recorded.

3. What procedures will be in place to ensure accuracy of observations.

4. How the relationship between observer and the observed is to be handled.

The successful participant observer will have some level of knowledge of the topic or issue being presented and an understanding of the vocabulary of the field. Blending in and remaining unobtrusive are important; however, this may not always be possible.

When using participant observation as a continuing education evaluation technique, the observer has multiple opportunities to observe the learning process. During both formal sessions and informal times, like meals and breaks, roaming around while watching and listening for participants' reactions becomes the order of the day. When possible, observation from the front of a room allows for gauging of facial expressions and group reactions to materials being presented. Some aspects of group interaction that should be taken into account include positive and negative observations regarding:

1. Apparent ability of all participants to be effective members of the group. Are they "getting" the message of the presentation? Are they discussing the topics presented? Taking notes?

2. Non-verbal communication. Have any participants shut down?

3. Reactions to the environmental factors. Too cold? Too warm? Can everyone hear?

4. Reactions to group dynamics. Does everyone have equal opportunity to participate?

5. Types of questions raised by participants.

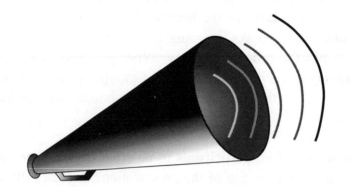

CHAPTER 19

Attitude Measurement

Ronald Powell

APPROACHES TO MEASURING ATTITUDES

Purposes for Measuring Attitudes

Attitudes are predispositions to feel, think, perceive, and perhaps, act in a particular way; they are an integral part of people's personalities. Attitudes are not opinions, although most people use the terms interchangeably because opinions arise from attitudes. Opinions are mental judgments that are yet open to dispute. Although attitudes can change, they tend to be more long term and more deeply held. An attitude related to evaluation could be: evaluation is generally a useful activity. An opinion related to evaluation could be: in this case, I think that conducting an evaluation could be politically dangerous.

It is desirable for library evaluators to measure attitudes of users, and nonusers.

- Attitudinal type data help to supplement and complement more factual kinds of data such as records.

- An assessment of users' attitudes toward a library's programs and services is central to measuring their level of satisfaction.

- Attitudes are believed to indicate predispositions to certain actions and reactions, and thus a knowledge of people's attitudes enables one to make more accurate predictions of their future behavior.

Problems in Measuring Attitudes

Unfortunately, attitudes are relatively difficult phenomena to measure. Some reasons for this difficulty are listed below.

- Individuals may not have an attitude regarding a specific issue because they had not thought about it until queried.

- Attitudes often are complex and multidimensional. A person may not have a single attitude toward a library service or a collection of materials but may feel differently about different aspects.

- The measurement of attitudes is affected by question wording, question sequence, interviewer behavior, etc.

- Attitudes cannot be directly measured. They can only be inferred from a person's words and behavior.

- Certain attitudes may change rapidly.

Methods for Measuring Attitudes

As is true of measuring most things, it is desirable to use already existing measurement techniques and tools if appropriate ones are available. Doing so tends to increase the reliability and validity of one's measurements, to save time, and to facilitate comparing the results of similar evaluations. In short, it's better not to reinvent the wheel unless necessary.

Some attitude measures have been published, are commercially available, and are considered to be "standardized." Others might have been used only a few times for in-house type studies and have not yet established their validity and reliability. In either case, the evaluator may have to modify previously used instruments in order to use them in a particular study. (See Henerson, 1987, Chapter 4, for information on identifying and obtaining existing measures of attitudes.)

Unfortunately, due in part to the lack of replicated research in library and information science, there are relatively few standardized tools available for measuring and evaluating library and information services. The evaluator may well have to develop his or her own measurement technique but certainly should draw upon the experiences of others as much as possible.

Questionnaire

The methodology often used for evaluating library and information services and programs is the survey. The specific data collection technique frequently used in surveys is the questionnaire.

In order for a questionnaire to adequately measure attitudes toward a program or service, it must employ appropriate *measurement scales*. The simplest scale is dichotomous, i.e., it gives the respondent only two choices such as "yes" or "no."

If it is desirable to give the respondent more than two choices, a checklist can be employed. For example,

> Select the statement that best represents how you feel about the story hour in which your child just participated.
>
> ☐ My child enjoyed most of the program.
>
> ☐ My child enjoyed some of the program.
>
> ☐ My child enjoyed little of the program.
>
> ☐ My child enjoyed none of the program.

Attitudinal questions often employ scaled responses. A popular type of attitude scale is the Likert scale. Such scales usually range from "strongly agree" to "strongly disagree" and provide four to seven choices. For example,

> The library's collection usually is adequate to meet my needs.
>
> Strongly Agree   Agree   Disagree   Strongly Disagree

Respondents may be asked to rank items in order of importance or on some other trait. An example (Powell, 1991, p. 92) of a rank-order or comparative rating scale is as follows:

> Please rank, in order of importance, the following library services.
> (Record "1" for the most important through "5" for the least important.)
>
> a. Library story hours   ☐
>
> b. Reference services   ☐
>
> c. Circulation services   ☐
>
> d. Audiovisual services   ☐
>
> e. Photocopy services   ☐

Due to the complexity of many attitudes, a set of questions may have to be utilized so as to measure an attitude adequately. Any of the previous formats may be applied to a complete set of questions, or a set of questions can incorporate several kinds of scaled responses. The semantic differential scale, for example, provides sets of paired adjectives, along with five- to seven-point rating scales (Powell, 1991, p. 94):

For each of the items below, what number comes closest
to describing the conditions of your public library?
(Circle one number on each line.)

	Extremely	Moderately	Neither	Moderately	Extremely	
a. Pleasant	1	2	3	4	5	Unpleasant
b. Clean	1	2	3	4	5	Dirty
c. Organized	1	2	3	4	5	Disorganized
d. Helpful	1	2	3	4	5	Unhelpful
e. Available when needed	1	2	3	4	5	Unavailable when needed

To obtain the respondent's overall attitude toward the library, the evaluator would sum the total values of the columns and divide by the number (five) of paired adjectives.

The evaluator should consider including at least one or two open-ended questions in an evaluation instrument. Such questions give the respondent an opportunity to volunteer information that the evaluator did not anticipate and to vent strong feelings.

Interview

Another data collection technique that is frequently used in a survey is the interview. A structured interview will look much like a questionnaire and will contain the types of questions described above.

An unstructured-type interview will employ mostly open-ended questions such as, "What do you like the most about the public library?" It will include probes for complete responses, such as, "Tell me more." or "Why aren't you satisfied with the library's reference services?" (See Chapter 15, "Interviewing.")

A type of interview that is especially popular today is the focus group interview. Such interviews are designed to focus attention on a given experience and its effects. The interviews usually involve eight to twelve respondents and a trained moderator who guides a discussion which lasts from one to two hours. (See Chapter 16, "Focus Groups.")

Observation

Observation of library users has the potential to measure attitudes as represented by behavior. Typically, "one or more observers are placed in a natural setting at a specified time and for a prescribed length of time" (Henerson, 1987, p. 109). They may or may not use predetermined sets of categories to record the observed behavior.

Observation has the advantages of 1) recording behavior as it occurs, 2) comparing actual behavior with recorded behavior, and 3) observing behavior that people may not think to report. On the other hand, in measuring attitudes, the results of observations tend to be relatively difficult to analyze and necessitate the assumption that behavior does indeed reflect attitude(s). (See Chapter 18, "Observation.")

QUALITATIVE METHODS

The measurement techniques described thus far have been primarily quantitative in nature. An evaluator might choose, however, to approach an evaluation in a more qualitative manner. Qualitative methods focus on viewing experiences more from the perspective of those involved and attempt to understand why individuals react or behave as they do. They tend to give more attention to the subjective aspects of human experience and behavior. In short, qualitative methods provide a more natural approach to evaluation.

A qualitative evaluation could utilize some of the data collection techniques already discussed, though in a more unstructured, open-ended fashion. For example, in a study of how senior citizens use a public library, the evaluators might well immerse themselves in the lives of the older library users and observe their behavior, attitudes, and beliefs from the inside (Glazier and Powell, 1992, p. xi).

VALIDITY AND RELIABILITY

Regardless of the measurement techniques used, it is critical that they be sufficiently valid and reliable. In essence, a data collection instrument is valid to the degree that it actually measures what it was designed to measure. For example, a questionnaire designed to measure individuals' level of satisfaction with a library's reference service might really be measuring their own confidence in their abilities to use reference materials and therefore would have little validity as a measure of satisfaction with the service.

Reliability reflects the degree to which an instrument accurately and consistently measures whatever it measures. A data collection tool may be high in validity and low in reliability, or vice versa, but ideally is strong in both.

UNDERSTANDING THE RESULTS

Having collected evaluative data, the evaluator must then analyze the data and interpret the findings. In doing so, he or she should keep in mind the purpose(s) for which the data have been collected and the stakeholders or audiences with whom they will be shared.

Organizing the Data

In order to organize and analyze data, it is necessary to first place them in categories. Responses to a question on level of satisfaction with a service, for example, could be placed in categories labeled strongly agree, agree, etc., as appropriate. In establishing the categories, the evaluator should take care that they are exhaustive, or represent all reasonable responses, and that they are mutually exclusive, meaning that a response cannot be placed correctly in more than one category.

Once the categories have been established, the data may be assigned to them. This process requires converting the raw data or responses to numerical codes so that they can be tabulated. If a computer is to be used for the analysis, the codes can be recorded on a coding sheet and then entered into a database, or they can be input directly into the computer. (See Chapter 20, "Making Sense of Narrative Responses.")

Analyzing the Data

Once the data are ready to be analyzed, the evaluator can employ a variety of statistical techniques. If the evaluative study has been designed to test a formal hypothesis, it will be necessary to use inferential, as well as descriptive, statistics. Otherwise, descriptive statistics will suffice. Descriptive statistics can be used to portray a variety of characteristics of the data through the use of tables, graphs, and charts and can be used to indicate central tendency (e.g., mean, median, mode); dispersion (e.g., range, standard deviation); and associations between or among categories of the data.

To analyze responses to open-ended questions, the evaluator can 1) produce a purely descriptive written summary, or 2) assign numerical values to different types of responses and then analyze those data (Henerson, 1987, p. 170). Even when using the second option, it may be worthwhile to quote some responses to open-ended questions (i.e., anecdotal data). (See Chapter 20, "Making Sense of Narrative Responses.")

Any analysis, however, is not complete until the results have been interpreted. While this interpretation should be done as objectively as possible, it may well reflect the perspective of the interpreter. For example, a head of collection development might interpret a low level of user satisfaction with the library's holdings as an indication that the library is selecting materials that are popular and thus frequently unavailable. The head of reference services might interpret such responses as meaning that the library needs to buy more copies of fewer titles.

AN EXAMPLE OF THE USE OF AN ATTITUDE MEASUREMENT TECHNIQUE

Margaret A. Wilkinson and Bryce Allen (1991, pp. 103–30) conducted a survey designed to address five problems:

1. Who are seniors?

2. Who are the activities and services in the public library reaching?

3. Is there general support for concentration on the senior user group?

4. Is there support for public library services or activities exclusive to seniors?

5. Where do library users find out about library activities?

Most of these research questions necessitated determining the opinions of library users. To that end, a questionnaire with ten structured and two open-ended questions was developed. The structured questions included checklists and scales ranging from "strongly disagree" to "strongly agree." Two of the questions were:

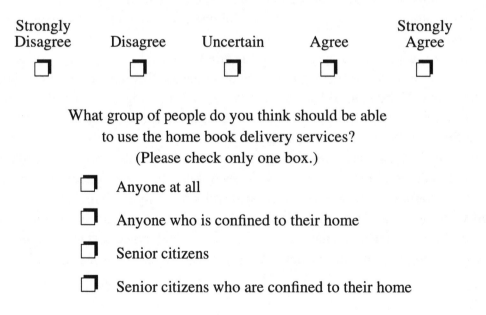

The library should have activities (such as films or talks) designed for seniors which only seniors may attend.

Strongly Disagree	Disagree	Uncertain	Agree	Strongly Agree
☐	☐	☐	☐	☐

What group of people do you think should be able to use the home book delivery services?
(Please check only one box.)

☐ Anyone at all

☐ Anyone who is confined to their home

☐ Senior citizens

☐ Senior citizens who are confined to their home

Library staff at each check-out desk offered questionnaires to adult users until 500 had been distributed. A total of 345 questionnaires (a 69% response rate) were completed and returned to a sealed box near the desk.

A combination of descriptive and inferential statistics was used to analyze the data. Results of the analysis were displayed in tables, bar graphs, line graphs, and pie charts. Some of the specific findings were:

> In the abstract, nearly everyone supported an increased level of service in an area traditionally associated with seniors: large-print books.

> When contrasted with services provided to another distinct user group, children, most respondents thought the needs of seniors should not be emphasized.

> Opposition to emphasizing seniors was particularly strong among those who defined seniors as older.

> There was support among younger seniors (50–65) for segregated programming.

EXAMPLES OF TRAINING SESSIONS

Designing and Conducting an Interview

Present a lecture/discussion on using interviews to measure attitudes. Then divide the learners into groups of four to six members each and ask the groups to do the following:

1. Identify an attitude to be measured; e.g., attitudes of adult members of the library's community to its hours of service. (The attitude could be assigned by the instructor.)

2. Decide on the format and approach of the interview, i.e., unstructured, open-ended, structured, face-to-face, telephone, etc.

3. Determine the number and sequence of the questions.

4. Draft questions and critique them.

5. Discuss how responses to the questions will be recorded, analyzed and reported.

If time permits, each group could select an interviewer and conduct trial interviews with other participants or individuals in an actual library setting. The groups could then share their experiences with the rest of the participants.

Analyzing Data

Present a lecture/discussion on descriptive data analysis. Then divide the learners into groups of four to six members each and give each group several completed structured questionnaires or interview schedules. (These could be questionnaires created and filled out by the evaluator or questionnaires generated by the groups in a previous training session.) Ask each group to:

1. Design a summary sheet—i.e., a form that contains the questions asked in the questionnaires and boxes or cells in which all of the responses to the questions can be recorded or tallied.

2. "Transfer" the data from the questionnaires to the summary sheet.

3. For each group of responses, calculate the number and percent of persons who answered each item a certain way and the average or mean response to each item and present those figures in a table.

As time permits, groups could present their findings and discuss how they could be used to evaluate a library.

REFERENCES AND FURTHER READING

Baker, Sharon, L., and Wilfrid F. Lancaster. *The Measurement and Evaluation of Library Services*. 2nd ed. Arlington, Va.: Information Resources Press, 1991.

Bookstein, Abraham. "Questionnaire Research in a Library Setting." *Journal of Academic Librarianship* 11 (March 1985): 24–28.

Hafner, Arthur W. *Descriptive Statistical Techniques for Librarians*. Chicago: American Library Association, 1982.

Henerson, Marlene E., Lynn L. Morris, and Carol J. Fitz-Gibbon. *How to Measure Attitudes*. Newbury Park, Calif.: Sage, 1987.

Powell, Ronald R. *Basic Research Methods for Librarians*. 2nd ed. Norwood, N.J.: Ablex, 1991.

Sandler, Mark. "Qualitative Research Methods in Library Decision-Making." In *Qualitative Research in Information Management,* ed. Jack D. Glazier and Ronald R. Powell. Englewood, Colo.: Libraries Unlimited, 1992.

Wilkinson, Margaret A., and Bryce Allen. "What are Users' Views on Seniors in the Public Library?" *Library and Information Science Research* 13 (1991): 103–30.

TRAINING CHECKLIST FOR ATTITUDE MEASUREMENT

Purpose: To enable the participants to:
- design a data collection instrument capable of measuring an attitude,
- conduct an interview, and
- organize and analyze the data gathered by an interview.

Rationale for approach: This type of training activity can:
- provide a hands-on experience in collection of data,
- give some sense of the difficulty of measuring attitudes, and
- give participants practice in conducting team research.

Number of participants: A maximum of 30 divided into six groups of five people each.

Estimated time for activity: Two hours for the lecture/discussion on using interviews to measure attitudes, two hours for the design of the interviews, two hours for the groups to practice conducting interviews, and at least fifteen minutes per group for reporting back.

Instructional approach: A combination of lecture, large group discussion, small group activity, and hands-on experience.

Room arrangement: A flexible room with chairs and small tables that can be arranged for a single lecturer as well as for small group activities. If only chairs are provided, they need to have arms for writing.

Special supplies needed: Pencils, notepads, chalkboard or newsprint pad and easel, overhead transparencies and projector, screen, marking pens, and handouts.

Advance preparation: Prepare lecture notes and handouts; assemble examples of interview schedules; assemble supplies; and, if desired, arrange for sites where participants can conduct practice interviews.

Directions:
1. Introductions of instructor and participants.
2. Overview of instructional objectives and timetable.
3. Lecture/discussion on using interviews to measure attitudes.
4. Small group design of interviews.
5. Practice interviews (optional).
6. Group reports to class (optional).
7. Final comments by instructor and participants.

The groups' interview schedules could be critiqued by the instructor and other participants. In lieu of groups' reporting their interviewing experiences, they could simply share their interview questions.

TELL IT! Tip Sheet

ATTITUDE MEASUREMENT

Purpose and Logic Behind Use of This Technique
- Gets information on what individuals think or feel about something
- Provides an indication of individuals' predispositions
- Can be a good supplement to other sources of information

Type(s) of Situation(s) for Which Technique Is Used
- Commonly used when determining levels of satisfaction with projects, services, policies, or the insitution as a whole

Components of Technique
- Identify specific attitude to be measured and population to query or observe
- Decide on a measurement scale and data collection method
- Develop questionnaire, interview, or observation guide
- Pre-test
- Collect data
- Tabulate and analyze results

Supplies Needed
- Varies with approach, but office equipment to create evaluation instrument and administer survey (e.g., phone, fax, word processing capability)
- Software to input results, or forms to tabulate by hand
- Computer, or writing implements

Personnel Needed
- Individuals to identify or create measurement scale(s), conduct study and analyze results

Time Factors
- Time varies widely depending on whether a new measure must be developed, the type of data collection, and level of detail of the analysis

Cost Factors
- Varies depending on: if an outside consultant is hired, equipment rented, prizes are offered to participants

Further Reading on This Technique
Marlene E. Henerson, Lynn Lyons Morris, and Carol Taylor Fitz-Gibbon. *How to Measure Attitudes*. Newbury Park, Calif.: Sage, 1987.

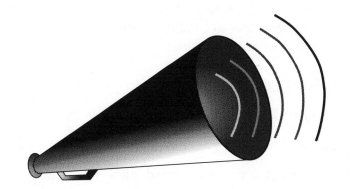

CHAPTER 20

Making Sense of Narrative Responses

Michele Besant

Narrative responses are textual answers to open-ended questions—those questions which require respondents to use their own language and do not limit answers to specified options. When facing the analysis of copious text, narrative responses can feel overwhelming. However, narrative responses are rich data. Remember: "If you knew all the answers, you wouldn't need to ask the questions." Also, there may be some information which can only be gathered with open-ended questions.

Making sense of narrative responses involves observing the patterns and contradictions in text. Meaning is made through a process of categorization, often called coding, and interpretation. The categorization, or coding, is an integral part of interpretation. In assigning codes, interpretation is begun. As patterns emerge, codes may be refined and regrouped to further reflect how the categories are related, i.e., another level of interpretation. In other words, the process is reiterative: categorizing, or coding, is interpretation leading to more interpretation leading to new categories/codes leading to interpretation—in as many loops as are useful to understanding the responses. While this process is essentially the same for any kind of text material (e.g., notes from observations or standardized interviews), the focus in this chapter is on text generated from open-ended questions in a written survey.

This chapter incorporates information from a presentation by Elizabeth Graue, Assistant Professor, Curriculum and Instruction, University of Wisconsin–Madison, at the Evaluating Library Programs and Services Clinic, January 8, 1994, Madison, Wisc.

Planning ahead is important for analysis. While you cannot anticipate exactly what will be written, being clear and staying focused on the purpose(s) of the survey will help frame questions that increase the clarity and focus of the responses as well.

Some questions to ask yourself include:

- Have you avoided jargon?

- Do your questions use bias-free language?

- Are any qualifying words vague (e.g.,"sometimes," "frequently")?

- Have you made conditional or qualified questions clear by stating the key idea last?

From the start examine the open-ended questions to get ideas about likely categories, or codes, that the responses will generate. These may be things you know you want to track through the data. These may be ideas from a hunch, speculation, or something you've read. You can always change your mind, but an initial list of categories may prove fruitful during the analysis. If you think you can predict most of the categories of responses, it is better to use a checklist (or close-ended) question instead. An open-ended question can then be used later in the questionnaire to help get information you may otherwise miss.

Be thinking about the mechanics of coding as well. If you're going to code directly on a questionnaire, make sure your form has plenty of space to allow for your scribbles beside, around and on the answers. If responses will be word processed before coding, print with large margins. When you have all the data in hand, consider making a copy so as to always have a clean original should you wish to reanalyze the responses another time (or just to assure a legible copy in case coding gets boisterous!).

Read through the responses at least once without a writing tool in hand. Given almost inevitable time pressures, this may feel hard to do. But even a very quick skim is useful for getting an overall picture of what is there. On the second, more careful reading, write down words or phrases that seem important or capsulate ideas well. For the first half dozen or so responses to a question, you will probably be noting many new potential categories, or codes. The growth of the list will slow rapidly after that as significant bits of information already have been noted. As soon as you hit a relative standstill in the growth of your list, decide on which words to use as codes. Usually there will be some overlaps that suggest groupings; you may decide to narrow the number of codes from these groupings. Ultimately the codes should each represent only one idea and in total cover all concepts, i.e., be both mutually exclusive and exhaustive.

Other codes may not be signaled by words in the data, but rather are descriptive of information you were planning to note. For instance, you may want a coding scheme that identifies comments as positive or negative. Or, you may want to always note descriptions of persons, activities and resources, and have a code that indicates "here's a description of a person (or activity or resource)." In other words, there may be different levels of coding. A good general rule is: keep it as simple as possible.

There is no magical number of codes. You have to have enough codes to capture and differentiate data in meaningful ways, but if you delineate answers too much, they will not be synthesized enough and the vast number of codes will take on the behemoth nature of raw data. The number of codes will also depend on what you're analyzing and why. For example, if you want to know the other agencies with which libraries in your system cooperate, you may code for each unique answer and get dozens. If you find they fall into three general groups and that level of identification suffices (e.g., public schools, businesses, community-based organizations), you might have only four codes (those three and "other") or perhaps five (those three, "other" and "none"). Think about why you asked the question and to whom the information will be useful.

Formalize the codes in a code list or codebook. While most people number the codes, whether you mark a response by number or word is up to you. How detailed is your analysis going to be? If you intend to do some quantitative analysis on a computer you will have to use numbers. Otherwise, think about which you will remember more easily. If the numbering indicates a meaningful sequence, using numbers could help you see patterns. If the numbers are arbitrary and will just jumble on you, having the memory aid of a word may be more to the point.

Test the codes to make sure they can be applied reliably. Mark copies of the same sample responses on different days and see if coding matches. If other people will be helping you code, train them by demonstration with many samples. Have them check their coding against each others' and yours on a sample and see how well they match. If time allows, doing your own coding can be advantageous: it gives the opportunity to refine codes and see more patterns as they emerge. Regardless of who does the coding, do a regular (every so many questionnaires) coding check for consistency.

Once all the responses are coded, manipulating the text by physically cutting it up and piling like pieces together, or by electronically rearranging it, will allow further categorization and pattern seeking across individual responses. Look at both frequent responses and atypical ones. In the rush to instill order, don't shut down your imagination. Some questions to consider:

- Are there other ways of looking at the text that provide a useful angle of vision?

- Are there metaphors that can expand (or focus) your thinking?

- What are differences or implications of an answer from the text if you ask your question in the negative instead of the positive?

- What does your "gut" tell you?

- How do the codes and patterns argue with, or agree with, what you expected?

It is good to remember that answers are always in relation to the question itself and the context of the question (though sometimes people will interpret what is being asked differently). Also remember you are looking at written responses: what people may be thinking does not always get communicated the same in writing as when it is spoken; or, it may change in the process of translation from thought to words on a page. Written, or spoken, responses do follow rules of discourse. Although these rules of discourse may be a level of analysis that is beyond what you need, linguistics and communication studies have taught us a lot about meaning embedded in the "form" of statements. Paying some attention to how something is expressed, as well as what is written, is prudent.

That wonderful and frightful amount of text will make sense. There is not a single right way to interpret it, however. You could interpret it several ways yourself at different times. Again, clarity on the purpose of collecting the information should help guide your decisions:

- Were the open-ended questions primarily a way to get supplemental information about "X"?

- Are you testing an idea?

- Are you conducting a reality check?

- Are you trying to "just listen" because you have little firm sense of what's working or not working?

- Are you giving people a chance to express what they find important?

How you ultimately go about finding the way the pieces fit will vary. Presumably some things will leap out at you. And some intricacies will only be discovered because you lined up different codes next to each other. You want to be "true to the data," but it is your knowledge, creativity, and thinking hard about the text that creates meaning from it.

EXAMPLE OF USING THE TECHNIQUE

Any data collection method that results in text instead of, or in addition to, numbers will require making sense of narrative responses. However, the process of categorizing, or coding can be simple or elaborate. You may have twenty short pieces of text from a questionnaire handed out at the end of a presentation which require one reading to note reactions to the facility, presenter, usefulness of material covered. Or you may have twenty long responses from interviews with department managers regarding the results of a reorganization plan which require several readings and "sortings" to find the points on which they agree. Or you may have several hundred responses of varying lengths to a survey mailed out about the library's role with regard to the Internet that require complex coding because the director wants one kind of information, the reference staff another. Users may be interested in yet different aspects of the results.

While the comprehensiveness and level of detail in an analysis is highly situational, the basics of coding are the same, regardless. At the end of this chapter, sample responses and codes are presented:
- open-ended question with sample responses;

- pieces of a codebook to illustrate how one might be set up;

- responses copied a second time with coding notations, to further demonstrate the process.

The question is: "In what ways have your evaluation results affected your family literacy program?" It was asked toward the end of a public library survey that was explicitly on evaluation of family literacy programs. The purpose behind the question was to find out as much as possible about what the informants perceived as the impact of evaluation on their programs.

The Coding List appears very detailed relative to the responses because the actual responses totaled over 150 questionnaires (the complete code list has 27 codes) and it is more elaborate than you may need. However, it is presented to demonstrate possibility and illustrate a variety of ways codes may be used. Some specifics to note include:

- variety of possible answers and how this gets reflected in the codes;

- range of answers receiving a specific code (e.g., check the responses coded "02" —"program adjustment");

- use of multiple codes for each response;

- possibility of a question being interpreted in different ways (e.g., 3rd response: informant provided information about evaluation of students' work).

The Coding Instructions in this example explain the rules for the machine readable data. If you are not inputting data for quantitative analysis you will not need to worry about the position of data in a file (column numbers). However, it may be useful to have a reminder of the question content. In this instance a succinct referent to the question was put in terms of "variable," or more specifically the variable, "AFFECT." (Because you are allowed up to two codes for each response, there is "AFFECT1" and "AFFECT2.") And you do need "decision rules" about how to apply the codes. For example, according to the rules in this codebook, if a respondent wrote "none," you would use the code "00," while using "99" indicates there was no response on the questionnaire.

USE OF RESULTS

The use to be made of the results will have some influence on what the results are. This is not to suggest making up results as convenient, but is a reminder that clarity about what kind of information is needed and why it is important to find out should be known from the beginning. In turn, the "why" is linked to the audience for the results. Think about the stakeholders. What pieces of the overall information are of most interest to whom? You could present:

- "consensus" themes and patterns,

- how the narrative responses support other data,

241

- discoveries of issues not reached by other data collection,

- a unique concern or fact that should be heard,

- and one or two good stories.

While an answer that comes repeatedly should not be ignored, a distinctive story can relate the importance of a program in very human terms. If you can combine summary of the data (with or without numbers) with striking answers, so much the better.

Open-ended questions allow people to share something *they* find significant and want you, the director, and your funders to know. Listen to them. They may explain how and why a service is important. They may make good suggestions for changes in a program. Their comments may contradict other findings, or "what everybody knows." They may well point to other questions that need asking.

An important last use of narrative responses is entertainment value. Often the very same piece of a program one person chooses to rave about another will rant about. And while you may be concerned about whether people can successfully access the Internet, they want to tell you about the temperature, or a screen-saver they find ugly, or, or, or. Are these access issues? You get to decide. And you may as well smile because you asked for it.

TRAINING SUGGESTIONS

A session on narrative analysis might most clearly follow a session on questionnaire design because thought regarding coding typically begins with the questions. Text to be analyzed could be from other sources (e.g., interviews, observation notes); however, for ease of presentation the examples here use questionnaire data.

Training on narrative analysis is usefully broken into four parts:

Description of the analysis process

Practice coding

Discussion of the sorting process

Discussion of presentation for different stakeholders

Describing the Process

The "Components of Technique" section of the tip sheet (page 246) can be used as an outline (perhaps on an overhead) to present an overview of the analysis process to the large group. It may be useful to include reminders:

- Narrative responses are rich data.

- Clarity regarding the "what" and "why" of your evaluation will help create good questions and answers.

- Narrative analysis is reiterative.

- Analysis is always an interpretive process, i.e., there is not a single, correct answer.

Practice Coding

While not every survey will require formal coding, going through the coding process is a good way to demonstrate categorization in a clear manner. You will need data with which to work. Sample data are included at the end of this chapter drawn from the U.S. Department of Education, Library Programs grant, *Public Library Family Literacy Services Survey*, conducted by Debra Wilcox Johnson, 1992. You can easily generate some data quickly by asking an open-ended question and having everyone in the room write a response. For example, they could respond to: What are the evaluation training needs in your library?, or, What causes stress at your workplace? So that an overhead can be prepared before discussion ask a question at the beginning of the presentation. No matter what your sources of data:

- Create an overhead of the open-ended question and 8–12 responses.

- Have the large group scan the responses and brainstorm key words.

- Record these in a list that everyone can see; number them.

- Go through one or two responses and "code" them with the appropriate number (or word[s]) on the overhead.

- Involve the participants in choosing codes for two more responses and discuss the adequacies of the code list and make adjustments as deemed necessary.

- Break into small groups of 4–5 people and have them each code more responses.

- Back in the large group, code the responses on the overhead together, discussing questions that arose in small groups and any disagreements between groups on the "right" code.

The Sorting Process

Facilitate a discussion of how to sort, or group, the coded responses. Remind participants that with this part of the process you are seeing how the chunks of data you've broken into coded parts, fit back together. You are making meaning across individual answers. Some possible questions include:

- Did respondents answer the question you thought you were asking? If not, what does this tell you?

- How are themes related? Contradictory?

- Are there unique responses that seem important?

- How do the answers to one question relate to the answers of another?

- In a summary statement, how do these responses tell the story of this issue?

Presentation to Stakeholders

You may wish to review Chapter 5, "Let People Know What Happened: Telling the Story," in preparation for this segment of the training. With participants, brainstorm who the stakeholders could be for the information gathered. If time allows, break into small groups again and assign each group a stakeholder group to receive a mini-presentation of the findings. Have a spokesperson from each group present to the large group. Or, facilitate a large group discussion about what strategies might be best for telling the story to various stakeholders. Good reminder questions include:

- What pieces of the information are of most interest to which stakeholders?

- Is the audience one for whom a "good story" will have impact? Or one for whom a story would be dismissed as "only anecdotal"?

REFERENCES AND FURTHER READING

Babbie, Earl. *The Practice of Social Research*. 6th ed. Belmont, Calif.: Wadsworth, 1992.

Glesne, Corrine, and Alan Peshkin. *Becoming Qualitative Researchers: An Introduction*. White Plains, N.Y.: Longman, 1992.

Lofland, John, and Lyn H. Lofland. *Analyzing Social Settings*. 2nd ed. Belmont, Calif.: Wadsworth, 1984.

Strauss, Anselm, and Juliet Corbin. *Basics of Qualitative Research*. Newbury Park, Calif.: Sage, 1990.

Tesch, Renata. *Qualitative Research: Analysis Types and Software Tools*. Bristol, Pa.: Falmer, 1990.

TRAINING CHECKLIST FOR NARRATIVE ANALYSIS

Purpose: To review the process of narrative analysis and create an opportunity for participants to get practice making sense of narrative responses.

Rationale for approach: A combination of presentation, discussion, and small group activity is used to create a cooperative teaching/learning environment that accommodates diverse learning styles.

Number of participants: No limit; however, once the group size goes beyond 25 it will be increasingly important to do most of the exercises in small groups.

Time required: If the intent is to raise awareness of issues related to coding, 1 1/2 hours should be sufficient. To allow more hands-on practice to build some skills will take 3–4 hours.

Instructional approach: A combination of lecture, discussion, and small group work are utilized to involve everyone as learner/teacher.

Room arrangement: Participants need to be able to move into groups easily as well as have tables at which to write. If you will have more than 3–4 small groups, having other rooms available for small group activities is a good idea.

Special supplies: Either multiple overhead projectors, or an overhead projector and newsprint pads and easels to enable showing sample data while brainstorming codes and to show code list while demonstrating coding the responses. If small groups will break out into other rooms, handouts of the data would be useful.

Advanced preparation: Handouts and/or overheads of sample data and codebook.

Directions:

1. Introductions

2. Presentation of overview of analysis process

3. Lecture/discussion on coding

4. Small group coding practice

5. Discussion of sorting process

6. Discussion (or small group presentation) regarding focusing results for stakeholders

TELL IT! Tip Sheet

NARRATIVE ANALYSIS

Purpose and Logic Behind Use of This Technique
- To interpret the meaning in text
- Narrative responses provide rich data

Type(s) of Situation(s) for Which Technique Is Used
- Most typically used with narrative responses to open-ended questions from written surveys or interviews
- May be used with any kind of text material, including notes from observations, field notes and memos

Components of Technique
- Plan ahead and ask clear and focused questions
- Read all the responses quickly
- Generate code list and decision rules for applying codes
- Mark responses with appropriate code(s)
- Group the responses to find themes, contradictions, good stories and to arrive at a general analysis of the data
- Develop interpretive summaries pertinent to particular stakeholder groups

Supplies Needed
- Writing implements or word processing capability
- Computer and statistical software, if needed for quantitative analysis

Personnel Needed
- One person may do the entire process, or the primary interpreter may get assistance with coding

Time Factors
- Will vary depending on amount of text and detail of analysis
- If coding alone, check reliability of codes by marking a sample of responses over again on a different day

Cost Factors
- Will vary depending on if you need to hire a consultant or coders, and/or wish to hire out having data put into machine readable form

Further Reading on This Technique
Corrine Glesne and Alan Peshkin. *Becoming Qualitative Researchers: An Introduction*. White Plains, N.Y.: Longman, 1992.

Anselm Strauss and Juliet Corbin. *Basics of Qualitative Research*. Newbury Park, Calif.: Sage, 1990.

Renata Tesch. *Qualitative Research: Analysis Types and Software Tools*. Bristol, Pa.: Falmer, 1990.

SAMPLE DATA

Question

After you started to offer your family literacy program, what circumstances or situations did you encounter that you had not expected?

Responses

We had not anticipated the need for funds to provide public transportation. In working with day-care providers and attempting to provide in-service orientation, we found we frequently had to do this during naptime—in the dark and using whispers! We had to become more adept at writing flyers that are easy to read.

The program was originally designed to reach non-English speaking and non-reading adults. We have been surprised at the number of educated parents who have attended classes to learn about child development, how to choose books for their children, how to interest children in books, etc.

After worrying that we would have more tutors than students, we had a great response to an article in a local Spanish paper and had to start a waiting list and step up tutor recruiting/training.

Retention and follow-through issues. Most families had several children. Transportation, illness and other conflicts often interfered with completion of a program. Even our six week cycle was too long for many.

The interest of parents with high level reading skills using program as supplement for their kids.

Need for childcare services—still do not have.

Difficulty for new readers and families to attend activities other than tutoring.

1) Program is very popular and demand is greater than our resources. 2) Even families expressing great enthusiasm often do not stay in the program because of life stresses. 3) It's hard to involve fathers, especially as many families are headed by a single mother.

We served almost three times the number of families as anticipated in our first year. Transportation was an unexpected challenge. Most of the families we served had limited English proficiency.

Adapted from the American Library Association 1993 Carroll Preston Baber Research Grant project, *Evaluation of Family Literacy Programs in Public Libraries*, conducted by Debra Wilcox Johnson with Sondra Cuban, Leah Langby, and Rhea Lawson, copyright © 1993 American Library Association. **Permission granted to reproduce for instructional purposes.**

QUESTION 15

In what ways have your evaluation results affected your family literacy program? [If none, please specify none.]

Sample Responses:

Redesigned program based on our findings

Useful with potential funder; useful to explain program to staff

Information received targets families where there is a need.
Enhanced at home reading activity.

Intensified recruiting of volunteer tutors.
Our program is new and only preliminary information is there.

We've been able to buy more materials based on circulation statistics. A local grant also came out of it. More programming, storytellers, etc. were funded.

Determine when more materials are needed—we realized a more creative "marketing" of collection was needed.

[answer space left blank]

Program will be terminated.

We've shifted collections, printed brochures and program fliers, created displays, developed job booklets & centers.

We were encouraged to continue our efforts.

Simply made us more aware of need for more staff

Constantly adjusting programs

Helps us in determining how to allocate resources ($, staff, materials)

Allows us to plan and set goals
Information and statistics for grant application

Adapted from the American Library Association 1993 Carroll Preston Baber Research Grant project, *Evaluation of Family Literacy Programs in Public Libraries*, conducted by Debra Wilcox Johnson with Sondra Cuban, Leah Langby, and Rhea Lawson, copyright © 1993 American Library Association. **Permission granted to reproduce for instructional purposes.**

QUESTION 15: AFFECT
(allows for 2 answers)

Coding List

01   showed need for more staff/volunteers

02   program adjustment (**write down specific examples)

03   program will be terminated

04   confirms their impressions

05   program enhancement/growth (**write down specific examples)

06   increased funding

07   received recognition/award (formal)

08   enhanced marketing

09   used as tool to increase staff understanding

10   used in soliciting potential funds

11   used to pursue/attract collaborative efforts

12   encouraged to continue effort

13   used in deciding how to allocate resources

14   helped with planning and goal setting

15   targeting particular populations

16   used to help students achieve goals

00   none   (These code numbers mean the same

99   missing or unusable info   thing across questions.)

Coding Instructions

Variable name	?#	Values	Column
AFFECT1	15	results affected prog 00 = none/01–98	140–141
AFFECT2	15	do not use 00 01–98	142–143

QUESTION 15: AFFECT
(allows for 2 answers)

Sample Responses Coded

Codes	Responses
02 99	Redesigned program based on our findings
10 09	Useful with potential funder; useful to explain program to staff
15 16	Information received targets families where there is a need. Enhanced at home reading activity.
00 99	none
01 99	Intensified recruiting of volunteer tutors. Our program is new and only preliminary information is there.
05 06	We've been able to buy more materials based on circulation statistics. A local grant also came out of it. More programming, storytellers, etc.,were funded.
02 08	Determine when more materials are needed—we realized a more creative "marketing" of collection was needed.
99 99	[answer space left blank]
03 99	Program will be terminated.
05 08	We've shifted collections, printed brochures and program fliers, created displays, developed job booklets & centers.
12 99	We were encouraged to continue our efforts.
01 99	Simply made us more aware of need for more staff
02 99	Constantly adjusting programs
13 99	Helps us in determining how to allocate resources ($, staff, materials)
14 10	Allows us to plan and set goals Information and statistics for grant application

---

Adapted from the American Library Association 1993 Carroll Preston Baber Research Grant project, *Evaluation of Family Literacy Programs in Public Libraries*, conducted by Debra Wilcox Johnson with Sondra Cuban, Leah Langby, and Rhea Lawson, copyright © 1993 American Library Association. **Permission granted to reproduce for instructional purposes.**

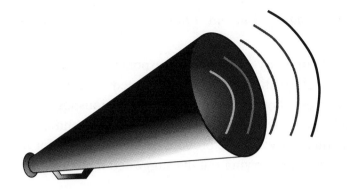

Evaluation:
A Selected Bibliography

The purpose of this bibliography is to provide references to some additional "user-friendly" material on evaluation of particular interest to librarians. There is a vast literature related to evaluation from many social science and human service fields. For a more comprehensive overview, see the reference lists in the books noted in "General Overviews." Additional titles are also cited in many chapters of this sourcebook.

GENERAL OVERVIEWS

Guba, Egon G., and Yvonna S. Lincoln. *Fourth Generation Evaluation.* Newbury Park, Calif.: Sage, 1989.

> Views evaluation as resting on "responsive focusing" and "constructivist methodology": information should be collected on a basis of stakeholder inputs and inquiry process should proceed with a consciousness that "reality" is created by people influenced by a variety of social, political, and cultural factors. Emphasis on evaluation as process, the product being an agenda for negotiation. Provides specific guidelines for carrying out the suggested methodology.

Herman, John L. ed. *Program Evaluation Kit.* Newbury Park, Calif.: Sage, 1987.

> Developed at the Center for the Study of Evaluation, UCLA, this kit consists of nine books. Each covers some aspect of evaluation in detail, from a basic overview to specific methods and write-up. The volumes stand independently; all contain suggested step-by-step procedures as well as many examples and are very good resources. (Some of the individual volumes are annotated separately.)
>
> Vol. 1 *Evaluator's Handbook*
> Vol. 2 *How to Focus an Evaluation*
> Vol. 3 *How to Design a Program Evaluation*
> Vol. 4 *How to Use Qualitative Methods in Evaluation*
> Vol. 5 *How to Assess Program Implementation*
> Vol. 6 *How to Measure Attitudes*
> Vol. 7 *How to Measure Performance and Use Tests*
> Vol. 8 *How to Analyze Data*
> Vol. 9 *How to Communicate Evaluation Findings*

Rossi, Peter H., and Howard E. Freeman. *Evaluation: A Systematic Approach.* 5th ed. Newbury Park, Calif.: Sage, 1993.

> Provides an introduction to evaluation from the perspective of appraising the utility of social programs. Pays much attention to wider political contexts and provides many examples from project reports. Includes chapters on tailoring evaluations and program monitoring. Good summaries of "key concepts" appear in the front of each chapter.

Scriven, Michael. *Evaluation Thesaurus.* 4th ed. Newbury Park, Calif.: Sage, 1991.

> An introductory essay discusses the nature of evaluation in general, setting out a "transdisciplinary paradigm." The almost 1,000 entries which follow the introduction analyze concepts, positions and techniques that illustrate the connections and developments in evaluation from a broad range of fields. All in a concise and witty manner!

Stufflebeam, Daniel L., and Anthony J. Shinkfield. *Systematic Evaluation: A Self-Instructional Guide to Theory and Practice.* Boston: Kluwer–Nijhoff, 1985.

> Provides an introduction to evaluation and an analysis of alternative approaches to designing evaluations—including objective-oriented, scientific, improvement-oriented, client-centered, adversarial, illuminative, and consumer-oriented approaches to evaluation. Self-scoring multiple choice questions, application exercises, and discussion questions are at the end of each unit for self-evaluation.

Worthen, Blaine R., and James R. Sanders. *Educational Evaluation: Alternative Approaches and Practical Guidelines.* New York: Longman, 1987.

> Designed as a basic text for courses in educational evaluation, this book also serves as a reference for practicing evaluators. Provides both an overview of a variety of approaches and practical guidelines for planning, conducting and using evaluations. Includes extensive references.

APPROACHES TO LIBRARY EVALUATION

Childers, Tom A., and Nancy A. Van House. *What's Good?: Describing Your Public Library's Effectiveness.* Chicago: American Library Association, 1993.

> Defines effectiveness broadly as "goodness," or the success and quality of an organization's performance. Provides guidelines for assessing a library's effectiveness and communicating it to the library's stakeholders, using a model, AMPLE, derived from the findings of the Public Library Effectiveness Study.

Hernon, Peter, and Charles R. McClure. *Evaluation and Library Decision Making.* Norwood, N.J.: Ablex, 1990.

> Presents evaluation from the perspectives of collection of research and management data. Includes chapters on evaluation design and data collection techniques, sampling, using a computer-based management information system, performance measures, political context and organizational change, and two study examples in academic library settings.

Lancaster, F. W. *If You Want to Evaluate Your Library....* 2nd ed. Champaign, Ill.: University of Illinois, Graduate School of Library and Information Science, 1993.

> Discusses methods of evaluation to determine both success rates and the reasons for successes and failures. In three sections: document delivery services; reference services; related evaluation topics, including cost effectiveness and cost benefit. Includes new material on the evaluation of bibliographic instruction.

Nichols, J. V. "Using Future Trends to Inform Planning/Marketing." *Library Trends* 43 (Winter 1995): 349–66.

> Explores the reasons for incorporating the identification of future trends of librarianship into library planning and marketing efforts. Reviews some key issues in financial and technological areas and uses them to illustrate the way this information can affect planning decisions. Focuses on environmental scanning and alternative scenario building.

A Stakeholder Evaluation Handbook: A Focus on Evaluation. (Prepared and revised by Sharon Granger, Donald Leaf, and Charles Wolfe and edited by Jeff Johnson of the Library of Michigan.) Lansing, Mich.: Library of Michigan, [1993].

> Using the stakeholder approach to evaluation, seven steps of the evaluation process are delineated, from the preliminary project plan to the final report. Developed specifically for use with evaluation of LSCA grant projects. (Available through John Rummel, Public Information Officer, Library of Michigan, 517-373-5578.)

Swisher, Robert, and Charles McClure. *Research for Decision Making: Methods for Librarians.* Chicago: American Library Association, 1984.

> Provides an introduction to statistics (including research design, data gathering, sampling, data description, and covariation) and makes suggestions about how to incorporate research findings into the decision making process.

EVALUATION METHODS

Qualitative Overview

Patton, Michael Q. *How to Use Qualitative Methods in Evaluation.* Newbury Park, Calif.: Sage, 1987.

> Provides a good general overview to qualitative methods. Discusses qualitative and quantitative data choices—pointing out that multiple methods and kinds of data are common. Includes chapters on designing qualitative evaluations and analyzing and interpreting qualitative data.

Questionnaires

Babbie, Earl. "Guidelines for Asking Questions." In *The Practice of Social Research*. 6th ed. Belmont, Calif.: Wadsworth Publishing Company, 1992.

> An overview of the problems to avoid when asking questions for social science research, addressing open vs. closed questions, clarification and relevancy of questions, and the avoidance of negatives or biased terminology.

Backstrom, Charles H., and Gerald Hursch-Cesar. *Survey Research*. 2nd ed. New York: John Wiley, 1981.

> Comprehensively covers the basics in very accessible language and format. Lots of checklists. Includes chapters: "Writing Questionnaires;" "Designing Questionnaires;" and "Conducting Interviews."

Dillman, Don. *Mail and Telephone Surveys: The Total Design Method*. New York: John Wiley, 1978.

> Total design method (TDM) consists of two parts: 1) identifies each aspect of a survey process that may affect quality or quantity of response; 2) provides a guide to assure attention to an administrative plan that will ensure a survey implemented in accordance with design intentions. Lots of detailed examples.

Foddy, William. *Constructing Questions for Interviews and Questionnaires*. New York: Cambridge University Press, 1993.

> Working with the principal thesis that most problems that arise from the construction of questions can be lessened by a clear specification of the kind of answers respondents should give, Foddy details question construction. Includes a useful chapter on "checks to ensure that questions work as intended."

Sudman, Seymour, and Norman M. Bradburn. *Asking Questions: A Practical Guide to Questionnaire Design*. San Francisco: Jossey–Bass, 1982.

> An excellent guide to asking better questions. Begins each chapter with a checklist of main points. Coverage includes asking threatening and non-threatening questions, measuring attitudes, order of questions, format of questionnaire.

Interviews

Fowler, Floyd J., Jr., and Thomas W. Mangione. *Standardized Survey Interviewing: Minimizing Interviewer-Related Error.* Newbury Park, Calif.: Sage, 1990.

> Defines and explores problems in the social science standardized survey interviewing process, including techniques, context, question design, and the selection, training, and supervising of interviewers. Includes index of tables.

Seidman, I. E. *Interviewing as Qualitative Research: A Guide for Researchers in Education and the Social Sciences.* New York: Teachers College Press, 1991.

> Provides a good talk through in-depth and unstructured interviewing. Even if you wish to use a structured interview format, the chapters, "Technique isn't Everything" and "Interviewing as a Relationship" are worth reading.

Focus Groups

Greenbaum, Thomas L. *The Practical Handbook and Guide to Focus Group Research.* Lexington, Mass.: D.C. Heath, 1988.

> The title is descriptive—a practical handbook and guide. Written from a marketing perspective.

Johnson, Debra Wilcox. "Keeping Things in Focus: Information for Decision Making." In *Keeping the Book$: Public Library Financial Practices,* edited by Jane B. Robbins and Douglas L. Zweizig, 405–20. Fort Atkinson, Wisc.: Highsmith, 1992.

> Walks one through the four major steps of doing a focus group interview: developing an interview guide, recruiting participants, conducting the interview, and preparing a report. Includes sample interview guides.

Krueger, Richard A. *Focus Groups: A Practical Guide for Applied Research.* Newbury Park, Calif.: Sage, 1988.

> Another very practical, hands-on guide to focus groups. Includes especially helpful chapters about analyzing results and reporting results.

Observation

Cartwright, Carol A., and G. Phillip. *Developing Observation Skills.* 2nd ed. New York: McGraw-Hill, 1984.

> Written for educators and psychologists observing children, but useful for its delineation of many possible note and record keeping devices. The many examples are easily transferable to a library setting.

King, Jean A., Lynn Lyons Morris, and Carol Taylor Fitz-Gibbon. "Methods: Observations." In *How to Assess Program Implementation*. Newbury Park, Calif.: Sage, 1987.

> Also uses the example of classroom observation, but includes clear instructions about structuring and recording observations. Delineates formal observation by recording technique: checklist, coded behavioral records, or delayed reports. Emphasizes training observers.

Webb, Eugene J., et al. *Nonreactive Measures in the Social Sciences*. Boston: Houghton Mifflin, 1981.

> A classic and a delight—only the title is dry. With great wit, the authors provide lots of information about many lesser used methodologies. Includes chapters: "Simple Observation" and "Contrived Observation: Hidden Hardware and Control." Makes one think about process and just how we create "knowledge."

Attitude Measurement

Henerson, Marlene E., Lynn L. Morris, and Carol J. Fitz-Gibbon. *How to Measure Attitudes*. Newbury Park, Calif.: Sage, 1987.

> Using a broad definition of attitude, "affect, feelings, values, or beliefs," this book is meant to introduce the decidedly complicated task of measuring it. Discusses both selecting and developing your own measurement instruments with emphasis on the latter (including development of questionnaires, attitude rating scales, interviews, observation procedures, sociometric instruments).

Oppenheim, A. N. *Questionnaire Design, Interviewing and Attitude Measurement*. New Edition. London: Pinter Publishers, 1992.

> While the new edition turned a specialized text dealing with questionnaire design and attitude measurement into a general survey research handbook, it still contains a lot of information on attitude measurement, including chapters on designing attitude statements and attitude scaling. Full of examples, practical advice and warnings.

Statistics

Novice

Fitz-Gibbon, Carol Taylor, and Lynn Lyons Morris. *How to Analyze Data*. Newbury Park, Calif.: Sage, 1987.

> Framed as methods to answer essential questions for evaluation, this book is a good way to gain a basic understanding of statistics. Chapters include: Summarizing a Single Set of Scores, Examining Differences Between Groups, Examining

Relationships Between Variables, Constructing Tests and Analyzing Questionnaires, Selecting Statistical Procedures, and Meta Analysis.

Simpson, Ian S. *Basic Statistics for Librarians*. 3rd ed. Chicago: American Library Association, 1988.

Provides an overview of statistics and their interpretation and applications. Covers basics of averages, sampling, probability, statistical tests, and correlation with the use of library examples and applications.

Intermediate

Jaeger, Richard M. *Statistics: A Spectator Sport*. 2nd ed. Beverly Hills, Calif.: Sage, 1990.

A detailed but understandable overview of statistics and how to interpret them, including topics such as terminology, correlation, variance, and inference. Provides a summary and problem set for each chapter.

Slonim, Morris James. *Sampling: A Quick, Reliable Guide to Practical Statistics*. New York: Simon and Schuster, 1967.

Intended for a general audience, this slim volume covers the sampling process in understandable language and uses many examples. Stratified, random, cluster, systematic, and other methods of sampling are described.

Advanced

Hernon, Peter, et al. *Statistics for Library Decision Making: A Handbook*. Norwood, N.J.: Ablex, 1989.

Explores theoretical issues involving research, statistics and library decision making as well as microcomputer applications. Overviews aspects of statistics, statistical tests, correlation, and statistical analysis. A final discussion centers on applications and communicating the findings of research.

EXAMPLES OF EVALUATION IN LIBRARY SETTINGS

Busch, Nancy, and Mary J. Ryan. *Nebraska Education Information Center Network: Final Evaluation Report to the Kellogg Foundation*. Lincoln, Nebr.: Nebraska Library Commission, 1993.

Describes the Nebraska Education Information Center Network and how it was implemented in six public libraries over a five-year period. Includes good information on how the project was evaluated using both extensive interviewing and a survey questionnaire. Positive outcomes and "lessons learned" are discussed in the context of how to strategize on future directions and services. (Available by interlibrary loan from: Document Distribution Office, Nebraska Library Commission, The Atrium, 1200 N St., Suite 120, Lincoln, NE 68508.)

Bunge, Charles. "Gathering and Using Patron and Librarian Perceptions of Question-Answering Success." In *Evaluation of Public Services and Public Services Personnel,* edited by Bryce Allen, 59–84. Urbana, Ill.: University of Illinois, Graduate School of Library and Information Science, 1991.

> Addresses the strengths and weaknesses of using patron and reference librarian responses in evaluating question-answering effectiveness. Provides a description of the Wisconsin-Ohio Reference Evaluation Program and includes relevant findings regarding relationships between patron-perceived answering success and factors such as staffing patterns and the types or sources of questions.

Hodges, Gerald G. "Evaluation and Measurement of Youth Services." In *Managers and Missionaries: Library Services to Children and Young Adults in the Information Age*, edited by Leslie Edmonds, 147–55. Urbana, Ill.: University of Illinois, Graduate School of Library and Information Science, 1989.

> Examines goal setting for youth library programs and examines four evaluative measurements for achieving them: instructional role quotient, access quotient, collection evaluation measurement, and reading guidance quotient.

Johnson, Debra Wilcox. "Measuring Up: Making Literacy Evaluation Meaningful." *Wilson Library Bulletin* 65 (November 1990): 35–39+.

> A succinct discussion of the whys and hows of evaluation for library literacy activities. Includes useful lists of possible measures and suggestions about the data collection in terms of sampling and periodic collection.

Lynch, Mary Jo, Pamela Kramer, and Ann Weeks. *Public School Library Media Centers in 12 States: Report of the NCLIS/ALA Survey.* Washington, D.C.: National Commission on Libraries and Information Science (NCLIS), 1994.

> Reports data collected by mailed questionnaire to present a "snapshot" of public school library media centers chosen to represent different regions and conditions. NCLIS and ALA/AASL encourage other states to use the questionnaire developed for this survey. (Copy of questionnaire included; AASL office should be contacted for revised instrument.)

McClure, Charles R., et al. *Connecting Rural Public Libraries to the Internet: Project GAIN—Global Access Information Network.* Liverpool, N.Y.: NYSERNet, 1994.

> This project evaluation report prepared for NYSERNet is of particular value not only for the information on the Internet, but for project design. The project used a variety of data collection strategies. Includes copies of instruments used. (Available from: Publications Office, NYSERNet, 200 Elwood Davis Rd., Suite 103, Liverpool, N.Y. 13088-6147. [$10.00, includes postage & handling])

McClure, Charles R., John Carlo Bertot, and Douglas L. Zweizig. *Public Libraries and the Internet: Study Results, Policy Issues and Recommendations.* Washington, D.C.: National Commission on Libraries and Information Science (NCLIS), 1994.

> The final report of a national survey. Provides ideas about just how much information can be generated with a questionnaire (copy included). Integrates both many numbers and qualitative data in the write-up. (Available from NCLIS: 202-606-9200.)

McDonald, Joseph A., and Lynda Baseney Micikas. *Academic Libraries: The Dimensions of their Effectiveness.* Westport, Conn.: Greenwood, 1994.

> Describes an approach to examining library effectiveness based on Kim Cameron's principles of researching organizational effectiveness. Chapters include: Assessing Organizational Effectiveness; Criteria for Assessing Academic Library Organizational Effectiveness; Research Methodology; Results and Discussion; The Grail of Library Goodness; Libraries and Information. Includes useful bibliography and appendices on such things as effectiveness critieria, sampling, questionnaires, variables, statistics.

McIntyre, B. "Measuring Excellence in Public Libraries." *Australian Public Libraries and Information Services* 7 (September 1994): 135–55.

> Explores current problems faced when measuring public library performance against the standards of the Australian Library and Information Association. Suggests a new measurement index, the "Excellence Index," consisting of a combination of input, internal efficiency, and output indicators.

Robins, Kikanza Nuri. "Culturally Competent Libraries." *California State Library Foundation Bulletin* 46 (January 1994): 8–15.

> "Cultural competence is a point on a continuum that represents the set of values and behaviors in an individual, or the policies, practices, and procedures in an organization that facilitate effective cross-cultural interaction ."(p. 9)
> Discusses assessing the cultures of libraries and their clients to have informa-

tion for appropriate program and service decisions. Provides a clear discussion of cultural competence in terms of five basic principles.

Rodger, Eleanor Jo, and Jane Goodwin. "To See Ourselves as Others See Us: A Cooperative, Do-It-Yourself Reference Accuracy Study." *The Reference Librarian* 18 (Summer 1987): 135–47.

Describes an evaluation study of reference service in several library systems using staff as unobtrusive callers. A clear discussion of process and implementation makes it easily reapplicable.

Shonrock, Diana D., ed. *Evaluating Library Instruction: Sample Questions, Forms, and Strategies for Practical Use.* Chicago: American Library Association, 1996.

Members of the Library Instruction Round Table Research Committee of ALA analyzed hundreds of evaluation forms from all types of libraries and selected the most consistently useful items to include in this guide. Divided into fourteen sections such as "Patrons' Library Background," "Supporting Materials," "Evaluating the Instructor," "Summative Evaluation" with brief introductory comments to walk one through creating an instrument.

Turock, Betty J. "Assessing Services to Special Populations." In *Evaluation of Public Services and Public Services Personnel*, edited by Bryce Allen, 125–46. Champaign, Ill.: University of Illinois, Graduate School of Library and Information Science, 1991.

Discusses how librarianship has failed to emphasize outcome-based measurement and how evaluation should be conducted with the question to be answered as the basis for selecting an evaluation model. Eight models are suggested as alternatives.

Walter, Virginia A. *Output Measures and More: Planning and Evaluating Public Library Services for Youth.* Chicago: American Library Association, 1995.

Intended to help librarians and library administrators understand, rationalize, and improve their services to young adults, this work offers a broad menu of options for planning and evaluation with a focus on meeting the competencies recommended by the Young Adult Library Services Association (YALSA). Output measures are organized in seven basic categories: library use, materials use, materials availability, information services, programming, community relations, youth participation.

Westbrook, Lynn. "Evaluating Reference: An Introductory Overview of Qualitative Methods." *Reference Services Review* 18 (1990): 73–78.

> Four methods of qualitative evaluation—observation, interviews, surveys, and unobtrusive observation—are examined, and suggested project guidelines are offered.

Widdows, Richard, Tia A. Hensler, and Marlaya H. Wyncott. "The Focus Group Interview: A Method for Assessing Users' Evaluation of Library Service." *College and Research Libraries* 52 (July 1991): 352–59.

> Demonstrates how focus groups were utilized in obtaining student opinions of Purdue University's library system and provides an explanation of the rationale and method of the focus group interview.

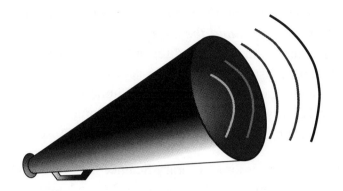

About the Contributors

Michele Besant is a doctoral student in the School of Library and Information Studies, University of Wisconsin–Madison. She has an M.A. in English Literature as well as an M.L.S from the University of Wisconsin–Madison. She has worked in academic and special libraries and was a feminist bookseller before entering library school. She enrolled in the Advanced Studies Program upon finishing the M.L.S to pursue an interest in doing research exploring the library–literacy connection. Other current interests include the impact of jail library service and the interaction of gays/lesbians and the library profession.

Debra Wilcox Johnson, Ph.D., of Johnson & Johnson Consulting, teaches, writes, and conducts research in the areas of evaluation, management, and public services. She is completing a national study on family literacy evaluation. This project, funded by an ALA Baber award, is developing measures for family literacy programs. Dr. Johnson has been hired by the Public Library Association to evaluate their Public Library Development Program. Her career has involved working with libraries of all sizes, including her first professional position at the Cleveland Public Library. She has worked throughout the United States conducting workshops on evaluation, management, and literacy. During the last 15 years, she has administered numerous research, demonstration, and consultant projects.

Keith Curry Lance, Ph.D., is the Director of the Library Research Service, a unit of the Colorado State Library that serves libraries and related organizations in that state and nationwide. Current national projects include a survey of state library agencies for the National Center for Education Statistics, workshops on the impact of school library media centers on academic achievement, and a statistical database for the Southeastern Library Network (SOLINET). Recent publications include: *The Impact of School Library Media Centers on Academic Achievement* (1993), articles in *Public Libraries* (1993) and *Colorado Libraries* (1992), and selections in *Applying Research to Pracice* (1992), *Politics and the Support of Libraries* (1991), and *The Whole Library Handbook* (1991). Dr. Lance is the owner/editor of the new Internet listserv, PLSRNET, the Public Library Research and Statistics Network. He is also a current member of the Steering Committee of the Federal-State Cooperative System for Public Library Data, the PLA Research Committee, and the Public Library Data Service Advisory Committee, and consults privately for the Consulting Librarians Group (Tallahassee, Florida) and JNR Associates (Golden, Colorado).

Ruby Licona is Associate Professor of Library Science at Weber State University, Ogden, Utah. Her library career includes considerable experience in academic, medical, and public libraries. She has taught library science at the undergraduate level at Weber State and at the graduate level at the University of Wisconsin–Madison. Her background also includes developing and conducting training, particularly in the area of automation. Currently she is also pursuing doctoral studies at the University of Wisconsin–Madison.

Amy Owen is Utah's State Librarian and Director of the Utah State Library Division of the Utah Department of Community and Economic Development. She was a member of the study team for the PLA Public Library Development Program and a joint author of *Planning and Role Setting for Public Libraries: A Manual of Options and Procedures* (American Library Association, 1987). She has also spoken widely and published a variety of articles on public library planning, standards, and evaluation. Professional activities include terms of service as President of the Board of Trustees for the Bibliographical Center for Research, member of the Board of the Association of Specialized and Cooperative Library Agencies, President of the Utah Library Association, Chair of the PLA Goals, Guidelines and Standards Committee, a member of the Board of Directors of the Chief Officers of State Library Agencies, Chair of the Utah Humanities Council, and membership on the NCLIS/NCES Task Force, which planned and established the FSCS program.

Ronald R. Powell is Professor in the Library and Information Science Program at Wayne State University, Detroit, Michigan. Prior to joining the faculty of Wayne State, he was a librarian in the acquisition and circulation departments at the University of Illinois, Urbana–Champaign; a research associate in the Library Research Center, University of Illinois; Library Director at the University of Charleston, West Virginia; and on the faculty at the Universities of Michigan and Missouri. He also served as Director of Graduate Studies and Chair of the Library Science Department while at the University of Missouri. Dr. Powell has taught, conducted research, and published in the areas of research methods, collection development, bibliographic instruction, academic libraries, the measurement and evaluation of library services, and education for librarianship. Among his publications are *Basic Reference Sources, Basic Research Methods for Librarians, Qualitative Research in Information Management, Problem Solving in Libraries*, and

The Relationship of Library User Studies to Performance Measures. He currently is conducting research on the impact of library use and library and informational needs of minority students. He is active in ALA, ACRL and ALISE.

Robert O. Ray is Professor in the Department of Continuing and Vocational Education at the University of Wisconsin–Madison. He received his Ph.D. from the University of Maryland–College Park in 1975 before joining the faculty of York College of Pennsylvania in York, Pennsylvania as an Assistant Professor in the Department of Behavioral Sciences. In 1976 he joined the faculty of the University of Wisconsin–Madison. His research and teaching focus on how individuals learn in non-formal educational settings and programs across the lifespan. Similarly, he is interested in how agencies use their educational mission as a learning resource for selected audiences. As a result he has focused on evaluating the educational effectiveness of programs delivered by agencies involved in non-school based education. Some of his activities include: the design and evaluation of community based natural resource management for education for the Republic of Thailand; effectiveness of learning and innovation within interdisciplinary health care teams; impact of training programs to prevent sexual misconduct among clergy. His publications have appeared in the *Journal of Leisure Research*, *The Alban Journal*, *Gerontology and Geriatrics Education*, and *Adult Education Quarterly*, among others.

Jane Robbins is a graduate of Wells College. She received her M.L.S from Western Michigan University and a Ph.D. from the University of Maryland. From 1981 through July 1994, she was the director of the School of Library and Information Studies at the University of Wisconsin–Madison. In August 1994, she became the Dean of the School of Library and Information Studies, Florida State University. She is co-principal investigator of the Department of Education, Library Program's Evaluating Library Programs & Services project. Her research interests include research and education for library and information science, organizational structure of information agencies, and education for librarianship; she is the author of books and articles in these interest areas.

Douglas Zweizig is Professor in the School of Library and Information Studies, University of Wisconsin–Madison, and co-principal investigator of the Evaluating Library Programs & Services project. Previously, he served as Senior Research Associate for King Research, Inc., and was on the faculty of the University of Washington and the University of Toledo. He earned his M.A. at Harvard, his M.L.S at Rutgers, and his Ph.D. at Syracuse University. He is a prolific author and research consultant specializing in evaluation and planning.

Index